Aspects and Impressions

By
Sir Edmund William Gosse

Essay Index Reprint Series

BOOKS FOR LIBRARIES PRESS
FREEPORT, NEW YORK

First Published 1922
Reprinted 1970

STANDARD BOOK NUMBER:
8369-1469-4

LIBRARY OF CONGRESS CATALOG CARD NUMBER:
77-105016

PRINTED IN THE UNITED STATES OF AMERICA

To
My Friend
JOHN C. SQUIRE
Poet, Editor, and Critic

Contents

Aspects and Impressions

GEORGE ELIOT

IN and after 1876, when I was in the habit of walking from the north-west of London towards Whitehall, I met several times, driven slowly homewards, a victoria which contained a strange pair in whose appearance I took a violent interest. The man, prematurely ageing, was hirsute, rugged, satyr-like, gazing vivaciously to left and right; this was George Henry Lewes. His companion was a large, thickset sybil, dreamy and immobile, whose massive features, somewhat grim when seen in profile, were incongruously bordered by a hat, always in the height of the Paris fashion, which in those days commonly included an immense ostrich feather; this was George Eliot. The contrast between the solemnity of the face and the frivolity of the headgear had something pathetic and provincial about it.

All this I mention, for what trifling value it may have, as a purely external impression, since I never had the honour of speaking to the lady or to Lewes. We had, my wife and I, common friends in the gifted family of Simcox —Edith Simcox (who wrote ingeniously and learnedly under the pen-name of H. Lawrenny) being an intimate in the household at the Priory. Thither, indeed, I was vaguely invited, by word of mouth, to make my appearance one Sunday, George Eliot having read some pages of mine with indulgence. But I was shy, and yet should probably have obeyed the summons but for an event which nobody foresaw. On the 18th of December, 1880, I was present at a concert given, I think, in the Langham Hall, where I sat just behind Mrs. Cross, as she had then

Aspects and Impressions

become. It was chilly in the concert-room, and I watched George Eliot, in manifest discomfort, drawing up and tightening round her shoulders a white wool shawl. Four days later she was dead, and I was sorry that I had never made my bow to her.

Her death caused a great sensation, for she had ruled the wide and flourishing province of English prose fiction for ten years, since the death of Dickens. Though she had a vast company of competitors, she did not suffer through that period from the rivalry of one writer of her own class. If the Brontës had lived, or Mrs. Gaskell, the case might have been different, for George Eliot had neither the passion of *Jane Eyre* nor the perfection of *Cranford,* but they were gone before we lost Dickens, and so was Thackeray, who died while *Romola* was appearing. Charles Kingsley, whose *Westward Ho!* had just preceded her first appearance, had unluckily turned into other and less congenial paths. Charles Reade, whose *It is Never Too Late to Mend* (1856) had been her harbinger, scarcely maintained his position as her rival. Anthony Trollope, excellent craftsman as he was, remained persistently and sensibly at a lower intellectual level. Hence the field was free for George Eliot, who, without haste or hesitation, built up slowly such a reputation as no one in her own time could approach.

The gay world, which forgets everything, has forgotten what a solemn, what a portentous thing was the contemporary fame of George Eliot. It was supported by the serious thinkers of the day, by the people who despised mere novels, but regarded her writings as contributions to philosophical literature. On the solitary occasion when I sat in company with Herbert Spencer on the committee of the London Library he expressed a strong objection to the purchase of fiction, and wished that for the London Library no novels should be bought, "except, of course, those of George Eliot." While she lived, critics compared her with Goethe, but to the disadvantage of the sage of Weimar. People who started controversies about evolutionism, a favourite Victorian pastime, bowed low at

George Eliot

the mention of her name, and her own strong good sense alone prevented her from being made the object of a sort of priggish idolatry. A big-wig of that day remarked that "in problems of life and thought which baffled Shakespeare her touch was unfailing." For Lord Acton at her death "the sun had gone out," and that exceedingly dogmatic historian observed, *ex cathedrâ,* that no writer had "ever lived who had anything like her power of manifold but disinterested and impartial sympathy. If Sophocles or Cervantes had lived in the light of our culture, if Dante had prospered like Manzoni, George Eliot might have had a rival." It is very dangerous to write like that. A reaction is sure to follow, and in the case of this novelist, so modest and strenuous herself, but so ridiculously overpraised by her friends, it came with remarkable celerity.

The worship of an intellectual circle of admirers, reverberating upon a dazzled and genuinely interested public, was not, however, even in its palmiest days, quite unanimous. There were other strains of thought and feeling making way, and other prophets were abroad. Robert Browning, though an optimist, and too polite a man to oppose George Eliot publicly, was impatient of her oracular manner. There was a struggle, not much perceived on the surface of the reviews, between her faithful worshippers and the new school of writers vaguely called pre-Raphaelite. She loved Matthew Arnold's poetry, and in that, as in so much else, she was wiser and more clairvoyant than most of the people who surrounded her, but Arnold preserved an attitude of reserve with regard to her later novels. She found nothing to praise or to attract her interest in the books of George Meredith; on the other hand, Coventry Patmore, with his customary amusing violence, voted her novels "sensational and improper." To D. G. Rossetti they were "vulgarity personified," and his brother defined them as "commonplace tempering the stuck-up." Swinburne repudiated *Romola* with vigour as "absolutely false." I dare say that from several of these her great contemporaries less harsh estimates of her work might be

3

Aspects and Impressions

culled, but I quote these to show that even at the height of her fame she was not quite unchallenged.

She was herself, it is impossible to deny, responsible for a good deal of the tarnish which spread over the gold of her reputation. Her early imaginative writings—in particular *Janet's Repentance, Adam Bede*, the first two-thirds of *The Mill on the Floss*, and much of *Silas Marner* —had a freshness, a bright vitality, which, if she could have kept it burnished, would have preserved her from all effects of contemporary want of sympathy. When we analyse the charm of the stories just mentioned, we find that it consists very largely in their felicity of expressed reminiscence. There is little evidence in them of the inventive faculty, but a great deal of the reproductive. Now, we have to remember that contemporaries are quite in the dark as to matters about which, after the publication of memoirs and correspondence and recollections, later readers are exactly informed. We may now know that Sir Christopher Cheverel closely reproduces the features of a real Sir Roger Newdigate, and that Dinah Morris is Mrs. Samuel Evans photographed, but readers of 1860 did not know that, and were at liberty to conceive the unknown magician in the act of calling up a noble English gentleman and a saintly Methodist preacher from the depths of her inner consciousness. Whether this was so or not would not matter to anyone, if George Eliot could have continued the act of pictorial reproduction without flagging. The world would have long gazed with pleasure into the camera obscura of Warwickshire, as she reeled off one dark picture after another, but unhappily she was not contented with her success, and she aimed at things beyond her reach.

Her failure, which was, after all (let us not exaggerate), the partial and accidental failure of a great genius, began when she turned from passive acts of memory to a strenuous exercise of intellect. If I had time and space, it would be very interesting to study George Eliot's attitude towards that mighty woman, the full-bosomed caryatid of romantic literature, who had by a few years

George Eliot

preceded her. When George Eliot was at the outset of her own literary career, which as we know was much belated, George Sand had already bewitched and thrilled and scandalized Europe for a generation. The impact of the Frenchwoman's mind on that of her English contemporary produced sparks or flashes of starry enthusiasm. George Eliot, in 1848, was "bowing before George Sand in eternal gratitude to that great power of God manifested in her," and her praise of the French peasant-idyls was unbounded. But when she herself began to write novels she grew to be less and less in sympathy with the French romantic school. A French critic of her own day laid down the axiom that "il faut bien que le roman se rapproche de la poésie ou de la science." George Sand had thrown herself unreservedly into the poetic camp. She acknowledged "mon instinct m'eût poussée vers les abîmes," and she confessed, with that stalwart good sense which carried her genius over so many marshy places, that her temperament had often driven her, "au mépris de la raison ou de la verité morale," into pure romantic extravagance.

But George Eliot, whatever may have been her preliminary enthusiasms, was radically and permanently anti-romantic. This was the source of her strength and of her weakness; this, carefully examined, explains the soaring and the sinking of her fame. Unlike George Sand, she kept to the facts; she found that all her power quitted her at once if she dealt with imaginary events and the clash of ideal passions. She had been drawn in her youth to sincere admiration of the Indianas and Lelias of her florid French contemporary, and we become aware that in the humdrum years at Coventry, when the surroundings of her own life were arduous and dusty, she felt a longing to spread her wings and fly up and out to some dim Cloud-Cuckoo Land the confines of which were utterly vague to her. The romantic method of Dumas, for instance, and even of Walter Scott, appealed to her as a mode of escaping to dreamland from the flatness and vulgarity of life under the "miserable reign of Mammon."

Aspects and Impressions

But she could not achieve such flights; her literary character was of a totally different formation. What was fabulous, what was artificial, did not so much strike her with disgust as render her paralysed. Her only escape from mediocrity, she found, was to give a philosophical interest to common themes. In consequence, as she advanced in life, and came more under the influence of George Henry Lewes, she became less and less well disposed towards the French fiction of her day, rejecting even Balzac, to whom she seems, strangely enough, to have preferred Lessing. That Lessing and Balzac should be names pronounced in relation itself throws a light on the temper of the speaker.

Most novelists seem to have begun to tell stories almost as early as musicians begin to trifle with the piano. The child keeps other children awake, after nurse has gone about her business, by reeling off inventions in the dark. But George Eliot showed, so far as records inform us, no such aptitude in infancy or even in early youth. The history of her start as a novel-writer is worthy of study. It appears that it was not until the autumn of 1856 that she, "in a dreamy mood," fancied herself writing a story. This was, I gather, immediately on her return from Germany, where she had been touring about with Lewes, with whom she had now been living for two years. Lewes said to her, "You have wit, description, and philosophy—those go a good way towards the production of a novel," and he encouraged her to write about the virtues and vices of the clergy, as she had observed them at Griff and at Coventry. *Amos Barton* was the immediate result, and the stately line of stories which was to close in *Daniel Deronda* twenty years later was started on its brilliant career. But what of the author? She was a storm-tried matron of thirty-seven, who had sub-edited the *Westminster Review,* who had spent years in translating Strauss's *Life of Jesus* and had sunk exhausted in a still more strenuous wrestling with the *Tractatus Theologico-Politicus* of Spinoza, who had worked with Delarive at Experimental Physics in Geneva, and who had censured,

6

George Eliot

as superficial, John Stuart Mill's treatment of Whewell's *Moral Philosophy*. This heavily-built Miss Marian Evans, now dubiously known as Mrs. Lewes, whose features at that time are familiar to us by the admirable paintings and drawings of Sir Frederick Burton, was in training to be a social reformer, a moral philosopher, an apostle of the creed of Christendom, an anti-theological professor, anything in the world rather than a writer of idle tales.

But the tales proved to be a hundredfold more attractive to the general public than articles upon taxation or translations from German sceptics. We all must allow that at last, however tardily and surprisingly, George Eliot had discovered her true vocation. Let us consider in what capacity she entered this field of fiction. She entered it as an observer of life more diligent and more meticulous perhaps than any other living person. She entered it also with a store of emotional experience and with a richness of moral sensibility which were almost as unique. She had strong ethical prejudices, and a wealth of recollected examples by which she could justify them. Her memory was accurate, minute, and well arranged, and she had always enjoyed retrospection and encouraged herself in the cultivation of it. She was very sympathetic, very tolerant, and although she had lived in the very Temple of Priggishness with her Brays and her Hennells and her Sibrees, she remained singularly simple and unaffected. Rather sad, one pictures her in 1856, rather dreamy, burdened with an excess of purely intellectual preoccupation, wandering over Europe consumed by a constant, but unconfessed, nostalgia for her own country, coming back to it with a sense that the Avon was lovelier than the Arno. Suddenly, in that "dreamy mood," there comes over her a desire to build up again the homes of her childhood, to forget all about Rousseau and experimental physics, and to reconstruct the "dear old quaintnesses" of the Arbury of twenty-five years before.

If we wish to see what it was which this mature philosopher and earnest critic of behaviour had to pro-

7

Aspects and Impressions

duce for the surprise of her readers, we may examine the description of the farm at Donnithorne in *Adam Bede*. The solemn lady, who might seem such a terror to ill-doers, had yet a packet of the most delicious fondants in the pocket of her bombazine gown. The names of these sweetmeats, which were of a flavour and a texture delicious to the tongue, might be Mrs. Poyser or Lizzie Jerome or the sisters Dodson, but they all came from the Warwick-shire factory at Griff, and they were all manufactured with the sugar and spice of memory. So long as George Eliot lived in the past, and extracted her honey from those wonderful cottage gardens which fill her early pages with their colour and their odour, the solidity and weight of her intellectual methods in other fields did not interfere, or interfered in a negligible way, with the power and intensity of the entertainment she offered. We could wish for nothing better. English literature has, of their own class, nothing better to offer than certain chapters of *Adam Bede* or than the beginning of *The Mill on the Floss*.

But, from the first, if we now examine coldly and in-quisitively, there was a moth sleeping in George Eliot's rich attire. This moth was pedantry, the result, doubtless, of too much erudition encouraging a natural tendency in her mind, which as we have seen was acquisitive rather than inventive. It was unfortunate for her genius that after her early enthusiasm for French culture she turned to Germany and became, in measure, like so many power-ful minds of her generation, Teutonized. This fostered the very tendencies which it was desirable to eradicate. One can but speculate what would have been the result on her genius of a little more Paris and a little less Berlin. Her most successful immediate rival in France was Octave Feuillet; the *Scenes of Clerical Life* answer in time to *Le Roman d'un Jeune Homme Pauvre*, and *Monsieur de Camors* to *Felix Holt*. There could not be a stronger or more instructive contrast than between the elegant fairy-land of the one and the robust realism of the other. But our admirable pastoral writer, whose inward eye was stored with the harmonies and humours of Shakespeare's

George Eliot

country, was not content with her mastery of the past. She looked forward to a literature of the future. She trusted to her brain rather than to those tired servants, her senses, and more and more her soul was invaded by the ambition to invent a new thing, the scientific novel, dealing with the growth of institutions and the analysis of individual character.

The critics of her own time were satisfied that she had done this, and that she had founded the psychological novel. There was much to be said in favour of such an opinion. In the later books it is an undeniable fact that George Eliot displays a certain sense of the inevitable progress of life which was new. It may seem paradoxical to see the peculiar characteristics of Zola or of Mr. George Moore in *Middlemarch,* but there is much to be said for the view that George Eliot was the direct forerunner of those naturalistic novelists. Like them, she sees life as an organism, or even as a progress. George Eliot in her contemplation of the human beings she invents is a traveller, who is provided with a map. No Norman church or ivied ruin takes her by surprise, because she has seen that it was bound to come, and recognizes it when it does come. Death, the final railway station, is ever in her mind; she sees it on her map, and gathers her property around her to be ready when the train shall stop. This psychological clairvoyance gives her a great power when she does not abuse it, but unfortunately from the very first there was in her a tendency, partly consequent on her mental training, but also not a little on her natural constitution, to dwell in a hard and pedagogic manner on it. She was not content to please, she must explain and teach as well.

Her comparative failure to please made its definite appearance first in the laboured and overcharged romance of *Romola.* But a careful reader will detect it in her earliest writings. Quite early in *Amos Barton,* for instance, when Mrs. Hackit observes of the local colliers that they "passed their time in doing nothing but swilling ale and smoking, like the beasts that perish," the author immediately spoils

9

this delightful remark by explaining, like a schoolmaster, that Mrs. Hackit was "speaking, we may presume, in a remotely analogical sense." The laughter dies upon our lips. Useless pedantry of this kind spoils many a happy touch of humour, Mrs. Poyser alone perhaps having wholly escaped from it. It would be entirely unjust to accuse George Eliot, at all events until near the end of her life, of intellectual pride. She was, on the contrary, of a very humble spirit, timorous and susceptible of discouragement. But her humility made her work all the harder at her task of subtle philosophical analysis. It would have been far better for her if she had possessed less of the tenacity of Herbert Spencer and more of the recklessness of George Sand. An amusing but painful example of her Sisyphus temper, always rolling the stone uphill with groans and sweat, is to be found in her own account of the way she "crammed up " for the composition of *Romola.* She tells us of the wasting toil with which she worked up innumerable facts about Florence, and in particular how she laboured long over the terrible question whether Easter could have been "retarded " in the year 1492. On this, Sir Leslie Stephen—one of her best critics, and one of the most indulgent—aptly queries, "What would have become of *Ivanhoe* if Scott had bothered himself about the possible retardation of Easter? The answer, indeed, is obvious, that *Ivanhoe* would not have been written."

The effect of all this on George Eliot's achievement was what must always occur when an intellect which is purely acquisitive and distributive insists on doing work that is appropriate only to imagination. If we read very carefully the scene preceding Savonarola's sermon to the Dominicans at San Marco, we perceive that it is built up almost in Flaubert's manner, but without Flaubert's magic, touch by touch, out of books. The author does not see what she describes in a sort of luminous hallucination, but she dresses up in language of her own what she has carefully read in Burlamacchi or in Villari. The most conscientious labour, expended by the most powerful brain, is incapable

George Eliot

of producing an illusion of life by these means. George Eliot may even possibly have been conscious of this, for she speaks again and again, not of writing with ecstasy of tears and laughter, as Dickens did, but of falling into "a state of so much wretchedness in attempting to concentrate my thoughts on the construction of my novel" that nothing but a tremendous and sustained effort of the will carried her on at all. In this vain and terrible wrestling with incongruous elements she wore out her strength and her joy, and it is heart-rending to watch so noble a genius and so lofty a character as hers wasted in the whirlpool. One fears that a sense of obscure failure added to her tortures, and one is tempted to see a touch of autobiography in the melancholy of Mrs. Transome (in *Felix Holt*), of whom we are told that "her knowledge and accomplishments had become as valueless as old-fashioned stucco ornaments, of which the substance was never worth anything, while the form is no longer to the taste of any living mortal."

The notion that George Eliot was herself, in spite of all the laudation showered upon her, consciously in want of some element essential for her success is supported by the very curious fact that from 1864 to 1869, that is to say through nearly one-quarter of her whole literary career, she devoted herself entirely to various experiments in verse. She was so preternaturally intelligent that there is nothing unlikely in the supposition that she realized what was her chief want as a writer of imaginative prose. She claims, and she will always be justified in claiming, a place in the splendid roll of prominent English writers. But she holds it in spite of a certain drawback which forbids her from ever appearing in the front rank as a great writer. Her prose has fine qualities of force and wit, it is pictorial and persuasive, but it misses one prime but rather subtle merit, it never sings. The masters of the finest English are those who have received the admonition *Cantate Domino!* They sing a new song unto the Lord. Among George Eliot's prose contemporaries there were several who obeyed this command. Ruskin, for instance, above all the Victorian prose-writers, shouts like the morning-star. It is the peculiar gift of all great prosaists. Take so rough an executant as Hazlitt : "Harmer Hill stooped with all its pines, to listen to a poet, as he passed!" That is the chanting faculty in prose, which all the greatest men possess; but George Eliot has no trace of it, except sometimes, faintly, in the sheer fun of her peasants' conversation. I do not question that she felt the lack herself, and that it was this which, subconsciously, led her to make a profound study of the art of verse.

She hoped, at the age of forty-four, to hammer herself into poetry by dint of sheer labour and will-power. She read the great masters, and she analysed them in the light of prosodical manuals. In 1871 she told Tennyson that Professor Sylvester's "laws for verse-making had been useful to her." Tennyson replied, "I can't understand that," and no wonder. Sylvester was a facetious mathematician who undertook to teach the art of poetry in so many lessons. George Eliot humbly working away at Sylvester, and telling Tennyson that she was finding him "useful," and Tennyson, whose melodies pursued him, like bees in pursuit of a bee-master, expressing a gruff good-natured scepticism—what a picture it raises! But George Eliot persisted, with that astounding firmness of application which she had, and she produced quite a large body of various verse. She wrote a Comtist tragedy, *The Spanish Gypsy,* of which I must speak softly, since, omnivorous as I am, I have never been able to swallow it. But she wrote many other things, epics and sonnets and dialogues and the rest of them, which are not so hard to read. She actually printed privately for her friends two little garlands, *Agatha* (1868) and *Brother and Sister* (1869), which are the only "rare issues" of hers sought after by collectors, for she was not given to bibliographical curiosity. These verses and many others she polished and re-wrote with untiring assiduity, and in 1874 she published a substantial volume of them. I have been reading them over again, in the intense wish to be pleased with them, but it is impossible—the root of the matter is not in them.

George Eliot

There is an *Arion*, which is stately in the manner of Marvell. The end of this lyric is tense and decisive, but there is the radical absence of song. George Eliot admired Wordsworth very much : occasionally she reproduces very closely the duller parts of *The Excursion*. In the long piece of blank verse called *A College Breakfast Party*, which she wrote in 1874, almost all Tennyson's faults are reconstructed on the plan of the Chinese tailor who carefully imitates the rents in the English coat he is to copy. There is a Goethe-like poem, of a gnomic order, called *Self and Life*, stuffed with valuable thoughts as a turkey is stuffed with chestnuts.

And it is all so earnest and so intellectual, and it does so much credit to Sylvester. After long consideration, I have come to the conclusion that the following sonnet, from *Brother and Sister*, is the best piece of sustained poetry that George Eliot achieved. It deals with the pathetic and beautiful relations which existed between her and her elder brother Isaac, the Tom Tulliver of *The Mill on the Floss*:

> His sorrow was my sorrow, and his joy
>   Sent little leaps and laughs through all my frame;
> My doll seemed lifeless, and no girlish toy
>   Had any reason when my brother came.
> I knelt with him at marbles, marked his fling,
>   Cut the ringed stem and made the apple drop,
> Or watched him winding close the spiral string
>   That looped the orbits of the humming-top.
> Grasped by such fellowship my vagrant thought
>   Ceased with dream-fruit dream-wishes to fulfil;
> My aëry-picturing fantasy was taught
>   Subjection to the harder, truer skill
> That seeks with deeds to grave a thought-tracked line,
> And by "What is" "What will be" to define.

How near this is to true poetry, and yet how many miles away !

At last George Eliot seems to have felt that she could never hope, with all her intellect, to catch the unconsidered music which God lavishes on the idle linnet and the frivolous chaffinch. She returned to her own strenuous business of building up the psychological novel. She wrote *Middlemarch*, which appeared periodically throughout 1872 and as a book early the following year. It was received with great enthusiasm, as marking the return of a popular favourite who had been absent for several years. *Middlemarch* is the history of three parallel lives of women, who "with dim lights and tangled circumstances tried to shape their thought and deed in noble agreement," although "to common eyes their struggles seemed mere inconsistency and formlessness." The three ineffectual St. Theresas, as their creator conceived them, were Dorothea, Rosamond, and Mary, and they "shaped the thought and deed " of Casaubon and Ladislaw and Fred Vincy. *Middlemarch* is constructed with unfailing power, and the picture of commonplace English country life which it gives is vivacious after a mechanical fashion, but all the charm of the early stories has evaporated, and has left behind it merely a residuum of unimaginative satire. The novel is a very remarkable instance of elaborate mental resources misapplied, and genius revolving, with tremendous machinery, like some great water-wheel, while no water is flowing underneath it.

When a realist loses hold on reality all is lost, and I for one can find not a word to say in favour of *Daniel Deronda,* her next and last novel, which came out, with popularity at first more wonderful than ever, in 1876. But her inner circle of admirers was beginning to ask one another uneasily whether her method was not now too calculated, her effects too plainly premeditated. The intensity of her early works was gone. Readers began to resent her pedantry, her elaboration of allusions, her loss of simplicity. They missed the vivid rural scenes and the flashes of delicious humour which had starred the serious pages of *Adam Bede* and *The Mill* like the lemon-yellow pansies and potentillas on a dark Welsh moor. They regretted the ease of the conversation in her early books, where it had always been natural, lively, and brief; it was

George Eliot

now heavy and doctrinaire. Tennyson rebelled against the pompousness, and said, in his blunt way, that Jane Austen knew her business better, a courageous thing to say in Victorian circles fifty years ago. Then came *Theophrastus Such,* a collection of cumbrous and didactic essays which defy perusal; and finally, soon after her death, her *Correspondence,* a terrible disappointment to all her admirers, and a blow from which even the worship of Lord Acton never recovered. Of George Eliot might have been repeated Swift's epitaph on Sir John Vanbrugh :

> Lie heavy on him, earth, for he
> Laid many a heavy load on thee.

It was the fatal error of George Eliot, so admirable, so elevated, so disinterested, that for the last ten years of her brief literary life she did practically nothing but lay heavy loads on literature.

On the whole, then, it is not possible to regard the place which George Eliot holds in English literature as so prominent a one as was rather rashly awarded her by her infatuated contemporaries. It is the inevitable result of "tall talk" about likeness to Dante and Goethe that the figure so unduly magnified fails to support such comparisons when the perspective is lengthened. George Eliot is unduly neglected now, but it is the revenge of time on her for the praise expended on her works in her lifetime. Another matter which militates against her fame to-day is her strenuous solemnity. One of the philosophers who knelt at the footsteps of her throne said that she was "the emblem of a generation distracted between the intense need of believing and the difficulty of belief." Well, we happen to live, fortunately or unfortunately for ourselves, in a generation which is "distracted" by quite other problems, and we are sheep that look up to George Eliot and are not fed by her ponderous moral aphorisms and didactic ethical influence. Perhaps another generation will follow us which will be more patient, and students yet unborn will read her gladly. Let us never forget, however, that she worked with all her heart in a spirit of perfect honesty, that she brought a vast intelligence to the service of literature, and that she aimed from first to last at the loftiest goal of intellectual ambition. Where she failed, it was principally from an inborn lack of charm, not from anything ignoble or impure in her mental disposition. After all, to have added to the slender body of English fiction seven novels the names of which are known to every cultivated person is not to have failed, but to have signally, if only relatively, succeeded.

HENRY JAMES

I

VOLUMINOUS as had been the writings of Henry James since 1875, it was not until he approached the end of his career that he began to throw any light on the practical events and social adventures of his own career. He had occasionally shown that he could turn from the psychology of imaginary characters to the record of real lives without losing any part of his delicate penetration or his charm of portraiture. He had, in particular, written the *Life of Hawthorne* in 1879, between *Daisy Miller* and *An International Episode;* and again in 1903, at the height of his latest period, he had produced a specimen of that period in his elusive and parenthetical but very beautiful so-called *Life of W. W. Story.* But these biographies threw no more light upon his own adventures than did his successive volumes of critical and topographical essays, in which the reader may seek long before he detects the sparkle of a crumb of personal fact. Henry James, at the age of seventy, had not begun to reveal himself behind the mask which spoke in the tones of a world of imaginary characters.

So saying, I do not forget that in the general edition of his collected, or rather selected, novels and tales, published from 1908 onwards, Henry James prefixed to each volume an introduction which assumed to be wholly biographical. He yielded, he said, "to the pleasure of placing on record the circumstances" in which each successive tale was written. I well recollect the terms in which he spoke of these prefaces before he began to write them. They were to be full and confidential, they were to throw to the winds all restraints of conventional reticence, they

Aspects and Impressions

were to take us, with eyes unbandaged, into the inmost sanctum of his soul. They appeared at last, in small print, and they were extremely extensive, but truth obliges me to say that I found them highly disappointing. Constitutionally fitted to take pleasure in the accent of almost everything that Henry James ever wrote, I have to confess that these prefaces constantly baffle my eagerness. Not for a moment would I deny that they throw interesting light on the technical craft of a self-respecting novelist, but they are dry, remote, and impersonal to a strange degree. It is as though the author felt a burning desire to confide in the reader, whom he positively button-holes in the endeavour, but that the experience itself evades him, fails to find expression, and falls stillborn, while other matters, less personal and less important, press in and take their place against the author's wish. Henry James proposed, in each instance, to disclose "the contributive value of the accessory facts in a given artistic case." This is, indeed, what we require in the history or the autobiography of an artist, whether painter or musician or man of letters. But this includes the production of anecdotes, of salient facts, of direct historical statements, which Henry James seemed in 1908 to be completely incapacitated from giving, so that really, in the introductions to some of these novels in the Collected Edition, it is difficult to know what the beloved novelist is endeavouring to divulge. He becomes almost chimæra bombinating in a vacuum.

Had we lost him soon after the appearance of the latest of these prefaces—that prefixed to *The Golden Bowl,* in which the effort to reveal something which is not revealed amounts almost to an agony—it would have been impossible to reconstruct the life of Henry James by the closest examination of his published writings. Ingenious commentators would have pieced together conjectures from such tales as *The Altar of the Dead* and *The Lesson of the Master,* and have insisted, more or less plausibly, on their accordance with what the author *must* have thought or done, endured or attempted. But, after all, these would have been "conjectures," not more definitely based than

Henry James

what bold spirits use when they construct lives of Shakespeare, or, for that matter, of Homer. Fortunately, in 1913, the desire to place some particulars of the career of his marvellous brother William in the setting of his "immediate native and domestic air," led Henry James to contemplate, with minuteness, the fading memories of his own childhood. Starting with a biographical study of William James, he found it impossible to treat the family development at all adequately without extending the survey to his own growth as well, and thus, at the age of seventy, Henry became for the first time, and almost unconsciously, an autobiographer.

He had completed two large volumes of *Memories,* and was deep in a third, when death took him from us. *A Small Boy and Others* deals with such extreme discursiveness as is suitable in a collection of the fleeting impressions of infancy, from his birth in 1843 to his all but fatal attack of typhus fever at Boulogne-sur-Mer in (perhaps) 1857. I say "perhaps" because the wanton evasion of any sort of help in the way of dates is characteristic of the narrative, as it would be of childish memories. The next instalment was *Notes of a Son and Brother,* which opens in 1860, a doubtful period of three years being leaped over lightly, and closes—as I guess from an allusion to George Eliot's *Spanish Gypsy*—in 1868. The third instalment, dictated in the autumn of 1914 and laid aside unfinished, is the posthumous *The Middle Years,* faultlessly edited by the piety of Mr. Percy Lubbock in 1917. Here the tale is taken up in 1869, and is occupied, without much attempt at chronological order, with memories of two years in London. As Henry James did not revise, or perhaps even re-read, these pages, we are free to form our conclusion as to whether he would or would not have vouchsafed to put their disjected parts into some more anatomical order.

Probably he would not have done so. The tendency of his genius had never been, and at the end was less than ever, in the direction of concinnity. He repudiated arrangement, he wilfully neglected the precise adjustment of parts. The three autobiographical volumes will always

Aspects and Impressions

be documents precious in the eyes of his admirers. They are full of beauty and nobility, they exhibit with delicacy, and sometimes even with splendour, the qualities of his character. But it would be absurd to speak of them as easy to read, or as fulfilling what is demanded from an ordinary biographer. They have the tone of Veronese, but nothing of his definition. A broad canvas is spread before us, containing many figures in social conjuncture. But the plot, the single "story" which is being told, is drowned in misty radiance. Out of this *chiaroscuro* there leap suddenly to our vision a sumptuous head and throat, a handful of roses, the glitter of a satin sleeve, but it is only when we shut our eyes and think over what we have looked at that any coherent plan is revealed to us, or that we detect any species of composition. It is a case which calls for editorial help, and I hope that when the three fragments of autobiography are reprinted as a single composition, no prudery of hesitation to touch the sacred ark will prevent the editor from prefixing a skeleton chronicle of actual dates and facts. It will take nothing from the dignity of the luminous reveries in their original shape.

Such a skeleton will tell us that Henry James was born at 2 Washington Place, New York, on April 15th, 1843, and that he was the second child of his parents, the elder by one year being William, who grew up to be the most eminent philosopher whom America has produced. Their father, Henry James the elder, was himself a philosopher, whose ideas, which the younger Henry frankly admitted to be beyond his grasp, were expounded by William James in 1884, in a preface to their father's posthumous papers. Henry was only one year old when the family paid a long visit to Paris, but his earliest recollections were of Albany, whence the Jameses migrated to New York until 1855. They then transferred their home to Europe for three years, during which time the child Henry imbibed what he afterwards called "the European virus." In 1855 he was sent to Geneva for purposes of education, which were soon abandoned, and the whole family began an aimless wander-

Henry James

ing through London, Paris, Boulogne-sur-Mer, Newport, Geneva, and America again, nothing but the Civil War sufficing to root this fugitive household in one abiding home.

Henry James's health forced him to be a spectator of the war, in which his younger brothers fought. He went to Harvard in 1862 to study law, but was now beginning to feel a more and more irresistible call to take up letters as a profession, and the Harvard Law School left little or no direct impression upon him. He formed a close and valuable friendship with William Dean Howells, seven years his senior, and the pages of the *Atlantic Monthly,* of which Howells was then assistant editor, were open to him from 1865. He lived for the next four years in very poor health, and with no great encouragement from himself or others, always excepting Howells, at Cambridge, Massachusetts. Early in 1869 he ventured to return to Europe, where he spent fifteen months in elegant but fruitful vagabondage. There was much literary work done, most of which he carefully suppressed in later life. The reader will, however, discover, tucked away in the thirteenth volume of the Collected Edition, a single waif from this rejected epoch, the tale called *A Passionate Pilgrim,* written on his return to America in 1870. This visit to Europe absolutely determined his situation; his arrival in New York stimulated and tortured his nostalgia for the old world, and in May, 1872, he flew back here once more to the European enchantment.

Here, practically, the biographical information respecting Henry James which has hitherto been given to the world ceases, for the fragment of *The Middle Years,* so far as can be gathered, contains few recollections which can be dated later than his thirtieth year. It was said of Marivaux that he cultivated no faculty but that *de ne vivre que pour voir et pour entendre.* In a similar spirit Henry James took up his dwelling in fashionable London lodgings in March, 1869. He had come from America with the settled design of making a profound study of English manners, and there were two aspects of the subject which stood out for him above all others. One of these was the rural beauty of ancient country places, the other was the magnitude—"the inconceivable immensity," as he put it —of London. He told his sister, "The place sits on you, broods on you, stamps on you with the feet of its myriad bipeds and quadrupeds." From his lodgings in Half Moon Street, quiet enough in themselves, he had the turmoil of the West End at his elbow, Piccadilly, Park Lane, St. James's Street, all within the range of a five minutes' stroll. He plunged into the vortex with incredible gusto, "knocking about in a quiet way and deeply enjoying my little adventures." This was his first mature experience of London, of which he remained until the end of his life perhaps the most infatuated student, the most "passionate pilgrim," that America has ever sent us.

But his health was still poor, and for his constitution's sake he went in the summer of 1869 to Great Malvern. He went alone, and it is to be remarked of him that, social as he was, and inclined to a deep indulgence in the company of his friends, his habit of life was always in the main a solitary one. He had no constant associates, and he did not shrink from long periods of isolation, which he spent in reading and writing, but also in a concentrated contemplation of the passing scene, whatever it might be. It was alone that he now made a tour of the principal English cathedral and university towns, expatiating to himself on the perfection of the weather—"the dozen exquisite days of the English year, days stamped with a purity unknown in climates where fine weather is cheap." It was alone that he made acquaintance with Oxford, of which city he became at once the impassioned lover which he continued to be to the end, raving from Boston in 1870 of the supreme gratifications of Oxford as "the most dignified and most educated" of the cradles of our race. It was alone that during these enchanting weeks he made himself acquainted with the unimagined loveliness of English hamlets buried in immemorial leafage and whispered to by meandering rivulets in the warm recesses of antiquity. These, too, found in Henry James a worshipper more

Henry James

ardent, it may almost be averred, than any other who had crossed the Atlantic to their shrine.

Having formed his basis for the main construction of his English studies, Henry James passed over to the Continent, and conducted a similar pilgrimage of entranced obsession through Switzerland and Italy. His wanderings, "rapturous and solitary," were, as in England, hampered by no social engagement; "I see no people to speak of," he wrote, "or for that matter to speak to." He returned to America in April, 1870, at the close of a year which proved critical in his career, and which laid its stamp on the whole of his future work. He had been kindly received in artistic and literary circles in London; he had conversed with Ruskin, with William Morris, with Aubrey de Vere, but it is plain that while he observed the peculiarities of these eminent men with the closest avidity, he made no impression whatever upon them. The time for Henry James to "make an impression" on others was not come yet; he was simply the well-bred, rather shy, young American invalid, with excellent introductions, who crossed the path of English activities, almost without casting a shadow. He had published no book; he had no distinct calling; he was a deprecating and punctilious young stranger from somewhere in Massachusetts, immature-looking for all his seven-and-twenty years.

Some further uneventful seasons, mainly spent in America but diversified by tours in Germany and Italy, bring us to 1875, when Henry James came over from Cambridge with the definite project, at last, of staying in Europe "for good." He took rooms in Paris, at 29 Rue de Luxembourg, and he penetrated easily into the very exclusive literary society which at that time revolved around Flaubert and Edmond de Goncourt. This year in Paris was another highly critical period in Henry James's intellectual history. He was still, at the mature age of thirty-two, almost an amateur in literature, having been content, up to that time, to produce scarcely anything which his mature taste did not afterwards repudiate. *The Passionate Pilgrim* (1870), of which I have spoken above, is the only waif and stray of the pre-1873 years which he has permitted to survive. The first edition of this short story is now not easy of reference, and I have not seen it; the reprint of 1908 is obviously, and is doubtless vigorously, re-handled. Enough, however, remains of what must be original to show that, in a rather crude, and indeed almost hysterical form, the qualities of Henry James's genius were, in 1869, what they continued to be in 1909. He has conquered, however, in *A Passionate Pilgrim*, no command yet over his enthusiasm, his delicate sense of beauty, his apprehension of the exquisite colour of antiquity.

From the French associates of this time he derived practical help in his profession, though without their being aware of what they gave him. He was warmly attracted to Gustave Flaubert, who had just published *La Tentation de St. Antoine*, a dazzled admiration of which was the excuse which threw the young American at the feet of the Rouen giant. This particular admiration dwindled with the passage of time, but Henry James continued faithful to the author of *Madame Bovary*. It was Turgenev who introduced him to Flaubert, from whom he passed to Guy de Maupassant, then an athlete of four-and-twenty, and still scintillating in that blaze of juvenile virility which always fascinated Henry James. In the train of Edmond de Goncourt came Zola, vociferous over his late tribulation of having *L'Assommoir* stopped in its serial issue; Alphonse Daudet, whose recent *Jack* was exercising over tens of thousands of readers the tyranny of tears; and François Coppée, the almost exact coeval of Henry James, and now author of a *Luthier de Crémone*, which had placed him high among French poets. That the young American, with no apparent claim to attention except the laborious perfection of his French speech, was welcomed and ultimately received on terms of intimacy in this the most exclusive of European intellectual circles is curious. Henry James was accustomed to deprecate the notion that these Frenchmen took the least interest in him: "they have never read a line of me, they have never even per-

suaded themselves that there was a line of me which anyone could read," he once said to me. How should they,
poor charming creatures, in their self-sufficing Latin intensity, know what or whether some barbarian had remotely
"written"? But this does not end the marvel, because,
read or not read, there was Henry James among them,
affectionately welcomed, talked to familiarly about "technique," and even about "sales," like a fellow-craftsman.
There must evidently have developed by this time something modestly "impressive" about him, and I cannot
doubt that these Parisian masters of language more or less
dimly divined that he too was, in some medium not by
them to be penetrated, a master.

After this fruitful year in Paris, the first result of which
was the publication in London of his earliest surviving
novel, *Roderick Hudson*, and the completion of *The
American*, Henry James left his "glittering, charming,
civilized Paris" and settled in London. He submitted
himself, as he wrote to his brother William in 1878, "without reserve to that Londonizing process of which the effect
is to convince you that, having lived here, you may, if
need be, abjure civilization and bury yourself in the country, but may not, in pursuit of civilization, live in any
smaller town." He plunged deeply into the study of
London, externally and socially, and into the production
of literature, in which he was now as steadily active as he
was elegantly proficient. These novels of his earliest
period have neither the profundity nor the originality of
those of his middle and final periods, but they have an
exquisite freshness of their own, and a workmanship the
lucidity and logic of which he owed in no small measure
to his conversations with Daudet and Maupassant, and to
his, at that time almost exclusive, reading of the finest
French fiction. He published *The American* in 1877, *The
Europeans* and *Daisy Miller* in 1878, and *An International
Episode* in 1879. He might advance in stature and
breadth; he might come to disdain the exiguous beauty of
these comparatively juvenile books, but now at all events
were clearly revealed all the qualities which were to

develop later, and to make Henry James unique among writers of Anglo-Saxon race.

His welcome into English society was remarkable if we reflect that he seemed to have little to give in return for what it offered except his social adaptability, his pleasant and still formal amenity, and his admirable capacity for listening. It cannot be repeated too clearly that the Henry James of those early days had very little of the impressiveness of his later manner. He went everywhere, sedately, watchfully, graciously, but never prominently. In the winter of 1878-79 it is recorded that he dined out in London 107 times, but it is highly questionable whether this amazing assiduity at the best dinner-tables will be found to have impressed itself on any Greville or Crabb Robinson who was taking notes at the time. He was strenuously living up to his standard, "my charming little standard of wit, of grace, of good manners, of vivacity, of urbanity, of intelligence, of what makes an easy and natural style of intercourse." He was watching the rather gross and unironic, but honest and vigorous, English upper-middle-class of that day with mingled feelings, in which curiosity and a sort of remote sympathy took a main part. At 107 London dinners he observed the ever-shifting pieces of the general kaleidoscope with tremendous acuteness, and although he thought their reds and yellows would have been improved by a slight infusion of the Florentine harmony, on the whole he was never weary of watching their evolutions. In this way the years slipped by, while he made a thousand acquaintances and a dozen durable friendships. It is a matter of pride and happiness to me that I am able to touch on one of the latter.

It is often curiously difficult for intimate friends, who have the impression in later years that they must always have known one another, to recall the occasion and the place where they first met. That was the case with Henry James and me. Several times we languidly tried to recover those particulars, but without success. I think, however, that it was at some dinner-party that we first met, and as the incident is dubiously connected with the publication

Henry James

of the *Hawthorne* in 1879, and with Mr. (now Lord) Morley, whom we both frequently saw at that epoch, I am pretty sure that the event took place early in 1880. The acquaintance, however, did not "ripen," as people say, until the summer of 1882, when in connexion with an article on the drawings of George Du Maurier, which I was anxious Henry James should write—having heard him express himself with high enthusiasm regarding these works of art—he invited me to go to see him and to talk over the project. I found him, one sunshiny afternoon, in his lodgings on the first floor of No. 3 Bolton Street, at the Piccadilly end of the street, where the houses look askew into Green Park. Here he had been living ever since he came over from France in 1876, and the situation was eminently characteristic of the impassioned student of London life and haunter of London society which he had now become.

Stretched on the sofa and apologizing for not rising to greet me, his appearance gave me a little shock, for I had not thought of him as an invalid. He hurriedly and rather evasively declared that he was not that, but that a muscular weakness of his spine obliged him, as he said, "to assume the horizontal posture" during some hours of every day in order to bear the almost unbroken routine of evening engagements. I think that this weakness gradually passed away, but certainly for many years it handicapped his activity. I recall his appearance, seen then for the first time by daylight; there was something shadowy about it, the face framed in dark brown hair cut short in the Paris fashion, and in equally dark beard, rather loose and "fluffy." He was in deep mourning, his mother having died five or six months earlier, and he himself having but recently returned from a melancholy visit to America, where he had unwillingly left his father, who seemed far from well. His manner was grave, extremely courteous, but a little formal and frightened, which seemed strange in a man living in constant communication with the world. Our business regarding Du Maurier was soon concluded, and James talked with increasing ease, but always with a

27

Aspects and Impressions

punctilious hesitancy, about Paris, where he seemed, to my dazzlement, to know even a larger number of persons of distinction than he did in London.

He promised, before I left, to return my visit, but news of the alarming illness of his father called him suddenly to America. He wrote to me from Boston in April, 1883, but he did not return to London until the autumn of that year. Our intercourse was then resumed, and, immediately, on the familiar footing which it preserved, without an hour's abatement, until the sad moment of his fatal illness. When he returned to Bolton Street—this was in August, 1883—he had broken all the ties which held him to residence in America, a country which, as it turned out, he was not destined to revisit for more than twenty years. By this means Henry James became a homeless man in a peculiar sense, for he continued to be looked upon as a foreigner in London, while he seemed to have lost citizenship in the United States. It was a little later than this that that somewhat acidulated patriot, Colonel Higginson, in reply to someone who said that Henry James was a cosmopolitan, remarked, "Hardly! for a cosmopolitan is at home even in his own country!" This condition made James, although superficially gregarious, essentially isolated, and though his books were numerous and were greatly admired, they were tacitly ignored alike in summaries of English and of American current literature. There was no escape from this dilemma. Henry James was equally determined not to lay down his American birthright and not to reside in America. Every year of his exile, therefore, emphasized the fact of his separation from all other Anglo-Saxons, and he endured, in the world of letters, the singular fate of being a man without a country.

The collection of his private letters, therefore, which has just been published under the sympathetic editorship of Mr. Percy Lubbock, reveals the adventures of an author who, long excluded from two literatures, is now eagerly claimed by both of them, and it displays those movements of a character of great energy and singular originality which circumstances have hitherto concealed from curiosity. There was very little on the surface of his existence to bear evidence to the passionate intensity of the stream beneath. This those who have had the privilege of seeing his letters know is marvellously revealed in his private correspondence. A certain change in his life was brought about by the arrival in 1885 of his sister Alice, who, in now confirmed ill-health, was persuaded to make Bournemouth and afterwards Leamington her home. He could not share her life, but at all events he could assiduously diversify it by his visits, and Bournemouth had a second attraction for him in the presence of Robert Louis Stevenson, with whom he had by this time formed one of the closest of his friendships. Stevenson's side of the correspondence has long been known, and it is one of the main attractions which Mr. Lubbock held out to his readers that Henry James's letters to Stevenson are now published. No episode of the literary history of the time is more fascinating than the interchange of feeling between these two great artists. The death of Stevenson, nine years later than their first meeting, though long anticipated, fell upon Henry James with a shock which he found at first scarcely endurable. For a long time afterwards he could not bring himself to mention the name of R. L. S. without a distressing agitation.

In 1886 the publication of *The Bostonians,* a novel which showed an advance in direct or, as it was then styled, "realistic" painting of modern society, increased the cleft which now divided him from his native country, for *The Bostonians* was angrily regarded as satirizing not merely certain types, but certain recognizable figures in Massachusetts, and that with a suggestive daring which was unusual. Henry James, intent upon making a vivid picture, and already perhaps a little out of touch with American sentiment, was indignant at the reception of this book, which he ultimately, to my great disappointment, omitted from his Collected Edition, for reasons which he gave in a long letter to myself. Hence, as his works now appear, *The Princess Casamassima,* of 1886, an essentially

Aspects and Impressions

London adventure story, takes its place as the earliest of the novels of his second period, although preceded by admirable short tales in that manner, the most characteristic of which is doubtless *The Author of Beltraffio* (1885). This exemplifies the custom he had now adopted of seizing an incident reported to him, often a very slight and bald affair, and weaving round it a thick and glittering web of silken fancy, just as the worm winds round the unsightly chrysalis its graceful robe of gold. I speak of *The Author of Beltraffio*, and after thirty-five years I may confess that this extraordinarily vivid story was woven around a dark incident in the private life of an eminent author known to us both, which I, having told Henry James in a moment of levity, was presently horrified and even sensibly alarmed to see thus pinnacled in the broad light of day.

After exhausting at last the not very shining amenities of his lodgings in Bolton Street, where all was old and dingy, he went westward in 1886 into Kensington, and settled in a flat which was both new and bright, at 34 De Vere Gardens, Kensington, where he began a novel called *The Tragic Muse*, on which he expended an immense amount of pains. He was greatly wearied by the effort, and not entirely satisfied with the result. He determined, as he said, "to do nothing but short lengths" for the future, and he devoted himself to the execution of *contes*. But even the art of the short story presently yielded to a new and, it must be confessed, a deleterious fascination, that of the stage. He was disappointed—he made no secret to his friends of his disillusion—in the commercial success of his novels, which was inadequate to his needs. I believe that he greatly over-estimated these needs, and that at no time he was really pressed by the want of money. But he thought that he was, and in his anxiety he turned to the theatre as a market in which to earn a fortune. Little has hitherto been revealed with regard to this "sawdust and orange-peel phase" (as he called it) in Henry James's career, but it cannot be ignored any longer. The memories of his intimate friends are stored with its incidents, his letters will be found to be full of it.

Henry James

Henry James wrote, between 1889 and 1894, seven or eight plays, on each of which he expended an infinitude of pains and mental distress. At the end of this period, unwillingly persuaded at last that all his agony was in vain, and that he could never secure fame and fortune, or even a patient hearing from the theatre-going public by his dramatic work, he abandoned the hopeless struggle. He was by temperament little fitted to endure the disappointments and delays which must always attend the course of a dramatist who has not conquered a position which enables him to browbeat the tyrants behind the stage. Henry James was punctilious, ceremonious, and precise; it is not to be denied that he was apt to be hasty in taking offence, and not very ready to overlook an impertinence. The whole existence of the actor is lax and casual; the manager is the capricious leader of an irresponsible band of egotists. Henry James lost no occasion of dwelling, in private conversation, on this aspect of an amiable and entertaining profession. He was not prepared to accept young actresses at their own valuation, and the happy-go-lucky democracy of the "mimes," as he bracketed both sexes, irritated him to the verge of frenzy.

It was, however, with a determination to curb his impatience, and with a conviction that he could submit his idiosyncrasies to what he called the "passionate economy" of play-writing, that he began, in 1889, to dedicate himself to the drama, excluding for the time being all other considerations. He went over to Paris in the winter of that year, largely to talk over the stage with Alphonse Daudet and Edmond de Goncourt, and he returned to put the finishing touches on *The American*, a dramatic version of one of his earliest novels. He finished this play at the Palazzo Barbaro, the beautiful home of his friends, the Daniel Curtises, in Venice, in June, 1890, thereupon taking a long holiday, one of the latest of his extended Italian tours, through Venetia and Tuscany. Edward Compton had by this time accepted *The American*, being attracted by his own chances in the part of Christopher Newman. When Henry James reappeared in London, and particularly when the rehearsals began, we all noticed how deeply the theatrical virus had penetrated his nature. His excitement swelled until the evening of January 3rd, 1891, when *The American* was acted at Southport by Compton's company in anticipation of its appearance in London. Henry James was kind enough to wish me to go down on this occasion with him to Southport, but it was not possible. On the afternoon of the ordeal he wrote to me from the local hotel : "After eleven o'clock to-night I *may* be the world's—you know—and I may be the undertaker's. I count upon you and your wife both to spend this evening in fasting, silence, and supplication. I will send you a word in the morning, a wire if I can." He was "so nervous that I miswrite and misspell."

The result, in the provinces, of this first experiment was not decisive. It is true that he told Robert Louis Stevenson that he was enjoying a success which made him blush. But the final result in London, where *The American* was not played until September, 1891, was only partly encouraging. Henry James was now cast down as unreasonably as he had been uplifted. He told me that "the strain, the anxiety, the peculiar form and colour of the ordeal (not to be divined in the least in advance) " had "sickened him to *death.*" He used language of the most picturesque extravagance about the "purgatory " of the performances, which ran at the Opera Comique for two months. There was nothing in the mediocre fortunes of this play to decide the questions whether Henry James was or was not justified in abandoning all other forms of art for the drama. We endeavoured to persuade him that, on the whole, he was not justified, but he swept our arguments aside, and he devoted himself wholly to the infatuation of his sterile task.

The American had been dramatized from a published novel. Henry James now thought that he should do better with original plots, and he wrote two comedies, the one named *Tenants* and the other *Disengaged,* of each of which he formed high expectations. But, although they were submitted to several managers, who gave them their

Henry James

customary loitering and fluctuating attention, they were in every case ultimately refused. Each refusal plunged the dramatist into the lowest pit of furious depression, from which he presently emerged with freshly-kindled hopes. Like the moralist, he never was but always to be blest. *The Album* and *The Reprobate*—there is a melancholy satisfaction in giving life to the mere names of these stillborn children of his brain—started with wild hopes and suffered from the same complete failure to satisfy the caprice of the managers. At the close of 1893, after one of these "sordid developments," he made up his mind to abandon the struggle. But George Alexander promised that, if he would but persevere, he really and truly would produce him infallibly at no distant date, and poor Henry James could not but persevere. "I mean to wage this war ferociously for one year more," and he composed, with infinite agony and deliberation, the comedy of *Guy Domvile*.

The night of January 5th, 1895, was the most tragical in Henry James's career. His hopes and fears had been strung up to the most excruciating point, and I think that I have never witnessed such agonies of parturition. *Guy Domvile*—which has never been printed—was a delicate and picturesque play, of which the only disadvantage that I could discover was that instead of having a last scene which tied up all the threads in a neat conclusion, it left all those threads loose as they would be in life. George Alexander was sanguine of success, and to do Henry James honour such a galaxy of artistic, literary, and scientific celebrity gathered in the stalls of the St. James's Theatre as perhaps were never seen in a London playhouse before or since. Henry James was positively storm-ridden with emotion before the fatal night, and full of fantastic plans. I recall that one was that he should hide in the bar of a little public-house down an alley close to the theatre, whither I should slip forth at the end of the second act and report "how it was going." This was not carried out, and fortunately Henry James resisted the temptation of being present in the theatre during the performance. All seemed

33

Aspects and Impressions

to be going fairly well until the close, when Henry James appeared and was called before the curtain—only to be subjected—to our unspeakable horror and shame—to a storm of hoots and jeers and catcalls from the gallery, answered by loud and sustained applause from the stalls, the whole producing an effect of hell broke loose, in the midst of which the author, as white as chalk, bowed and spread forth deprecating hands and finally vanished. It was said at the time, and confirmed later, that this horrible performance was not intended to humiliate Henry James, but was the result of a cabal against George Alexander.

Early next morning I called at 34 De Vere Gardens, hardly daring to press the bell for fear of the worst of news, so shattered with excitement had the playwright been on the previous evening. I was astonished to find him perfectly calm; he had slept well and was breakfasting with appetite. The theatrical bubble in which he had lived a tormented existence for five years was wholly and finally broken, and he returned, even in that earliest conversation, to the discussion of the work which he had so long and so sadly neglected, the art of direct prose narrative. And now a remarkable thing happened. The discipline of toiling for the caprices of the theatre had amounted, for so redundant an imaginative writer, to the putting on of a mental strait-jacket. He saw now that he need stoop no longer to what he called "a meek and lowly review of the right ways to keep on the right side of a body of people who have paid money to be amused at a particular hour and place." Henry James was not released from this system of vigorous renunciation without a very singular result. To write for the theatre the qualities of brevity and directness, of an elaborate plainness, had been perceived by him to be absolutely necessary, and he had tried to cultivate them with dogged patience for five years. But when he broke with the theatre, the rebound was excessive. I recall his saying to me, after the fiasco of *Guy Domvile*, "At all events, I have escaped for ever from the foul fiend Excision!" He vibrated with the

34

Henry James

sense of release, and he began to enjoy, physically and intellectually, a freedom which had hitherto been foreign to his nature.

II

THE abrupt change in Henry James's outlook on life, which was the result of his violent disillusion with regard to theatrical hopes and ambitions, took the form of a distaste for London and a determination, vague enough at first, to breathe for the future in a home of his own by the sea. He thought of Bournemouth, more definitely of Torquay, but finally his fate was sealed by his being offered, for the early summer months of 1896, a small house on the cliff at Point Hill, Playden, whence he could look down, as from an "eagle's nest," on the exquisite little red-roofed town of Rye and over the wide floor of the marsh of Sussex. When the time came for his being turned out of this retreat, he positively could not face the problem of returning to the breathless heat of London in August, and he secured the Vicarage in the heart of Rye itself for two months more. Here, as earlier at Point Hill, I was his guest, and it was wonderful to observe how his whole moral and intellectual nature seemed to burgeon and expand in the new and delicious liberty of country life. We were incessantly in the open air, on the terrace (for the Vicarage, though musty and dim, possessed, like the fresher Point Hill, a sea-looking terrace), sauntering round the little town, or roving for miles and miles over the illimitable flats, to Winchelsea, to Lydd, to the recesses of Walland Marsh—even, on one peerless occasion, so far afield as to Midley Chapel and the Romneys.

Never had I known Henry James so radiant, so cheerful or so self-assured. During the earlier London years there had hung over him a sort of canopy, a mixture of reserve and deprecation, faintly darkening the fullness of communion with his character; there always had seemed to be something indefinably non-conductive between him and those in whom he had most confidence. While the play-writing fit was on him this had deepened almost into

35

fretfulness; the complete freedom of intercourse which is the charm of friendship had been made more and more difficult by an excess of sensibility. Henry James had become almost what the French call a *buisson d'épines.* It was therefore surprising and highly delightful to find that this cloud had ceased to brood over him, and had floated away, leaving behind it a laughing azure in which quite a new and charming Henry James stood revealed. The summer of 1896, when by a succession of happy chances I was much alone with him at Rye, rests in my recollection as made exquisite by his serene and even playful uniformity of temper, by the removal of everything which had made intercourse occasionally difficult, and by the addition of forms of amenity that had scarcely been foreshadowed. On reflection, however, I find that I am mixing up memories of June at Point Hill and of September at the Vicarage with the final Rye adventure, which must now be chronicled. When he was obliged to turn out of his second refuge, he returned to London, but with an ever-deepening nostalgia for the little Sussex town where he had been happy. In the following summer the voice of Venice called him so loudly that he stayed in London longer than usual, meaning to spend the autumn and winter in Italy. He thought meanwhile of Bournemouth and of Saxmundham. He went on his bicycle round the desolate ghost of Dunwich, but his heart was whispering "Rye" to him all the while. Nothing then seemed available, however, when suddenly the unexpected vacancy of the most eligible residence conceivable settled, in the course of a couple of days, the whole future earthly pilgrimage of Henry James. The huge fact was immediately announced in a letter of September 25th, 1897 :

I am just drawing a long breath from having signed—a few moments since—a most portentous parchment : the lease of a smallish, charming, cheap old house in the country—down at Rye—for 21 years. (It was built about 1705.) It is exactly what I want and secretly and hopelessly coveted (since knowing

Henry James

it) without dreaming it would ever fall. But it *has* fallen—and has a beautiful room for you (the King's Room—George II's —who slept there); together with every promise of yielding me an indispensable retreat from May to October (every year). I hope you are not more sorry to take up the load of life that awaits, these days, the hunch of one's shoulders than I am. You'll ask me what I mean by "life." Come down to Lamb House and I'll tell you.

There were the most delightful possibilities in the property, which included a small garden and lawn, the whole hemmed in by a peaceful old red wall, plentifully tapestried with espaliers. The noble tower of Rye church looked down into it, and Henry James felt that the chimes sounded sweetly to him as he faced his garden in monastic quiet, the little market-town packed tightly about him, yet wholly out of sight.

Meanwhile the intellectual release had been none the less marked than the physical. The earliest result of his final escape from the lures of the Vivian of the stage had been the composition of a novel, *The Spoils of Poynton,* in a manner entirely different from that of his earlier long romances. This was published in 1897, and in the meantime he had set to work on a longer and more ambitious romance, *What Maisie Knew.* In these he began the exercise of what has been called his "later manner," which it would be out of proportion to attempt to define in a study which purports to be biographical rather than critical. It is enough to remind the reader familiar with Henry James's writings that in abandoning the more popular and conventional method of composition he aimed at nothing less than a revolution in the art of the novelist. While thus actively engaged in a new scheme of life, he found it more and more difficult to break "the spell of immobility" which enveloped him. He who had been so ready to start on any call of impulse in any direction found it impossible to bring himself to respond, at Christmas, 1897, to the appeal of Madame Alphonse Daudet to come over to Paris to grace the obsequies of her illustrious husband. The friends—

and the author of *Jack* was the most intimate of James's Parisian acquaintances—had not met after 1895, when Daudet had spent a month in London mainly under the charge of Henry James, since which time the French novelist's life had been sapped and drained from him by a disease the symptoms of which were beginning to be painfully manifest when he was with us in London. The old French friends were now disappearing. Their places in Henry James's affection were partly filled by Paul Bourget and by Maurice Barrès, whose remarkable and rather "gruesome" book, *Les Déracinés*, now supplied James with an endless subject of talk and reflection.

The first novel actually completed at Lamb House was *The Awkward Age,* which was ready for the printers early in 1898. The ecstasy with which he settled down to appreciate his new surroundings is reflected in that novel, where the abode of Mr. Longdon is neither more nor less than a picture of Lamb House. It was a wonderful summer and autumn, and, as Henry James said : "The air of the place thrilled all the while with the bliss of birds, the hum of little lives unseen, and the flicker of white butterflies." The MS. of *The Awkward Age* was no sooner finished than he took up the germ of an incident dimly related to him years before at Addington, by Archbishop Benson, and wove it into *The Turn of the Screw,* a sort of moral (or immoral) ghost story which not a few readers consider to be the most powerful of all his writings, and which others again peculiarly detest. I admit myself to be a hanger-on of the former group, and I have very vivid recollections of the period when *The Turn of the Screw* was being composed. The author discussed it with a freedom not usual with him. I remember that when he had finished it he said to me one day : "I had to correct the proofs of my ghost story last night, and when I had finished them I was so frightened that I was afraid to go upstairs to bed ! "

By the close of 1898 he had got rid of the flat in De Vere Gardens, which had become a mere burden to him, and had taken what he called an "invaluable south-looking,

Henry James

Carlton-Gardens-sweeping bedroom " at the Reform Club in Pall Mall, which served his brief and sudden pilgrimages to town for many seasons. Lamb House, in the course of this year, became his almost exclusive residence, and it is to be noted that at the same time a remarkable change came over the nature of his correspondence. He had been a meticulous but not very inspired letter-writer in early youth; his capacity for epistolary composition and his appetite for it had developed remarkably in the middle years (1882-1890). During the hectic period of his theatrical ambition it had dwindled again. But when he settled finally at Rye, spreading himself in luxurious contentment within the protection of his old brick garden-wall, the pink and purple surface of which stood in his fancy as a sort of bodyguard of security passed down for that particular purpose through mild ages of restfulness, as soon as he sat, with his household gods about him, in the almost cotton-woolly hush of Lamb House, he began to blossom out into a correspondent of a new and splendid class. The finest and most characteristic letters of Henry James start with his fifty-fifth year, and they continue to expand in volume, in richness and in self-revelation almost to the close of his life. On this subject Mr. Percy Lubbock, than whom no one has known better the idiosyncrasies of Henry James, has described his method of correspondence in a passage which could not be bettered:

The rich apologies for silence and backwardness that preface so many of his letters must be interpreted in the light, partly indeed of his natural luxuriance of phraseology, but much more of his generous conception of the humblest correspondent's claim on him for response. He could not answer a brief note of friendliness but with pages of abounding eloquence. He never dealt in the mere small change of intercourse; the postcard and the half-sheet did not exist for him; a few lines of enquiry would bring from him a bulging packet of manuscript, overwhelming in its disproportion. No wonder that with this standard of the meaning of a letter he often groaned under his postal burden. He discharged himself of it, in general, very late at night; the morning's work left

39

him too much exhausted for more composition until then. At midnight he would sit down to his letter-writing and cover sheet after sheet, sometimes for hours, with his dashing and not very readable script. Occasionally he would give up a day to the working off of arrears by dictation, seldom omitting to excuse himself to each correspondent in turn for the infliction of the "fierce legibility" of type.

This amplitude of correspondence was the outcome of an affectionate solicitude for his friends, which led him in another direction, namely, in that of exercising a hospitality towards them for which he had never found an opportunity before. He did not, however, choose to collect anything which might remotely be called "a party"; what he really preferred was the presence of a single friend at a time, of a companion who would look after himself in the morning, and be prepared for a stroll with his host in the afternoon, and for a banquet of untrammelled conversation under the lamp or on the expanse of the lawn after the comfortable descent of nightfall.

His practice in regard to such a visitor was always to descend to the railway station below the town to welcome the guest, who would instantly recognize his remarkable figure hurrying along the platform. Under the large soft hat would be visible the large pale face, anxiously scanning the carriage-windows and breaking into smiles of sunshine when the new-comer was discovered. Welcome was signified by both hands waved aloft, lifting the skirts of the customary cloak, like wings. Then, luggage attended to, and the arm of the guest securely seized, as though even now there might be an attempt at escape, a slow ascent on foot would begin up the steep streets, the last and steepest of all leading to a discreet door which admitted directly to the broad hall of Lamb House. Within were, to right and left, the pleasant old rooms, with low windows opening straight into the garden, which was so sheltered and economized as to seem actually spacious. Further to the left was a lofty detached room, full of books

Henry James

and lights, where in summer Henry James usually wrote, secluded from all possible disturbance. The ascent of arrival from the railway grew to be more and more interesting as time went on, and as the novelist became more and more a familiar and respected citizen, it was much interrupted at last by bows from ladies and salaams from shopkeepers; many little boys and girls, the latter having often curtsied, had to be greeted and sometimes patted on the head. These social movements used to inspire in me the inquiry : "Well, how soon are you to be the Mayor-Elect of Rye? " a pleasantry which was always well received. So obviously did Henry James, in the process of years, become the leading inhabitant that it grew to seem no impossibility. Stranger things had happened! No civic authority would have been more conscientious and few less efficient.

His outward appearance developed in accordance with his moral and intellectual expansion. I have said that in early life Henry James was not "impressive"; as time went on his appearance became, on the contrary, excessively noticeable and arresting. He removed the beard which had long disguised his face, and so revealed the strong lines of mouth and chin, which responded to the majesty of the skull. In the breadth and smoothness of the head—Henry James became almost wholly bald early in life—there was at length something sacerdotal. As time went on, he grew less and less Anglo-Saxon in appearance and more Latin. I remember once seeing a Canon preaching in the Cathedral of Toulouse who was the picture of Henry James in his unction, his gravity, and his vehemence. Sometimes there could be noted—what Henry would have hated to think existing—a theatrical look which struck the eye, as though he might be some retired *jeune premier* of the Français, *jeune* no longer; and often the prelatical expression faded into a fleeting likeness to one or other celebrated Frenchman of letters (never to any Englishman or American), somewhat of Lacordaire in the intolerable scrutiny of the eyes, somewhat of Sainte-Beuve, too, in all except the mouth, which,

Aspects and Impressions

though mobile and elastic, gave the impression in rest of being small. All these comparisons and suggestions, however, must be taken as the barest hints, intended to mark the tendency of Henry James's radically powerful and unique outer appearance. The beautiful modelling of the brows, waxing and waning under the stress of excitement, is a point which singularly dwells in the memory.

It is very difficult to give an impression of his manner, which was complex in the extreme, now restrained with a deep reserve, now suddenly expanding, so as to leave the auditor breathless, into a flood of exuberance. He had the habit of keeping his friends apart from one another; his intimacies were contained in many watertight compartments. He disliked to think that he was the subject of an interchange of impressions, and though he who discussed everybody and everything with the most penetrating and analysing curiosity must have known perfectly well that he also, in his turn, was the theme of endless discussion, he liked to ignore it and to feign to be a bodiless spectator. Accordingly, he was not apt to pay for the revelations, confidences, guesses and what not which he so eagerly demanded and enjoyed by any coin of a similar species. He begged the human race to plunge into experiences, but he proposed to take no plunge himself, or at least to have no audience when he plunged.

So discreet was he, and so like a fountain sealed, that many of those who were well acquainted with him have supposed that he was mainly a creature of observation and fancy, and that life stirred his intellect while leaving his senses untouched. But every now and then he disclosed to a friend, or rather admitted such a friend to a flash or glimpse of deeper things. The glimpse was never prolonged or illuminated, it was like peering down for a moment through some chasm in the rocks dimmed by the vapour of a clash of waves. One such flash will always leave my memory dazzled. I was staying alone with Henry James at Rye one summer, and as twilight deepened we walked together in the garden. I forget by what meanders we approached the subject, but I suddenly found

Henry James

that in profuse and enigmatic language he was recounting to me an experience, something that had happened, not something repeated or imagined. He spoke of standing on the pavement of a city, in the dusk, and of gazing upwards across the misty street, watching, watching for the lighting of a lamp in a window on the third storey. And the lamp blazed out, and through bursting tears he strained to see what was behind it, the unapproachable face. And for hours he stood there, wet with the rain, brushed by the phantom hurrying figures of the scene, and never from behind the lamp was for one moment visible the face. The mysterious and poignant revelation closed, and one could make no comment, ask no question, being throttled oneself by an overpowering emotion. And for a long time Henry James shuffled beside me in the darkness, shaking the dew off the laurels, and still there was no sound at all in the garden but what our heels made crunching the gravel, nor was the silence broken when suddenly we entered the house and he disappeared for an hour.

But the gossamer thread of narrative must be picked up once more, slight as it is. Into so cloistered a life the news of the sudden loss of Edward Burne-Jones in June, 1898, fell with a sensation; he had "seen the dear man, to my great joy, only a few hours before his death." In the early spring of the next year Henry James actually summoned resolution to go abroad again, visiting at Hyères Paul Bourget and the Vicomte Melchior de Vogüé (of whose *Le Roman Russe* and other essays he was a sturdy admirer), and proceeding to Rome, whence he was "whirled by irresistible Marion Crawford off to Sorrento, Capri, Naples," some of these now seen for the first time. He came back to England and to Lamb House at the end of June, to find that his novel of *The Awkward Age*, which was just published, was being received with a little more intelligence and sympathetic comprehension than had been the habit of greeting his productions, what he haughtily, but quite justly, called "the lurid asininity " of the Press in his regard now beginning to be sensibly affected by

43

the loyalty of the little clan of those who saw what he was
"driving at" in the new romances, and who valued it as a
pearl of price. Nevertheless, there was still enough thick-
witted denunciation of his novels to fill his own "clan"
with anger, while some even of those who loved him best
admitted themselves bewildered by *The Awkward Age*.
Nothing is more steadily cleared away by time than the
impression of obscurity that hangs over a really fine work
of imagination when it is new. Twenty years have now
passed, and no candid reader any longer pretends to find
this admirable story "bewildering."

The passing of old friends was partly healed by the
coming of new friends, and it was about this time that
Mr. H. G. Wells, Mr. Rudyard Kipling, and Mr. W. E.
Norris began to be visited and corresponded with. In
1900 and 1901 Henry James was slowly engaged, with
luxurious throes of prolonged composition, in dictating
The Ambassadors, which he "tackled and, for various
reasons, laid aside," only to attack it again "with intensity
and on the basis of a simplification that made it easier" until
he brought it successfully through its voluminous career.
In the summer of 1902 Mrs. Wharton, who had dedicated
to him, as a stranger, her novel of *The Valley of Decision*,
became a personal acquaintance, and soon, and till the
end, one of the most valued and intimate of his friends.
This event synchronized with the publication of his own
great book, *The Wings of a Dove*. It was followed by
The Golden Bowl. He now turned from such huge
schemes as this—which in his fatigue he described as "too
inordinately drawn out and too inordinately rubbed in"
—to the composition of short stories, in which he found
both rest and refreshment.

On this subject, the capabilities of the *conte* as a form of
peculiarly polished and finished literature, he regaled me
—and doubtless other friends—at this time with priceless
observations. I recall a radiant August afternoon when
we sallied from his high abode and descended to the mud
of the winding waters of the Brede, where, on the shaky
bridge across the river, leaning perilously above the flood,

Henry James

Henry James held forth on the extraordinary skill of Guy de Maupassant, whose posthumous collection, *Le Colporteur*, had just reached him, and on the importance of securing, as that inimitable artist so constantly secured, one straight, intelligible action which must be the source of all vitality in what, without it, became a mere wandering anecdote, more or less vaguely ornamented. Henry James was at this time, I think, himself engaged upon the series of short stories which ultimately appeared under the title of *The Better Sort*, each one, as he said, being the exhibition of a case of experience or conduct. He collected and published in these years several such volumes of short compositions, in which he endeavoured, and admirably effected his endeavour, to combine neatness of handling with that beauty of conception which became more and more the object of his passionate desire. The reader naturally recalls such perfect specimens of his craft as *The Real Right Thing* and *The Beast in the Jungle*.

For many years he had let his fancy toy with the idea of returning, on a visit only, to America. In 1904 this project really took shape, and the long-debated journey actually took place. He terminated another extended romance, *The Golden Bowl*, and in August set sail for New York, ostensibly for the purpose of writing a book of American impressions. The volume called *The American Scene*, published in 1906, gives his account of the adventure, or rather of certain parts of it. He lived through the first autumn with his family in the mountains of New Hampshire, and, after a sojourn in Cambridge, spent Christmas in New York. He then went south in search of warmth, which he found at last in Florida. By way of Chicago, St. Louis, and Indianapolis he reached California in April, 1905. He delivered in various American Colleges two lectures, specially written for the purpose, which came out as a little volume in the United States, but have not yet appeared in England. His impressions of America, in the volume which he published after his return, stop with Florida, and give therefore no record of the extreme pleasure which he experienced in California, of which his private letters were full. He declared, writing on April 5th, 1905, from Coronado Beach, that "California has completely bowled me over. . . . The flowers, the wild flowers, just now in particular, which fairly *rage* with radiance over the land, are worthy of some purer planet than this. . . . It breaks my heart to have so stinted myself here"; but return eastward was imperative, and in August, 1905, he was back again safe in the silence of Lamb House.

Throughout the following autumn and winter he was, as he said, "squeezing out" his American impressions, which did not flow so easily as he had hoped they would. Many other enterprises hung temptingly before him, and distracted his thoughts from that particular occupation. Moreover, just before his plan for visiting the United States had taken shape, he had promised to write for a leading firm of English publishers "a romantical-psychological-pictorial-social" book about London, and in November, 1905, he returned to this project with vivacity. There is a peculiar interest about works that great writers mean to compose and never succeed in producing, and this scheme of a great picturesque book about London is like a ghost among the realities of Henry James's invention. He spoke about it more often and more freely than he did about his solid creations; I feel as though I had handled and almost as though I had read it. Westminster was to have been the core of the matter, which was to circle out concentrically to the City and the suburbs. Henry James put me under gratified contribution by coming frequently to the House of Lords in quest of "local colour," and I took him through the corridors and up into garrets of the Palace where never foreign foot had stepped before. There was not, to make a clean breast of it, much "local colour" to be wrung out, but Henry James was indefatigable in curiosity. What really did thrill him was to stand looking down from one of the windows of the Library on the Terrace, crowded with its motley afternoon crew of Members of both Houses and their guests of both sexes. He liked that better than to mingle with the throng itself, and he should have written a superb page on the scene, with its background of shining river and misty towers. Alas! it will not be read until we know what songs the Sirens sang.

All through the quiet autumn and winter of 1906 he was busy preparing the collective and definite, but far from complete, edition of his novels and tales which began to appear some twelve months later. This involved a labour which some of his friends ventured to disapprove of, since it included a re-writing into his latest style of the early stories which possessed a charm in their unaffected immaturity. Henry James was conscious, I think, of the arguments which might be brought against this reckless revision, but he rejected them with violence. I was spending a day or two with him at Lamb House when *Roderick Hudson* was undergoing, or rather had just undergone, the terrible trial; so the revised copy, darkened and swelled with MS. alterations, was put into my hands. I thought—I dare say I was quite mistaken —that the whole perspective of Henry James's work, the evidence of his development and evolution, his historical growth, were confused and belied by this wholesale tampering with the original text. Accordingly I exclaimed against such dribbling of new wine into the old bottles. This was after dinner, as we sat alone in the garden-room. All that Henry James—though I confess, with a darkened countenance—said at the time was, "The only alternative would have been to put the vile thing"— that is to say the graceful tale of *Roderick Hudson*— "behind the fire and have done with it!" Then we passed to other subjects, and at length we parted for the night in unruffled cheerfulness. But what was my dismay, on reaching the breakfast-table next morning, to see my host sombre and taciturn, with gloom thrown across his frowning features like a veil. I inquired rather anxiously whether he had slept well. "Slept!" he answered with dreary emphasis. "Was I likely to sleep when my brain was tortured with all the cruel and—to put it plainly to you—monstrous insinuations which you

47

had brought forward against my proper, my necessary, my absolutely inevitable corrections of the disgraceful and disreputable style of *Roderick Hudson?* " I withered, like a guilty thing ashamed, before the eyes that glared at me over the coffee-pot, and I inly resolved that not one word of question should ever escape my lips on this subject again.

Early in 1907 he was tempted once more, after so long absence, to revisit France. While in America he had acquired the habit of motoring, which he learned to enjoy so much that it became the greatest physical pleasure of his life, and one which seemed definitely to benefit his health. He motored through a great part of France, and then proceeded to his beloved Italy, where he spent some radiant summer days under the pines near Vallombrosa, and later some more with his lifelong friend Mrs. Curtis in her wonderful Palazzo Barbaro in Venice. Ten weeks in Paris must be added to the foreign record of this year, almost the last of those which Henry James was able to dedicate to the Latin world that he loved so well and comprehended so acutely. The "nightmare," as he called it, of his Collected Edition kept him closely engaged for months after his return—it ultimately ran into a range of twenty-four volumes—but he was also sketching a novel, *The Ivory Tower*, which was to embody some of his American recollections; this was never finished. He met new friends of the younger generation, such as Hugh Walpole and Rupert Brooke, and they gave him great happiness.

He seemed to be approaching old age in placidity and satisfaction when, towards the end of 1909, he was seized by a mysterious group of illnesses which "deprived him of all power to work and caused him immeasurable suffering of mind." Unfortunately his beloved brother William was also failing in health, and had come to Europe in the vain search for recovery; their conditions painfully interacted. The whole year 1910 was one of almost unmitigated distress. Henry accompanied Mr. and Mrs. William back to their home in New Hampshire, where in

Henry James

the autumn not only the eminent philosopher, but a third brother, Robertson James, died, leaving Henry solitary indeed, and weighed upon by a cloud of melancholy which forbade him to write or almost to speak. Out of this he passed in the spring of 1911, and returned to Lamb House, where he had another sharp attack of illness in the autumn of 1912. It was now felt that the long pale winters over the marsh at Rye were impossible for him, and the bedroom at the Reform Club insufficient. He therefore rented a small flat high up over the Thames in Cheyne Walk, where he was henceforth to spend half of each year and die. He sat, on the occasion of his seventieth birthday, to Mr. Sargent for the picture which is now one of the treasures of the National Portrait Gallery; this was surprisingly mutilated, while being exhibited at the Royal Academy, by a "militant suffragette"; Henry James was extraordinarily exhilarated by having been thus "impaired by the tomahawk of the savage," and displayed himself as "breasting a wondrous high-tide of postal condolence in this doubly-damaged state." This was his latest excitement before the war with Germany drowned every other consideration.

The record of the last months of Henry James's life is told in the wonderful letters that he wrote between the beginning of August, 1914, and the close of November, 1915. He was at Rye when the war broke out, but he found it absolutely impossible to stay there without daily communication with friends in person, and, contrary to his lifelong habit, he came posting up to London in the midst of the burning August weather. He was transfigured by the events of those early weeks, overpowered, and yet, in his vast and generous excitement, himself overpowering. He threw off all the languor and melancholy of the recent years, and he appeared actually grown in size as he stalked the streets, amazingly moved by the unexpected nightmare, "the huge horror of blackness" which he saw before him. "The plunge of civilization into the abyss of blood and darkness by the wanton feat of these two infamous autocrats" made him suddenly

realize that the quiet years of prosperity which had preceded 1914 had been really, as he put it, "treacherous,"
and that their perfidy had left us unprotected against the
tragic terrors which now faced our world. It was astonishing how great Henry James suddenly seemed to become;
he positively loomed above us in his splendid and disinterested faith. His first instinct had been horror at the
prospect; his second anger and indignation against the
criminals; but to these succeeded a passion of love and
sympathy for England and France, and an unyielding but
anxious and straining confidence in their ultimate success.
Nothing could express this better than the language of a
friend who saw him constantly and studied his moods
with penetrating sympathy. Mr. Percy Lubbock says:

> To all who listened to him in those days it must have
> seemed that he gave us what we lacked—a voice; there was
> a trumpet note in it that was heard nowhere else and that
> alone rose to the height of the truth.

The impression Henry James gave in these first months
of the war could not be reproduced in better terms. To
be in his company was to be encouraged, stimulated and
yet filled with a sense of the almost intolerable gravity
of the situation; it was to be moved with that "trumpet
note " in his voice, as the men fighting in the dark defiles
of Roncevaux were moved by the sound of the oliphant
of Roland. He drew a long breath of relief in the thought
that England had not failed in her manifest duty to
France, nor "shirked any one of the implications of the
Entente." When, as at the end of the first month, things
were far from exhilarating for the Allies, Henry James
did not give way to despair, but he went back to Rye,
possessing his soul in waiting patience, "bracing himself
unutterably," as he put it, "and holding on somehow
(though to God knows what!) in presence of the per-
petrations so gratuitously and infamously hideous as the
destruction of Louvain and its accompaniments."
At Lamb House he sat through that gorgeous tawny

Henry James

September, listening to the German guns thundering just across the Channel, while the advance of the enemy through those beautiful lands which he knew and loved so well filled him with anguish. He used to sally forth and stand on the bastions of his little town, gazing over the dim marsh that became sand-dunes, and then sea, and then a mirage of the white cliffs of French Flanders that were actually visible when the atmosphere grew transparent. The anguish of his execration became almost the howl of some animal, of a lion of the forest with the arrow in his flank, when the Germans wrecked Reims Cathedral. He gazed and gazed over the sea south-east, and fancied that he saw the flicker of the flames. He ate and drank, he talked and walked and thought, he slept and waked and lived and breathed only the War. His friends grew anxious, the tension was beyond what his natural powers, transfigured as they were, could be expected to endure, and he was persuaded to come back to Chelsea, although a semblance of summer still made Rye attractive.

During this time his attitude towards America was marked by a peculiar delicacy. His letters expressed no upbraiding, but a yearning, restrained impatience that took the form of a constant celebration of the attitude of England, which he found in those early months consistently admirable. In his abundant and eloquent letters to America he dealt incessantly on the shining light which events were throwing on "England's moral position and attitude, her predominantly incurable good-nature, the sublimity or the egregious folly, one scarcely knows which to call it, of her innocence in face of the most prodigiously massed and worked-out intentions of aggression." He admitted, with every gesture of courtesy, that America's absence from the feast of allied friendship on an occasion so unexampled, so infinitely momentous, was a bitter grief to him, but he was ready to believe it a necessity. For his own part, almost immediately on his return to London in October, 1914, Henry James began to relieve the mental high pressure by some kinds of practical work for which nothing in his previous life had fitted him, but into which he now threw himself with even exhausting ardour. He had always shrunk from physical contact with miscellaneous strangers, but now nothing seemed unwelcome save aloofness which would have divided him from the sufferings of others. The sad fate of Belgium particularly moved him, and he found close to his flat in Cheyne Walk a centre for the relief of Belgian refugees, and he was active in service there. A little later on he ardently espoused the work of the American Volunteer Motor Ambulance Corps. His practical experiences and his anxiety to take part in the great English movement for relief of the Belgians and the French are reflected in the essays which were collected in 1919 under the title of *Within the Rim*.

We were, however, made anxious by the effect of all this upon his nerves. The magnificent exaltation of spirit which made him a trumpeter in the sacred progress of the Allies was of a nature to alarm us as much as it inspirited and rejoiced us. When we thought of what he had been in 1911, how sadly he had aged in 1912, it was not credible that in 1915 he could endure to be filled to overflowing by this tide of febrile enthusiasm. Some of us, in the hope of diverting his thoughts a little from the obsession of the war, urged him to return to his proper work; and he responded in part to our observations, while not abandoning his charitable service. He was at work on *The Ivory Tower* when the war began, but he could not recover the note of placidity which it demanded, and he abandoned it in favour of a novel begun in 1900 and then laid aside, *The Sense of the Past*. He continued, at the same time, his reminiscences, and was writing the fragment published since his death as *The Middle Years*. But all this work was forced from him with an effort, very slowly; the old sprightly running of composition was at an end, the fact being that his thoughts were now incessantly distracted by considerations of a far more serious order.

The hesitations of Mr. Wilson, and Henry James's conviction that in the spring of 1915 the United States

Henry James

government was "sitting down in meekness and silence under the German repudiation of every engagement she solemnly took with" America, led to his taking a step which he felt to be in many respects painful, but absolutely inevitable. His heart was so passionately united with England in her colossal effort, and he was so dismally discouraged by the unending hesitation of America, that he determined to do what he had always strenuously refused to do before, namely, apply for British naturalization. Mr. Asquith (then Prime Minister), Sir George Prothero (the Editor of the *Quarterly Review*), and I had the honour and the gratification of being chosen his sponsors. In the case of so illustrious a claimant the usual formalities were passed over, and on July 26th, 1915, Henry James became a British subject. Unhappily he did not live to see America join the Allies, and so missed the joy for which he longed above all others.

But his radiant enthusiasm was burning him out. In August he had a slight breakdown, and his autumn was made miserable by an affection of the heart. He felt, he said, twenty years older, but "still, I cultivate, I at least attempt, a brazen front." He still got about, and I saw him at Westminster on the evening of November 29th. This was, I believe, the last time he went out, and two days later, on the night between the 1st and the 2nd of December, he had a stroke. He partly rallied and was able to receive comfort from the presence of his sister-in-law, Mrs. William James, who hurried across the Atlantic to nurse him. At the New Year he was awarded the highest honour which the King can confer on a British man of letters, the Order of Merit, the insignia of which were brought to his bedside by Lord Bryce. On February 28th, 1916, he died, within two months of his 73rd birthday. His body was cremated, and the funeral service held at that "altar of the dead" which he had loved so much, Chelsea Old Church, a few yards from his own door.

1920.

SAMUEL BUTLER

LET it be said at once that Mr. Henry Festing Jones's *Life of Samuel Butler* tells the history of a very remarkable man with a vividness which leaves nothing to be desired. This is not a vain compliment; it is a tribute which common justice demands on an unusual occasion. There were ninety-nine chances in a hundred that Butler's life would never be adequately, or even intelligently, recorded. Nature and circumstance had done their best to make him obscure and incomprehensible. The situation has been saved by two facts: the first, that Butler was excessively interested in himself; the second, that Mr. Jones was always—not merely since Butler's death, but always—excessively interested in Butler. These are not conditions which are essential to the success of biography in every case, especially when the general unanimity of admiration has made all the contemporaries of a great man in some sort his biographers, but they are absolutely required to preserve for us the features of an eccentric and isolated person who failed almost all through his life to attract admiration, and who laid himself out to be completely misunderstood when the tide should at last turn in his favour. We are preserved from such a loss by the meticulous attention which Samuel Butler paid to himself, and by the infatuated zeal with which Mr. Jones adopted, continued, and developed that attention. Butler lives twice over, or rather has never ceased to live, in the mind and humour of Mr. Henry Festing Jones.

We move in an age which prides itself more and more on being able to see the mote in the eye of its immediate predecessor. But Samuel Butler was the precursor of this rebellion, and is historically notable as the earliest anti-Victorian. He was born at a moment which was to prove less rich than almost any other of the remarkable nineteenth century, in producing men who were to be eminent for intellectual talent. It almost looks as though Nature, which had been so profuse, and was presently to become so liberal again, paused for a few years, while she prepared to let the Victorian Age proper wear itself out. The immediate contemporaries of Butler were Shorthouse, whose *John Inglesant* started a new sentimentality, and William Morris, who combined a fresh aspect of romance with an investigation of the bases of society which was essentially revolutionary; with these were T. H. Green, who introduced a new Hegelian spirit into philosophical speculation, and John Richard Green, who re-examined the foundations of our history. But none of these men displayed any real parallelism with Butler, by whose work they were none of them at any time affected, and of whom perhaps none of them ever heard. The only other name which can be quoted in this connexion is that of Lecky, who may indeed be regarded as the exact opposite of Butler in almost every respect—successful from earliest youth, at peace with the world, reverently acceptive of every Victorian formula, and blandly unconscious that everything was not permanently for the best in the best of all possible worlds.

Butler is a curious example of a man of something very like genius, who passed through a long life in the midst of intelligent fellow-men, not rebuffing their attentions, but encouraging them; not escaping by a mordid modesty from criticism, but doing everything in his power to exasperate it; and yet failing to be observed. The strange thing about his case is that he lived, mostly in London, for sixty-six years, and that until nearly the close of that time scarcely anyone felt more than the most tepid and casual curiosity about him. The only similar case that occurs to the memory in the history of nineteenth-century literature is Borrow, who in like manner, but not with a like desolating completeness, simply was unable to catch

Samuel Butler

the eye of criticism. When each of these writers died, it seemed impossible that either of them would ever occupy half a page in any history of literature. It now seems equally difficult to suppose that any such history, if possessing the least pretension to completeness, will in future omit either of them. This is quite apart from any question which may present itself as to the probability of a decline in the present "fashion" for them both. It merely expresses the fact that while Borrow and Butler alike walked all through their lives invisible, for the rest of time they must both be patent, whether liked or disliked.

Borrow affected a certain disdain for the laudation which would not come his way, and in later life seemed to have relinquished any desire to move in the mouths of men. But Butler never ceased to long for fame, and probably to expect it. Towards the close of his life, whenever he was asked what new work might be expected from his ingenious pen, he used to look demure and answer, "I am editing my remains; I wish ' to leave everything in order for my executors.' " This was looked upon as a joke, but it turns out to have been strictly true. No one ever laboured more to appear at his best—in strict accordance with truth, but still, at his best—to the world after his decease. His assiduities were like those of the dying Narcissa—

And Betty, give those cheeks a little red,
One wouldn't, sure, look horrid when one's dead!

He recovered as many of his own letters as he could and annotated them; he arranged the letters of his friends; he copied, edited, indexed, and dated all this mass of correspondence, and he prepared those "Notes" which have since his death provided his admirers with their choicest repast. In doing all this he displayed an equal *naïveté* and enthusiasm. Mr. Festing Jones, to whom all this industry has of course been invaluable, puts the matter in a nutshell when he says that Butler "was not contemplating publication, but neither was he contemplating oblivion." He was simply putting the rouge-pot within Betty's reach.

Here is Butler's own account of the matter, and it throws a strong light upon his character:

> People sometimes give me to understand that it is a piece of ridiculous conceit on my part to jot down so many notes about myself, since it implies a confidence that I shall one day be regarded as an interesting person. I answer that neither I nor they can form any idea as to whether I shall be wanted when I am gone or no. The chances are that I shall not.

But he was not inclined to take any risks. He was the residuary of his own temperament, and if by chance posterity were to wake up and take a violent interest in him, he personally would be to blame, and would incur a very serious responsibility, if there were no documents forthcoming to satisfy the curiosity of the new generation. It is to his frank response to this instinct of self-preservation that we owe the very exhaustive and faithful narrative of Mr. Festing Jones, as we did the precious "Note-books" of 1912.

In consideration of the eagerness and sympathy with which Butler is followed by an active group of admirers among the young writers of to-day, it may be doubtful whether the extraordinary minuteness of Butler's observation, continued as it is with an equally extraordinary fullness by his biographer, may not have an evil effect in encouraging a taste for excessive discursiveness in authorship of this class. There have been very distinguished examples lately of abandonment to an unchecked notation of detail. It is scarcely necessary to refer to the texture of the later novels of Henry James, or to the amazing *Côté de chez Swann* of M. Marcel Proust, which latter is one of the most characteristic successes of the moment. This widespread tendency to consider every slight observation, whether phenomenal or emotional, worthy of the gravest and tenderest analysis, develops at an epoch when

Samuel Butler

the world is becoming congested with printed matter, and
when one might imagine that conciseness and selection
would be the qualities naturally in fashion.   Neither
Samuel Butler nor his biographer conceives it possible
that anything can be negligible; to them the meanest
flower that blows by the wayside of experience gives
thoughts that cannot be brought to lie within one or even
within ten pages.   The complacency with which Butler
annotates his own childish letters to his mother is equalled
only by the gravity with which Mr. Jones examines those
very annotations.

Not without a qualm, however, do I note this re-
dundancy, since it is a source of pleasure to all but the
hasty reader, who, indeed, should be advised not to
approach Butler at all.   The charm of his mind lies in its
divagations, its inconsistencies, its puerile and lovable
self-revelations, and all these are encouraged by the wandering style common to the author and to his biographer.
One of the most clear-sighted of his friends, trying to
sum up his character at his death, said that "he was too
versatile a genius ever to be in the front rank of one
particular line, and he had too much fun in him to be
really serious when he ought to have been."   But why
ought he to have been "really serious," and why should
he have sought "front rank " in one particular line?
This is the inevitable way in which a man of ingenious
originality is misjudged by those who have loved him
most and who think they understood him best.   Butler
was not remarkable, and does not now deserve the reputation which his name enjoys, on account of the subjects
about which he chose to write, nor on account of the
measure of decorum with which he approached those
themes, but in consequence of the sinuous charm, the
irregular and arresting originality of his approach itself,
his fame having been indeed rather delayed, and the
purgatory of his obscurity prolonged, by the want of
harmony between most of the subjects he selected and the
manner in which it was native to himself to treat those
subjects.   In other words, what makes Butler a difficult

theme for analysis is that, unlike most authors, his genius is not illuminated, but positively obscured for a student of to-day, by the majority of his controversial writings. He was not a prophet; he was an inspired "crank." He is most characteristic, not when he is discussing Evolution, or Christianity, or the Sonnets of Shakespeare, or the Trapanese Origin of the "Odyssey," but when he is meandering along, endlessly, paradoxically, in the act of written conversation about everything at large and nothing in particular, with himself as the central theme.

The most valuable of Butler's imaginative writings, and indeed the most important from almost every point of view, are the two romances which stand respectively at the opening and at the close of his career, like two golden pillars supporting the roof of his reputation. His earliest publication (for the slight and brief budget of letters from New Zealand was not published by himself) was *Erewhon* —or "Nowhere"—a fantastic Utopia of the class started a century and a half ago by Paltock in his fascinating adventures of *Peter Wilkins*. Like Wilkins, the hero of *Erewhon* flies from civilization, and discovers in the Antarctic world a race of semi-human beings, who obey a strict code of morals consistent in itself, but in complete divergence from ours on many important points. I discover no evidence that Butler ever saw Paltock's romance, and he would probably have been scornful of the Glums and Gowries, and of the gentle winged people wrapped in throbbing robes of their own substance. But I think some dim report of an undiscovered country where ethics were all turned topsy-turvy may have started him on *Erewhon*. The other novel, that which closes Butler's career as a writer, is *The Way of All Flesh*, without a careful consideration of which, by the light of information now supplied by Mr. Festing Jones, no sketch of Butler's career can, for the future, be attempted.

As early as 1873, Butler confided to Miss Savage—of whose place in his life and influence upon his genius I shall presently have to speak—that he was contemplating the composition of an autobiographical novel. She read

Samuel Butler

the opening, and wrote, "as far as it goes it is perfect, and if you go on as you have begun, it will be a beautiful book." In case he got tired of it, what he had already written might make "a very nice finished sketch for a magazine." Evidently Miss Savage, who had an almost uncanny penetration into Butler's nature, had little confidence in his perseverance in the conduct of so large a design. She urged him on, however, and it very early occurred to her that the value of the story would consist in its complete veracity as an autobiography. She faced Butler with the charge that he was not being faithful to himself in this matter, and she said, "Is the narrator of the story to be an impartial historian or a special pleader?" Butler wriggled under her strictures, but failed to escape from them. Finally she faced him with a direct question:

> You have chosen the disguise of an old man of seventy-three [exactly double Butler's real age at that time], and must speak and act as such. An old man of seventy-three would scarcely talk as you do, unless he was constantly in your company, and was a very docile old man indeed—and I don't think the old man who is telling the story is at all docile.

Young or old, Butler was never "docile," and he was not inclined to give up his idealism without a struggle. But Miss Savage was indomitable. She continued to undermine what she called "the special pleader," on the ground that "I prefer an advocate in flesh and blood." Under this pressure, and stimulated by Miss Savage's ingenuous annotations, Butler adopted more and more a realistic tone, and kept the story more and more closely on autobiographic lines. It was progressing steadily when Butler had to go to Canada on the business expedition which cost him so many months of his life, and when he returned to London he did not resume the novel. He took it up again in 1878, and disliked it; it needed Miss Savage's energy to start him again with proper gusto. Mr. Festing Jones was by this time upon the spot, and though he does not say so, he probably supported Miss Savage. They were the Aaron and Hur who held up the arms of this incorrigible "special pleader," and insisted that he should stick to the truth, and not embroider it. In 1884 *The Way of All Flesh* was finished; in 1885 it underwent some revision, and after that was not touched again.

So long as Butler was alive, the uncompromising revelations of his family life, and the bitterness of the censure of living persons, which the novel contained, made it impossible to dream of issuing it. To do so would have been to break a nest of hornets over Butler's pate. But the moment he was dead, his executor, the late Mr. R. A. Streatfeild, acting upon the author's known wishes, published *The Way of All Flesh*. This was in 1903, and the publication synchronized with the surprising burst of critical appreciation which the announcement of Butler's death had awakened in the Press. In almost all unprejudiced quarters the value of *The Way of All Flesh* as a sincere and masterly contribution to imaginative literature, was acknowledged, although it took five years more for a second edition of the book to be called for. Butler, however, was recognized at last as an author of distinguished merit, and there was a reverberation of curiosity concerning so remarkable a man who had walked about among us for nearly seventy years without attracting any particular attention. This curiosity, it was indicated by his admirers, could now be assuaged by a study of *The Way of All Flesh*, which was a faithful portrait of the writer, and of all the persons who had checked his growth or encouraged his development. So the legend was started that no real *Life of Samuel Butler* was required, because in *The Way of All Flesh* we already possessed a complete one.

Apart from the fact that the best of autobiographies can never be the "real life," because it can never depict the man quite as others saw him, it now transpires—and this is perhaps the most important feature of Mr. Festing Jones's admirable volumes — that the novel cannot be

Samuel Butler

accepted as an autobiography sound at all points. In spite of the warnings of Miss Savage, and, oddly enough, most of all in the person of Miss Savage herself, Butler was incapable of confronting the incidents of his own life without colouring them, and without giving way to prejudice in the statement of plain facts. He disliked excessively the atmosphere of middle-class Evangelicism in which he had been brought up, and we must dislike it too, but we need not dislike the persons involved so bitterly as Butler did. It was narrow, sterile and cruel, and it deserved no doubt the irony which Butler expended upon it. So long as we regard *The Way of All Flesh* as a story, invented with the help of recollections which the novelist was at liberty to modify in any way he thought desirable, there is no quarrel to be picked with any part of it. But when we are led, as we have been, to take it as a full and true record of Butler's own life, with nothing changed but the names of the persons, we see by the light of Mr. Festing Jones that this is an absolutely untenable position. *The Way of All Flesh* is not an autobiography, but a romance founded on recollection.

The author of *Erewhon*, who was christened Samuel, not in honour of the author of *Hudibras*, but in memory of his own grandfather, the Bishop of Lichfield and Coventry, was the son of Canon Thomas Butler, incumbent of Langor-with-Branston, in Nottinghamshire, where the younger Samuel was born on the 4th of December, 1835. Readers of *The Way of All Flesh* may recognize the Butler family at Langor in the very unflattering picture of the Pontifexes in that novel. The Bishop's grandson disliked him very much indeed— "bullying, irritable, stupid old turkey-cock "—until 1887, when he got hold of the Bishop's letters and papers, "and fell over head and ears in love with him." He excused his earlier sarcasms by saying—"When I wrote harshly describing him, I knew nothing about my grandfather except that he had been a great schoolmaster—and I do not like schoolmasters; and then a bishop—and I do not like bishops; and that he was supposed to be like my father." For the latter, who is Theobald Pontifex in *The Way of All Flesh*, he never expressed any leniency whatever, yet it is impossible to avoid hoping that if he had studied his father, as at the age of fifty he studied his grandfather, he might have relented a little in that instance also.

Ernest Pontifex says, in *The Way of All Flesh*, that he could remember no feeling towards his parents during his childhood except fear and shrinking. To Butler, fathers in general, as a class, were "capable de tout," like the prophet Habakkuk. Mr. Festing Jones prints a very explicit paper he has found on this subject, the least distressing paragraph in which is the last, where Butler says, "An unkind fate never threw two men together who were more naturally uncongenial than my father and myself." Canon Butler was an evangelical clergyman of the Simeonite type, which flourished so intensely before and during the development of the High Church revival. He believed in bringing up children rigidly, from their infancy, in the strict practice of external religion. If they were recalcitrant, the love of God must be driven into them by their being whipped or shut up in a cupboard, or docked of some little puerile pleasure. Samuel Butler secretly rebelled, from babyhood, against this stern evangelical discipline, and the Canon, who had no imagination, simply redoubled his severities. It is an amusing touch, in this record of a dismal childhood, to learn that Samuel was excessively pleased, at the age of eight, by hearing an Italian lady in Naples say that a dear young friend of hers—poor unfortunate fellow, *povero disgraziato!*—had been obliged to murder his uncle and his aunt. Probably the pleasure the little boy felt in hearing of this "misfortune" was the earliest expression of that rebellious and fantastic dislike of conventionality which was to run through the whole series of the man's works.

In the letters from Butler to his family, written at school and at college, there is, however, no trace of the violent antagonism which he afterwards believed that he

Samuel Butler

had always felt. It is true that a boy who writes to his father and mother, and indeed in similar circumstances a man too, is constrained to resign himself to a certain innocent hypocrisy. Very few children are able to send to their parents, and very few parents are able to endure from their children, a perfectly sincere description of their crude sentiments during adolescence. But if Samuel Butler was really tormented at home, as Ernest Pontifex was, it is odd that some note of hostility should not have crept into his juvenile correspondence. However, Mr. Festing Jones, who is as judicious as a Lord of Appeal, seems to entertain no doubt that Canon Butler was a holy horror, so that we must bow to his opinion.

The earliest overt evidence of a falling out between father and son is delayed until, in Mr. Jones's unfaltering narrative, we reach the son's twenty-third year. He does not seem, at first, to have combated his father's obstinate demand that he should take orders in the Church of England. That Canon Butler, a clergyman of clergymen, should have desired to see his Samuel take this step, ought not to seem unreasonable, though it certainly proved unlucky. In the novel, it will be remembered, Ernest Pontifex actually was ordained, but to this length Samuel Butler never proceeded. He went to a parish in the east of London to work with a parson who had been one of his grandfather's pupils at Shrewsbury. There his faith in the efficacy of infant baptism was shaken, and presently falling, brought down about his ears the whole fabric of Simeonite Christianity in which he had so assiduously been trained. He suddenly, and no doubt abruptly, wrote to the Canon and said that he "declined to be ordained." From a carnal as well as a spiritual point of view this must have been a nasty shock for his parents, and Mr. Festing Jones tells us "there was a long and painful correspondence." This he mercifully spares us, but refers us to *The Way of All Flesh,* where Butler made dauntless use of it.

The financial situation was difficult. Canon Butler was fairly well-to-do, but he had other children to provide for, and Samuel, who refused to be a clergyman, went on refusing, as it must have seemed to his father, to be anything at all. Like the poet Cowley, he

> neither great at Court nor in the War,
> Nor at the Exchange would be, nor at the wrangling Bar.

All professions were suggested, and each in vain. At last it was decided that Samuel should emigrate to New Zealand, and become a sheep farmer. Only nine years earlier, a Church of England colony had been founded at Canterbury, in the South Island, and the town of Christchurch had been founded. It had enjoyed a great success, and by the year 1859, when Butler landed, almost all the sheep lands had been already taken up. At last he found an unoccupied run at the "back of beyond," and built a little homestead for himself, which he called Mesopotamia. It is needless to dwell on this episode of Butler's life, further than to point out that it proved him capable of sustained physical industry and of considerable financial adroitness. The remainder of his career hardly suggests the possession of either. The New Zealand episode is sufficiently dealt with in Butler's own book, *A First Year in Canterbury Settlement,* which, by the way, shows no trace of the author's subsequent merit as a writer. In June, 1864, he sailed homeward from the port of Lyttelton, but not alone, and we now approach the strangest incident of his life.

It was to be expected that the £4,400 which Butler had received from his father in 1859 would by this time have dwindled to zero. Not at all; it had swelled to £8,000. But just before he left New Zealand a young man, called Charles Pauli, whom he had known but very slightly as a journalist in Christchurch, and who had no claim upon Butler of any sort or species, came to him and asked him to pay for his passage back to England, and to advance him £200 a year for three years. "To me," wrote Butler in 1897, "in those days this seemed perfectly easy; and Pauli, I have not the smallest doubt, intended

Samuel Butler

and fully believed—for his temperament was always sanguine—that he should be able to repay me." Butler had very little insight into the "temperament" of Pauli, and the whole of the extraordinary story increases our conviction that this sardonic and sarcastic analyst of imaginary life was as powerless as a child in face of reality. The dreadful Pauli adventure, told for the first time by Mr. Festing Jones, in his deliberate, unimpassioned way, is the most amazing revelation of simplicity traded upon by fraud that it is possible to imagine.

There soon proved to be a complete absence of harmony in the tastes of Butler and Pauli, who had really nothing in common. Yet they settled together, when they arrived in London, in rooms in Clifford's Inn, Fleet Street. There Butler lived for all the rest of his life, thirty-eight years; but presently Pauli went elsewhere. Then the relations of the two became incomprehensible. Pauli was very irritable, and constantly found fault with Butler. He refused to let Butler know his address, and yet was continually sponging upon him. He said that he could get no help from his own parents, and that Butler stood between him and starvation. For three years Pauli did not attempt to work. At last, in 1867, he was called to the Bar. He lunched with Butler three times a week, when he always said that he was earning nothing. Butler's own statement, written in 1898, the year after Pauli's death, is as follows:

I have no means of ascertaining how much Pauli had from me between the years 1864 and 1881 (but it exceeded £3,500). I kept no accounts; I took no receipts from him; the understanding was that he would repay me when he came into his reversion. . . . In 1879 I only admitted to my father having helped Pauli from time to time; the fact was, I had done everything. . . . I had more than shared every penny I had with him, but I believed myself to be doing it out of income, and to have a right to do it.

Throughout the long periods in which Butler was hard pressed for sufficient money to exist—times in which there were painful and unseemly squabbles about an allowance between his father and himself—he was supporting Pauli, whose means of subsistence he took no pains to investigate, and who, in full cognition of Butler's attenuated sources of income, punctually took half for himself. Mr. Festing Jones's statement is amazing:

Pauli was called to the Bar in 1867, and took chambers in Lincoln's Inn for his work. He told Butler where they were, so that he could write if he had any communication to make to him that would not wait till they met; *but Butler was not to go there.* Of course, he could have gone, but he did not. He could have found out in a hundred ways where Pauli lived if he had set about it; but, knowing that Pauli did not wish it, he did nothing.

At last, in 1897, after having shared his poverty with this strange friend for thirty-three years, Butler read in *The Times* that Pauli was dead. Then, at last, he made inquiries, and found that for a great many years past Pauli's income from the law had exceeded £700 a year, and for nearly twenty had been over £1,000. Pauli left £9,000, not a penny of it to Butler, whose parasite he had been for the greater part of his life, when every five-pound note was of consequence to Butler. One knows not which to be more astounded at—heartless greediness on the one side, or fatuous simplicity on the other. When all the evidence came out at last beyond all further concealment, Butler wrote: "I understand now why Pauli preserved such an iron silence when I implored him to deal with me somewhat after the fashion in which I had dealt with him." [That is to say, in telling him precisely what Butler's exact financial position was.] "The iniquity of the whole thing, as it first struck me in full force, upset me."

This "squalid and miserable story" is told with inexorable fullness by Mr. Festing Jones. What is very remarkable about it is the evidence it gives of Butler's irregular penetration into character. He could be extremely acute in one direction and absolutely obtuse in

Samuel Butler

another. The incredible indulgence which permitted him to be the dupe and victim of a scoundrel like Pauli for more than thirty years seems incompatible with the intense and suspicious analysis which he expended on the motives of his father. After all, when the worst of Canon Butler is admitted, he was a Christian and a gentleman by the side of the appalling Pauli. Yet Butler would sacrifice his father, and actually tell falsehoods, for the purpose of screening and enriching Pauli (see Vol. I., p. 114), of whose villainy he could at any moment have assured himself, and with whom he practically admits that he had nothing in common.

The Pauli episode is valuable in supplying light on certain defects in Butler's intellectual composition. In measure, it tends to explain the inconsistencies, the irregularities of his mental life, and of his action as a scholar. He was the opposite of those who see life steadily, and see it whole. He had no wide horizons, but he investigated a corner or a section of a subject with a burning glass which left all other parts of the surface in darkness. There were Paulis on his mental horizon; there were in almost everything he approached passages where his want of appreciation, his want (let us boldly say) of elementary insight, produced the oddest effect of imperfection. His literary judgments were *saugrenu* to the last extreme. What are we to think of a man who lays it down that "Blake was no good because he learnt Italian to study Dante, and Dante was no good because he was so fond of Virgil, and Virgil was no good because Tennyson ran him; and as for Tennyson, well, Tennyson goes without saying"? There is no critical meaning in such outbursts; they would be almost imbecile in their aimless petulance if we did not understand that Virgil and Dante and Blake lay in the dark segment of Butler's vision, and that he had not so much formed an adverse opinion of their merits as no opinion at all. If, as surprisingly he did on every occasion, he heaped contempt on Virgil, it was simply because he wanted to get Virgil well out of the way of Homer, on whom his enthusiasm was concentrated.

Aspects and Impressions

It was so in all things. Butler despised the great Venetian painters, not because he had devoted attention to their faults, but because they stood in the way of Giovanni and Gentile Bellini, to whom he had dedicated a frenzied cult. "Titian, Leonardo, Raffaelle and Michel Angelo, well, to speak quite plainly, I like none of them," he wrote in the last year of his life. In music it was just the same. Butler attached himself, from early youth to the grave, to Handel in an almost maniacal infatuation. In order to clear a space, as it were, round this solitary object of his worship, he covered Beethoven and Bach with contempt; and if anyone forced him to listen to the "Requiem" of Mozart, he stopped his ears and hummed "Loathsome urns, disclose your treasure," to drown the hideous Austrian discord. For Butler, "Bach wriggles; Wagner writhes." All the masterpieces of the world of music he sweeps together in a universal disapproval as "heartless failures," whereas of Handel's least remarkable passages he calls out, "Can human genius do more?" The result is that Butler is interesting and sometimes valuable when he praises; when he blames, he is sometimes amusing, but more often impertinent and tiresome. What is the point of calling Plato one of the "Seven Humbugs of Christendom," or of talking of "that damned Republic"? To pretend to admire these peevish outbursts, however much we may be stimulated by the better sides of Butler's intelligence, is abject.

No section of Mr. Festing Jones's biography is more interesting than that in which, in the patient, judicious manner in which he so eminently excels, he depicts the relation of Butler to Miss Savage. Readers of *The Way of All Flesh* are familiar with the figure of Alethea Pontifex, who occupies the position of heroine in that novel. It has long been known that this was the portrait of a friend whom Butler had studied, confided in, and deeply valued. In what degree it was an accurate portrait has not hitherto been known. I have no hesitation in saying that the chapters which deal with this situation—and they are executed with as much delicacy as realism—form the

70

Samuel Butler

most unhackneyed and the most exciting section of Mr. Jones's volumes. They illuminate in portions, and they leave darker than ever in other parts, the rugged surface of Butler's extraordinary character; and I regret that exigencies of space do not permit me to do justice to documents so remarkable. But yet, something I must say.

The Alethea of the novel was so far from being an exact portrait that the sitter, after studying every line and touch of it, is supposed, was supposed by Butler himself, not to have perceived that it was intended for her. This, however, we must regard as hardly possible in the case of one so passionately clear-sighted, but there were many reasons why she should adopt such an attitude. Eliza Mary Ann Savage was a governess, whom Butler met about 1870, when he and she were art students together at Heatherley's. They were nearly of the same age, which at that time would be thirty-four. They were immediately drawn together by a singular parallelism in temper and sympathy. Miss Savage read the MS. of *Erewhon*, and minutely criticized it. From this time, 1871 to 1885, when she died, Butler submitted to her everything he wrote, and, obstinate as he was in the face of all other censures, invariably remodelled his work in accordance with her criticisms and suggestions. She supported him in all his enthusiasms, and shared all his prejudices. She was a very well-read woman, and was able to follow Butler into the remotest recesses of his studies. She responded to his lightest touch like a delicate musical instrument, and yet was rigid in opposing any divergence from what she conceived to be the normal line his talent ought to take. She was as stringently hostile to Christianity, as contemptuous of Darwin and Huxley, as infatuated about Handel, as haughtily an *enfant terrible* of the intelligence as he was, and the degree to which the admirers of Butler's books are indebted to her can never be definitely known, but is certainly very great.

Alethea Pontifex, in *The Way of All Flesh*, is tall, handsome, with fine blue eyes. Miss Savage was short,

71

insignificant, and plain, with brown eyes; she suffered from hip disease; physically, she was quite unattractive. This introduces into the real history an element of pathos and of pain which raises it to a far higher level of human interest than the novel has to offer us. To Miss Savage, in her isolated state, Butler was the whole world; and it is perfectly evident—Mr. Festing Jones need not hesitate so conscientiously in admitting it — that she was absorbingly, unalterably in love with Butler. She lived, quite unupbraiding, in the intermittent light of his countenance. For nearly twenty years they were, mentally, like a devoted husband and wife, yet the anomaly of their relations never struck Butler, to whom Miss Savage was a comrade of perfect sympathy, and no more. He did not observe, until Miss Savage was dead, that she had felt towards him otherwise than he felt towards her. He wrote, "I valued her, but she perfectly understood that I could do no more." Did she? Mr. Festing Jones prints a sonnet of Butler's, written in 1901, which seems to me to be one of the most amazing pieces of self-revelation that I know:

And now, though twenty years are come and gone,
　　That little lame lady's face is with me still;
Never a day but what, on every one,
　　She dwells with me as dwell she ever will.
She said she wished I knew not wrong from right;
　　It was not that; I knew, and would have chosen
Wrong if I could, but, in my own despite,
　　Power to choose wrong in my chilled veins was frozen.
'Tis said that if a woman woo, no man
　　Should leave her till she have prevailed; and, true,
A man will yield for pity if he can,
　　But if the flesh rebels, what can he do?
　　　　I could not; hence I grieve my whole life long
　　　　The wrong I did in that I did no wrong.

Such fragments of Miss Savage's letters as Mr. Festing Jones prints show that she was an admirable correspondent. Butler put her letters together in a separate collection,

Samuel Butler

edited, annotated, and ready for the Press. This is to be published some day in a volume by itself, and will have a pathetic value. But I confess to a certain feeling of regret that the inner being of this obscure, pathetic, and self-sacrificing woman should be immolated any further on the altar of Butler's egotism. My own instinct would be to say: Let poor Miss Savage, out of whose painful and imperfect existence so much "copy" has already been made, sleep on undisturbed under her mouldering headstone at Finchley. But Mr. Festing Jones knows best.

The most agreeable parts of this biography, at all events those which give us the most genial impression of Butler as a companion, deal with his repeated visits to Italy. These tours inspired, or were used to produce material for, a very pleasant section of his literary work. If we distinguish between the wit and picturesqueness of the ornament in Butler's controversial writings, and the actual basal texture of those writings, I do not see how a reasonable criticism can any longer pretend to set high value on his angry denunciations of the whole Darwinian theory of evolution, or on his diatribes about Unconscious Memory. There is a terrible work of his, published in 1887, called *Luck or Cunning as the Main Means of Organic Modification;* there is another, of 1882, called *Evolution, Old and New.* They are unreadable. His religious polemic was even more disagreeable than his scientific, and the lumbering sarcasm of the attack on Christianity, called *The Fair Haven,* is an epitome of all that is most unpleasing in the attitude of Butler. Unctuous sarcasm so sustained as to deceive the very elect, and "affectation of the tone of indignant orthodoxy," have a tendency to grow rancid in the passage of years, and to become exceedingly unappetizing. Samuel Butler, whose rashness was astounding, had the courage to call his homonym of the *Analogy* a "poor creature"! What would Joseph Butler, revisiting the glimpses of the moon, think of the author of *The Fair Haven?*

There is nothing of this incongruity in the books which

73

are founded on memories of Italian travel. Here the charm of Butler's style is expended, with a thousand oddities and playfulnesses, on subjects which blossom in its atmosphere. It is very strange that *Alps and Sanctuaries* (1882), and *Ex Voto* (1888), should share the neglect which was so unbrokenly the fate of Butler's publications, for these were charming and original to a high degree, and they illustrate, without any disadvantage, the whimsical penetration of his mind and the playful melody of his style at its best. *The Authoress of the Odyssey* (1897), which Hellenists found it impossible to take as a serious contribution to scholarship, was another of these by-products of travel in Sicily, and contained very numerous pages, which, whether convincing or no, were exceedingly picturesque and entertaining. No cultivated man or woman will, in the future, visit Trapani or ascend to the platforms of Mount Eryx without remembering how Butler was taken to the grotto where Ulysses hid his treasure, or how the Sicilian descendants of the Cyclopes treated him as a royal personage.

Not much new light is thrown on the purely literary characteristics of Butler by Mr. Festing Jones's biography. He has not dwelt at length on the individual works, nor at all on the general position of their author among his contemporaries. He left himself no space to go into such questions, being fully occupied with the task of interpreting and illuminating the personal characteristics of his subject. He is an unflinching portraitist, and in a painting of Oliver Cromwell from the life would be sure to do full justice to the wen. The rugged surface of Samuel Butler lends itself to such realism—and I will not say that Mr. Jones does not approach the confines of the superfluous in the excessive minuteness of his notes. We are assured that Butler took eight handkerchiefs and three pairs of socks with him when he went abroad, and that he very wisely carried diarrhœa pills in the handle half of his Gladstone bag. When Butler bought himself a new wash-hand basin, in 1887, the fact is duly recorded. We are told that once, in 1886, he swept every corner of

Samuel Butler

every room of his lodgings with tea-leaves, and that it made him perspire freely. That there will be readers who do not care how many times Butler brushed his hair every day, nor on what occasion he wore "the high hat which appears in the corner of the picture in his room," I am not inclined to deny, but I am not of them. These little things, recounted with Mr. Festing Jones's humorous serenity, are my delight. If some contemporary had recorded the fact that Shakespeare habitually soaked the crust of his manchet in his last mouthful of sack, or that he wore out his left shoe faster than his right, how grateful we should be for the information. Only, there must come into our consideration : Are Butler and Shakespeare figures of equal significance, apart from their shoes and their hair-brushes ?

There is less room for divergence of judgment on the question of the way in which Mr. Jones has revealed the moral and social characteristics of his hero. Here he could hardly be excessive. The amiability, the ruggedness, the nervous instability, the obstinacy as of a rock, the tenderness and the sardonic bitterness which made up so strange an amalgam, are all frankly revealed. It is for us to arrange them, if we can, into a consistent portrait of a most inconsistent figure. Here is, taken at random, an entry of Butler's own, which gives a good example of several of his characteristics :

17th April 1895. I travelled from Patros to Athens with a young Turk, about thirty years old, and his dog—an English terrier. We were alone in the carriage the greater part of the time, and I suppose the poor dog was bored; at any rate, after a while, he made up to me. He licked me all over my face, and then began to pretend that my coat pocket had got a rat in it which he must catch. I was so flattered at being made up to by anyone or anything who seemed to tell me I was a nice person, that I let him go on and hunt for rats all over me, till at last his master interposed in beautiful English, and then we talked. He was a Secretary to the Turkish Legation, and was very clever and nice.

75

Aspects and Impressions

The incident could hardly be more trifling, but it is inimitably told; and it reveals not merely a mastery of minute description, but the self-tormenting temperament of a man of extraordinary talent who, for some unfathomable reason, though love was in his heart, was for ever out of harmony with the world, and suspicious of those whom he would fain have ingratiated. Those are the main lineaments which Mr. Festing Jones's biography reveals, and they are those of a miniaturist touching his ivory with a fastidious brush, and of a "born orphan" who could not find a home in the wilderness of jarring humanity.

A NOTE ON CONGREVE

CONGREVE'S principal Continental critic has remarked that literary history has behaved towards
him in a very stepmotherly fashion (*sehr stiefmütterlich*). There is no other English poet of equal
rank of the last two centuries and a half whose biography
has been so persistently neglected. When, in 1888, I
wrote my *Life of Congreve* I had had no predecessor since
John Oldmixon, masquerading under the pseudonym of
"Charles Wilson," published that farrago of lies and nonsense which he called *Memoirs of The Life, Writings and
Amours of William Congreve, Esq.,* in 1730. In this
kingdom of the blind, however one-eyed, I continue to
be king, since in the thirty-three years succeeding the issue
of my biography no one has essayed to do better what I
did as well as I could. The only exception is the *William
Congreve, sein Leben und seine Lustspiele,* published in
1897 by Dr. D. Schmid, who was, I believe, and perhaps
still is, a professor in the University of Graz in Austria.
I darted, full of anticipation, to the perusal of Dr.
Schmid's volume, but was completely disappointed. He
reposes upon me with a touching uniformity; he quotes
me incessantly and with courteous acknowledgment; but
I am unable to discover in his whole monograph one grain
of fact, or correction of fact, not known to me in 1888.

In spite of this, I have always believed that someone
with more patience and skill than I possess would be able
to add much to our knowledge of a man who lived with
the Pope and Swift and Addison of whom we know so
much. The late George A. Aitken, who seemed to carry
about with him a set of Röntgen rays which he applied
to the members of the Age of Anne, would have been the

man to do it. Not very long before his lamented death I urged the task upon Aitken; but his mind was set on other things, on Prior in particular. I do not know why it is that Congreve, one of the great dramatists of the world, perhaps our greatest social playwright, seems to lack personal attractiveness. It is a scandal that he has never been edited. His plays are frequently, but always imperfectly, reprinted, and without any editorial care. I was rejoiced to see that Mr. Montague Summers, than whom no one living is more competent to carry out such a labour, proposed to edit Congreve's plays. But even he did not intend to include the poems, the novel, or the letters; and I have heard no more of his project. To the book collector the folio publications of Congreve in verse are precious and amusing, but they have never attracted the notice of a bibliographer. Scholarship has, indeed, been *stiefmütterlich* towards Congreve, as the Austrian critic said.

My excuse for recalling this subject is the fact that I am able, through the kindness of Mr. Thos. J. Wise, to announce the existence of a work by Congreve hitherto unknown and unsuspected in its original form. In the matchless library of Mr. Wise there lurks an anonymous quarto of which the complete title is: "*An Impossible Thing*. A Tale. London: Printed: And Sold by J. Roberts in Warwick-Lane, MDCCXX." This was shown by Mr. Wise to several of our best authorities, who combined in the conjecture that it must be a hitherto unknown work by Prior. Yet since the poet's death—and this shows how little anybody reads Congreve—the contents of Mr. Wise's quarto have appeared in each successive edition of the Poems. But before this was perceived the truth had dawned upon Mr. Wise, who, turning over the *Historical Account of the English Poets*, a publication by Curll in 1720, found that the following entry occurs in the "Corrigenda":

Mr. Congreve. This Gentleman has lately oblig'd us with two Tales from Fontaine, entitled,

A Note on Congreve

I. *The Impossible Thing.*
II. *The Man That lost his Heifer.*

These form his pamphlet of the same year, 1720. When
Mr. Wise was kind enough to point this out to me it
was only left for me to add that the anonymous *Historical
Account* was the work of Giles Jacob, the friend whose
notes on Congreve's life form the nucleus of all we know
about him. Thus the authorship of the two poems was
proved. And it was only after that proof that I turned
to the index of the old editions and found there the two
poems, lurking unsuspected. I blush to recall the painful
incident.

However, the separate publication of the two poems
in a quarto of 1720 is a wholly unrecorded fact, and
important to bibliographers. *The Peasant in Search of
his Heifer* is added apparently as an after-thought, to fill
up the sheet. *An Impossible Thing* opens with these
lines :

> To thee, Dear *Dick,* this Tale I send,
> Both as a Critick and a Friend.
> I tell it with some Variation
> (Not altogether a Translation)
> From *La Fontaine;* an Author, *Dick,*
> Whose Muse would touch thee to the quick.
> The Subject is of that same kind
> To which thy Heart seems most inclin'd.
> How Verse may alter it, God knows ;
> Thou lov'st it well, I'm sure, in Prose.
> So without Preface, or Pretence,
> To hold thee longer in Suspense,
> I shall proceed, as I am able,
> To the Recital of my Fable.

He does proceed, not without considerable indelicacy, but
in excellent running verse. The "Dick" who was to
enjoy it I conjecture—and in this Mr. Austin Dobson
confirmed me—to have been Richard Shelton, who is connected with Prior's *Alma* and *A Case Stated*. Prior and
Congreve have so much in common that it is tantalizing

79

not to be able to persuade them to throw light upon one another; they were haunting the same coffee-houses when Swift was writing to Stella in 1710.

The discovery, after 200 years, of a unique copy of an unsuspected separate publication by Congreve confirms a suspicion of mine that other such pamphlets may exist. The earliest attempt at a bibliography was made by Giles Jacob, evidently under the poet's own eye, in 1720. Jacob gives a list of poems, with which "the ingenious Mr. Congreve, besides his excellent Dramatick Works, has oblig'd the Publick," but he adds no dates. Of these poems the first is *An Epistle to the Right Honourable Charles Lord Halifax,* and the six next are odes of each of which we possess the text in folio form. But of the *Epistle to Halifax* no separate edition is known, and it appears first in the octavo of 1710. But I cannot help suspecting that Giles Jacob possessed, or could refer to, a folio sheet of (probably) 1694, the year in which Halifax, to reward Congreve for the dedication of *The Double Dealer,* is supposed to have appointed him a Commissioner for licensing hackney coaches. But I have shown how confused is all the evidence with regard to Congreve's offices, which roused Thackeray to such superfluous indignation. Perhaps the shilly-shallying of Charles Montague had something to do with the suppression of an original folio of the *Epistle,* if it ever existed. In any case, a single sheet with, or more likely without, the signature of Mr. Congreve is worth looking out for.

As thirty-three years have passed since my *Life of Congreve* was published I venture to take occasion to mention here one or two slight matters which I should like any possessors of that volume to interpolate. If I had the opportunity to issue a new edition I should further enlarge on a matter which I did make prominent, the very leading part which the veteran Dryden took in advancing the fortunes of his young and hitherto unknown rival. The episode is a charming one, and I have now some instances of it which escaped me in 1888. As is known, Congreve came up from the country some time in 1692.

A Note on Congreve

He was introduced by Southerne to Dryden, who took a great fancy to him at once. Dryden was preparing a composite translation of *Juvenal,* and he gave the young man the Eleventh Satire to turn. Next came Dryden's *Persius,* to which Congreve prefixed a splendid poem of compliment: the triumph of *The Old Bachelor* followed in January. All this, and more, I worked out; but one very interesting evidence of Dryden's assiduous kindness escaped me. In 1705 was published as a folio pamphlet the *Ode on Mrs. Arabella Hunt singing,* and I supposed that this was the original appearance of this pindaric, which is one of Congreve's best. But my attention has been arrested by observing that 1705 was the year in which Arabella Hunt died, and also that so early as 1693 Dryden published this ode in his *Third Miscellany.* The Arabella Hunt ode therefore belongs to the beginning, and not, as I supposed, to the close, of Congreve's brief poetic career. It is a beautiful thing:

> Let all be hushed, each softest motion cease;
> Be every loud tempestuous thought at peace;
> And every ruder gasp of breath
> Be calm, as in the arms of Death,

and ends with a Keats-like couplet:

> Wishing forever in that state to lie,
> For ever to be dying so, yet never die.

It is now plain that this ode was published as a book at the death of the singer, but had been composed at least twelve years earlier. Another instance of Dryden's connexion with Congreve, which I observed too late to record it, is the fact that the latter contributed a song to the *Love Triumphant* of the former in 1694. In the dedication of that play Dryden speaks of "my most ingenious friend, Mr. Congreve," who has observed "the mechanic unities" of time and space strictly. *Love Triumphant* was Dryden's last play, and its failure was complete. A spiteful

Aspects and Impressions

letter-writer of the time gloats over its damnation because it will "vex huffing Dryden and Congreve to madness." All this confirms the idea that the elder poet's complaisance in the younger was matter of general knowledge, and Dryden's withdrawal from the ungrateful theatre must have been a blow to Congreve, who, however, practically stepped at once into Dryden's shoes.

Another biographical crumb. Charles Hopkins, one of the poet-sons of Ezekiel Hopkins, the once-famous Bishop of Derry, was a *protégé* of Dryden, and in 1697 brought out his second play, *Boadicea,* which he dedicated to Congreve in a long poem, from which we learn that Hopkins was an intimate friend and disciple of the author of *The Double Dealer.*

> You taught me first my Genius and my Power,
> Taught me to know my own, but gave me more.

He praises Congreve's verses, and then goes on to say, in lines of conspicuous warmth and sincerity:

> Nor does your Verse alone our Passions move;
> Beyond the Poet, we the Person love.
> In you, and almost only you, we find
> Sublimity of Wit and Candour of the Mind.
> Both have their Charms, and both give that delight.
> 'Tis pity that you should, or should not write.

He proceeds, enthusiastically, in this strain, and closes at last in words which still carry a melodious echo:

> Here should I, not to tire your patience, end,
> But who can part so soon, with such a Friend?
> You know my Soul, like yours, without design,
> You know me yours, and I too know you mine.
> I owe you all I am, and needs must mourn
> My want of Power to make you some return.
> Since you gave all, do not a part refuse,
> But take this slender Offering of the Muse.
> Friendship, from servile Interest free, secures
> My Love, sincerely, and entirely yours.

A Note on Congreve

This is by no means the only occasion on which Charles Hopkins proclaimed his gratitude and affection. As early as 1694 he paid a tribute of friendship to Congreve, who wrote a prologue to Hopkins's first tragedy, *Pyrrhus King of Epirus* (1695). I think we may presume that it was owing to the greater poet's influence that *Pyrrhus* was put on the stage, for Congreve wrote a prologue, in which he warmly recommended it, saying :

> 'Tis the first Flight of a just-feather'd Muse,

adding, to the audience :

> Then spare the Youth; or if you'll damn the Play,
> Let him but first have his, then take your Day,

words which Congreve would hardly have used unless he had been responsible for the production.

It is odd that Hopkins should speak so humbly and Congreve dwell on his friend's inexperience, since Hopkins was at least six years older than Congreve, who was now twenty-seven and pretended to be only twenty-five. He enjoyed no further advantage from the devoted attachment of Charles Hopkins, who retired immediately to his father's home in Londonderry. Already he felt the decay of "a weak and sickly tenement," and his last play, pathetically entitled *Friendship Improv'd* (1697), was sent to London from Londonderry with a preface that bewailed his broken health. According to Giles Jacob, he was "a martyr to the cause of hard drinking, and a too Passionate fondness for the fair Sex." The same authority says that Hopkins "was always more ready to serve others than mindful of his own Affairs," and we can well believe it. An hour before his death, which took place in 1700, Charles Hopkins, "when in great pain," wrote a last copy of verses, which have been preserved. And so Congreve lost this most faithful henchman at the very moment when his own last and perhaps greatest play, *The Way of the World*, failed on the stage, and when he was most in need of sympathy.

Aspects and Impressions

Now for a white sheet to wrap both Congreve and myself. In 1888 I took credit, and not unjustly, for having discovered that Congreve prefixed verses to the first edition of a little rare book called *Reliquæ Gethinianæ*, which were never reprinted until I restored them, and that these were entirely different from those he prefixed to the third edition of the same book in 1703, the latter alone having been always since reprinted among Congreve's verses. Both poems are conceived in a Donne-like spirit of hyperbole. Grace, Lady Gethin, about whom I have found out more since my *Life of Congreve* was published, was a young Irish lady, Miss Norton, who married an Irish baronet, Sir Richard Gethin, and died at the age of twenty-one in 1697. She secured a wide reputation for learning and piety, and she was actually buried in Westminster Abbey. Her essays —with mortuary folding-plates, again in the spirit of Donne—were posthumously published and produced a favourable sensation. But to my great confusion Leslie Stephen, who had (marvellously) studied Lady Gethin, pointed out to me, when he read my biography, that she was a fraud, conscious or unconscious. Her so-called works were cribbed out of several seventeenth-century writers of morality, but particularly out of Bacon. She had copied them into her commonplace book, doubtless without guile. My dear friend and master grimly remarked, "I wonder neither you nor Congreve spotted ' reading makes a full man ' ! " But he never said a word in print about our negligence, which deepens my remorse. I suspect that Congreve, like myself, did not read the *Reliquiæ* very carefully, but it is strange that no other of Lady Gethin's numerous contemporary admirers discovered the mare's-nest.

In 1888 I was not able to describe Congreve's ode on the Taking of Namur in its original form, but since then I have secured a copy of the first edition of 1695. The title is *A Pindarique Ode, Humbly Offer'd to the King, On His Taking Namure. By Mr. Congreve.* There are many differences of text, showing that the poet subjected

A Note on Congreve

the poem to careful revision. In this first form, the King, afterwards spoken of as "William," is described and addressed as "Nassaw"; perhaps the poet was advised that His Majesty did not care to be incessantly reminded of his Dutch origin. Here is a cancelled passage, describing the horrors of the attack :

Cataracts of Fire Precipitate are driv'n
On their Adventurous Heads, as Ruin rain'd from Heaven . . .
    Echoes each scalding step resound,
And horrid Flames, bellowing to be unbound,
Tumble with hollow rage in Cavern'd Ground.

Perhaps Congreve thought this was too boisterous. In the Namur ode there are curious reminiscences of the battle of the angels in *Paradise Lost*. There was no half-title to this folio, let collectors take notice.

The complete neglect which has overtaken the minor writings of Congreve is regrettable. His odes and pastorals are deformed by a too-conscious rhetoric, and his imagery is apt to be what is called "artificial," that is to say, no longer in fashion. But they bear evidence of high cultivation and an elevated sense of style. When Dr. Johnson said that *The Mourning Muse of Alexis* (1695) was "a despicable effusion" he fell into the sin of over-statement. I admit that this agony of regret for the death of good Queen Mary II may not have been very sincere, and that the imagery is often vapid. Yet the poem is an interesting and a skilful exercise in a species of art which has its place in the evolution of our literature. It is not so good as Marvell would have made it earlier or as Collins later. But in 1695 I know not who could have done it better except Dryden, and even he, if more vigorous, was not commonly so melodious. That Congreve could not write a tolerable song I frankly admit. To book-collectors, however, the separate minor publications of our poet seem to offer a field which is still unharvested. With Mr. Wise's new discovery, and with the posthumous *Letter to Viscount Cobham*, there are

Aspects and Impressions

some nine or ten separate publications, besides the four (or five, with *The Judgment of Paris* of 1701) quarto plays. When to these we add the controversial pamphlets and *Squire Trelooby,* in its two forms of 1704 and 1734, we have quite an interesting little body of first editions for the bibliophile to expend his energy in collecting.

Lovers of pleasure will think small beer of these desultory annotations. But in the case of a great dramatist like Congreve, whose career is very imperfectly known to us, I hold that all information is welcome, even though the separate details of it seem to be trivial. I present these glimmerings in the hope that they may not be useless to the future editor and biographer, whoever he may be, whose lamp will throw my taper into the shade.

THE FIRST DRAFT OF SWINBURNE'S
ANACTORIA

NO modern poet offers a more interesting field for critical examination in his MSS. than Swinburne does, and in perhaps no other can the movement of mind, under changes of mood, be so accurately followed. His prose MSS. have a somewhat heavy uniformity, from which little is to be gathered, but the aspect of his written verse is so diverse as to be almost bewildering in its changes of form, not merely from one group of years to another, but even in the effusions of a single day. After long consideration, and a study of a multitude of MSS. written between 1857 and 1909, I have come to the conclusion that the critical value of Swinburne's drafts depends very much upon the spirit in which he happened to compose his poems. There were evidently three methods in his use. Some time ago there turned up a large number of dramatic and lyrical exercises, written by Swinburne as an undergraduate. These have greatly modified our conception of his early work, and they reveal in the apparently idle youth an amazing persistence in self-apprenticeship to the craft of verse. I hope to find leisure on a future occasion to describe these interesting and voluminous papers : in the meantime I only mention them here, in order to point out that they are written, with curious uniformity, and with very few corrections, in a hard, angular handwriting which Swinburne presently abandoned, but which resembles the formal script in which his later Putney poems appear to be composed.

I say "appear to be," because I am convinced, and my conviction is supported by the evidence of those who lived with him, that he adopted in later life the practice of composing and practically finishing his poems in his head before he put anything down on paper. He used to be heard walking up and down his room at The Pines, and then pausing awhile, evidently to write down what he had polished in his head. This accounts for the "clean " look of most of his later MSS., which appear to be first drafts, and yet have few corrections. What we now discover from the undergraduate MSS. of which I have spoken above is that, apparently, he adopted in early youth the plan to which he was to revert in old age. But of this plan there might be two varieties; Swinburne might work up his stanzas to perfection in his brain before writing anything, or he might be inspired with such a flow of language that the finished poem would slip smoothly from his brain. Doubtless there was something of both these in his practice, but I incline to think the former by far the most frequent. From neither can we obtain much impression of the mechanism of his invention.

But there was a third method, of which I am about to describe a peculiarly interesting example, which the poet adopted in the hey-day of his poetical career. Soon after he left Oxford, perhaps in 1860, his handwriting changed its character; it became less boyish, but more crabbed and careless. I think that the weakness of his wrist may have been the cause of this alteration. It is particularly marked in the period from 1862 to 1870. His later writing was emphatic in its stiff inelegance, but usually legible; the script of his middle period was, at its best, lax and straggling, at its worst almost indecipherable. But it varied extravagantly, so much so that it is often difficult to believe that the same pen, and still more that the same hour, could have produced such violently diverse exhibitions. It has gradually dawned upon me, while helping Mr. Wise to disentangle an accumulation of rough copies and fragments, that the cause of this diversity lay in the degree of excitement which Swinburne put into the act of composition. He was always paroxysmal, always the victim of excruciating intellectual excitement which descended upon him like the beak of the Promethean

The First Draft of Swinburne's *Anactoria*

vulture. To discover the points at which, in a particular composition, this fury of inspiration fell upon him, is to get a little closer to the secret of Swinburne's astonishing virtuosity, and is my excuse for the following observations.

So many of Swinburne's MSS. have been preserved, principally in the newspaper bundles which he so oddly carried with him, without ever examining, through all his peregrinations from Oxford to Putney, that it is particularly vexatious that those which we could least afford to spare, those of his blossoming period from 1861 to 1868, are very exiguously represented. No scrap of *The Queen Mother* has turned up, nor of the published form of *Rosamond* (an undergraduate sketch of this play remains). The original MS. of *Chastelard* exists only in a few fragments, the MS. sold in New York in 1913 being a clean copy for the press. According to the evidence of George Meredith, the first draft of *Laus Veneris* was written in red ink; the existing version, though containing corrections and cancelled passages, is written in black ink, and shows no sign of the frenzy of composition; it is evidently a transcript. Of *Poems and Ballads* no general MS. exists, but portions of the "copy" sent to the printers are in various collections. Most of these are transcripts, and show no sign of emotion or excitement. Several first drafts of *Poems and Ballads*, however, have been preserved, and of these the most remarkable that I have examined is that of *Anactoria*, of which I will now give some account.

Swinburne's first drafts offer none of the attractions which collectors of autographs commonly desiderate. They are never signed and rarely headed. That of the long poem afterwards called *Anactoria* has neither a title nor the Greek epigraph from Sappho. It is written, or rather wildly scribbled, on both sides of six sheets of blue foolscap, the water-mark of one of which is 1863, doubtless the date of the composition of the poem. These sheets were thrown away, and came into our hands in a great disorder of papers, mostly worthless, which left The Pines

after Watts-Dunton's death.   As we turned them over, in
the welter of manuscript, my eye caught the line

> Lilies, and languor of the Lesbian air,

and I realized what lay before us.   Scattered through the
bundle, five sheets were identified, but unfortunately one
sheet was missing.   By a happy chance, this also turned
up in another parcel three years later, and the first draft is
now, I believe, complete, although one passage in the
published poem, as I shall presently show, is absent.

The text begins high up on the first sheet, and offers no
peculiarity in the opening eight lines, which, with the
slight exception of "Sting" instead of "Blind" in line 2,
are identical with the published version of 1866.   The
handwriting is the usual script of Swinburne in the 60's,
crabbed, but plain and calm.   Suddenly, with line 7, a sort
of frenzy takes the poet's pen, and at the side of the paper,
in lines that slope more and more rapidly downwards, and
in such a stumbling and trembling hand that they are with
great difficulty to be spelt out, are interpolated the lines :

> Severed the bones that bleach, the flesh that cleaves,
> And let our sifted ashes drop like leaves.
> I feel thy blood against my blood; my pain
> Pains thee, and lips bruise lips, and vein stings vein.

Then, in very small clear script, opposite this outburst, is
written, by itself, like a solo on a flute :

> Let fruit be crushed on fruit, let flower on flower,
> Breast kindle breast and either burn one hour.

To this immediately follows :

> In her high place in Paphos,

which is the opening of line 64 in the published version.
But the first draft stops here, leaving that half-line un-
cancelled, and proceeds quietly, in a large hand,

> Saw love, a burning flame from crown to feet,

The First Draft of Swinburne's *Anactoria*

and so on for six lines which are now to be found in the middle of the poem. Thereupon follows a breathless interlude of six couplets, scribbled with extreme violence and so curiously interwoven that the only way to explain their relation is to quote them :

> I would my love could *slay* thee; I am satiated
> With seeing thee live, and fain would have thee dead,
> Vex thee with amorous agonies, and shake
> Life at thy lips, and leave it there to ache;
> Strain out thy soul with pangs too soft to kill,
> Intolerable interludes, and infinite ill;
> I would earth had thy body as fruit to eat,
> And no mouth but some serpent's found thee sweet.
> I would find grievous ways to have thee slain,
> Intense device, and superflux of pain,
> Relapse and reluctation of the breath,
> Dumb tunes and shuddering semitones of death.

If this passage be compared with the published text, it will be observed that firstly, there are, with the single alteration of "kill" for "slay," no verbal modifications whatever : and that secondly the couplets are shifted about like counters in a game, or as if they were solid objects which might be put here, there, or anywhere in a liquid setting. The first draft of *A Song of Italy*, now in the possession of Mr. Thos. J. Wise, presents the same characteristics, though in a less degree.

We are still on the opening sheet of the draft of *Anactoria*, and it now presents to us, quietly and conscientiously written in the middle of the page :

> For I beheld in sleep the light that is
> In her high place in Paphos, heard the kiss
> Of body and soul that mix with eager tears,
> And laughter stinging thro' the eyes and ears,

a sort of *tessera* evidently left there to be fitted in whenever a favourable blank presented itself; we find it, without the smallest change of language, fixed in the middle of the poem. It is noticeable that the fragment "In her high place in Paphos" is now utilized.

A storm of excitement presently ruffles the poet, and he turns the sheet in such agitation that he holds it upside-down. Without leading up to it in any way, he starts a passage

She came and touched me, saying "Who doth thee wrong, Sappho?"

which closes abruptly with lines which may be cited because they contain several of the very rare instances in which the draft slightly differs verbally from the text of 1866:

Ah, wilt thou slay me lest I kiss thee dead?
"*Be of good cheer, wilt thou forget?*" *she* said:
"*For* she that flies shall follow for thy sake,
For she shall give thee gifts that *will* not take,
Shall kiss that *will* not kiss thee" (yea, kiss me)
"When *I would* not, etc."

We presently come across the only couplet in the whole poem which was cancelled in the first draft, and yet re-appears in the published text. This is:

Bound with her myrtles, beaten with her rods,
The young men and the maidens and the gods,

now very effectively introduced into the argument, but in the first draft destroyed with a whirling movement of the pen, so that it looks as if a dust-storm involved it. Written with frenzied violence, almost perpendicularly, the draft then presents a couplet:

Taught the sun ways to travel, woven most fine
The moonbeams, shed the starbeams forth as wine,

for which a place is now found immediately before the "Bound with her myrtles" couplet. The ecstasy of the poet seems to have suddenly flagged here, and there follows

The First Draft of Swinburne's *Anactoria*

immediately, in sedate script, with even lines, the passage

> Alas, that neither moon nor sun nor dew
> Nor all cold things can purge me wholly through,
> Assuage me nor allay me nor appease,
> Till supreme sleep shall bring me bloodless ease,
> Till time wax faint in all his periods,

which now takes its place near the very close of the poem. The actual closing lines are, in like fashion, appended to the third page of the draft. They read as follows :

> Till fate undo the bondage of the gods,
> And lay to slake *the unquenchable desire*
> *Lethean lotus on a lip of fire,*
> And *pour* around and over and under me
> *The wake of* the insuperable sea.

There was evidently on the poet's part no original intention of utilizing these lines as a conclusion to the poem. I give them here because they present the solitary instance of important verbal alteration to be found in the whole text of 1866.

It would baffle the most meticulous investigation to restore the innumerable false starts, broken lines, and rejected readings which underlie the text of the Draft. There is no question here of Swinburne's creating or polishing anything in his mind, the whole work of composition proceeds on the paper itself, and what is very curious is the fact that nothing of any merit or technical beauty seems, so far as it is possible to decipher the cancelled verses, to be lost. As soon as ever the expression became adequate the line was left, and was never modified; as long as it was inadequate, it was pitilessly rejected, and the verse not passed till it satisfied the ear and imagination of the poet. What is interesting is that this work was carried out with the pen, and not, as was the practice in Swinburne's later years, with the mind; and nothing could be more opposed to the popular notion of Swinburne as the inspired improvisatore than all this evidence of intense laborious application to his creative task. In fact the more the original MSS. of Swinburne are examined, the more clearly is he revealed to us as an artist equally sedulous and sensitive, working by fits and starts, in gusts of overwhelming emotion, but always sufficiently master of himself to recognize, with finality, when the exact form of expression had been reached. Having recognized it, he did not, like Tennyson, Landor and other poets, fidget any further with it, but left it verbally permanent.

On the other hand, the draft of *Anactoria* proves, what we might have suspected, that if Swinburne completed his verbal text in his first movement of laboured inspiration, he made no effort then to build up his poem. It may be observed that *Dolores* is a rosary of stanza-beads on an invisible string; in other words, that the string might be broken, the beads shaken together, and the stanzas arranged in an entirely new sequence, without any injury to the effect of the poem. In other cases, and these some of Swinburne's finest lyrics, the same want of progression is to be noted. But we have not been able to witness the process before, nor were we prepared to find it working in a poem which is so elegiacal as *Anactoria*. Yet the evidence of the First Draft is positive. It is now clear that Swinburne forged his brilliant Dryden-like couplets as though each one were a stanza, and practically treated them as bits of mosaic to be fitted, in cooler blood, into a scheme not present to his mind when his inspiration seized him.

We seem, therefore, to be in the presence of a curious phenomenon. Whereas in the case of most poets the general outline of the work precedes the execution of it in detail, Swinburne offers us the paradox of an execution carried to the utmost finish before the act of evolution begins. He takes a bag-ful of couplets, all polished to the finest point, and—on some subsequent occasion—he builds these up into a poem which has the aspect of inevitable growth. The First Draft of *Anactoria*, which I have attempted to describe, is totally unintelligible, a chaos of

The First Draft of Swinburne's *Anactoria*

Rodin-like fragments, unless we accept this theory of the poet's method.

One point remains to be stated. The published text of *Anactoria* contains 304 lines. Of these I have found, scattered over the tract of delirious manuscript, 270. It is curious that not a single verse should have been added by the poet when he came to distribute and arrange his cluster of couplets, the solitary accession to the text being the solid passage of 34 lines in the middle of the poem, beginning

> Or say what God above all gods and years
> With offering and blood-sacrifice of tears.

Of this, not a single trace is to be found in the Draft. My first supposition was that the sheet containing these lines was lost, as might well be when we consider the accidental and fortuitous way in which the rest was retrieved. But I have come to the conclusion that this is not the case. The text in the Draft stops at the line

> The mystery of the cruelty of things

without any sign that the idea of the impassive harshness of Fate was to be expanded. The 34 lines which now follow have, moreover, a character that distinguishes them from the rest of *Anactoria*, with which they are not quite in keeping. They leave the individual passion of Sappho entirely out of sight, and they are instinct with an order of theological ideas which occupied Swinburne in 1864 and 1865, when he was writing *Atalanta in Calydon* and the earliest of *Songs before Sunrise*. They are on a higher philosophical plane than the melodious ravings of the love-sick poetess, and the more we read them, the more may we be persuaded that they are an after-thought.

THE HÔTEL DE RAMBOUILLET

THE fashion of the moment, whether in literature or in art, whether in England or in France, favours what is rough, vivid and undisciplined. A new generation of readers welcomes the lyrical effusions of the cowboy, the lumberman, the tramp, and even the apache. It accepts Bubu de Montparnasse as a hero and does not shrink from overhearing the confidences of a burglar. There is no reason why we should exercise our sarcasm over these *naïvetés* of taste, while indeed, as social beings, we are even entitled to rejoice at them, since, in the language of practical æstheticism, a positive always involves a negative. If this age dotes on the dirtiness of tramps, it is because every one of us is obliged to be occupied and clean ; and if the apache is the object of our poetry, it is because, in our extremely settled, confident and comfortable lives, we miss the excitement of being in personal danger. But let the delicate social balance of our existence be again disturbed, let us become practically accustomed to starvation and outrage and murder, and not another strophe would our poets address to the drunken navvy or the grimy bathchair-man. If London or Paris were to burn, if only for a fortnight, literature and art would hurry back to the study of princesses and to the language of the Golden Age.[1]

No more striking instance of this oscillation is to be found in history than is afforded by France at the opening of the seventeenth century, in the creation of what is called the *vie de salon*. This movement, the most civilizing, the most refining in the intellectual life of France,

[1] I leave these airy words of prophecy as they stood in 1912 before the cataclysm ! (1922.)

Aspects and Impressions

was the direct outcome of the convulsion of the civil wars It was the ugliness, the wickedness, the brutality of the reigns of the later Valois which made the best minds of Paris determine to be gentle, beautiful and delicate under Louis XIII. Forty years of savage rapine had laid a severe embargo upon civilization, and no picture of France in 1625 can be complete without a glance at the background of 1575. In that half-century of administrative disorder, in the bitter and distracted state of country life, the population had lost confidence in virtue, and had become rude and dishonest. One of the Venetian ambassadors, travelling through France, declared of the Frenchmen whom he met, that "the sight of blood had made them cunning, coarse and wild." If such was the condition of the countryside, the towns were even worse. There resulted from the misery after the siege of Paris a universal weariness, a longing for tolerance in man to man, a yearning for refinement in private life, for security, for cultivation, for repose of mind and body and estate.

That Henri IV was a Protestant has led, perhaps, to some injustice being done to his memory in a Catholic country. But he deserved well of France in this critical moment. Every necessity of life had become extravagantly dear, every branch of industry depressed, if not extinct, when he came to the throne. He set himself to be the guardian of trade, and of the arts. He rebuilt cities, and a contemporary reported of him that "no sooner was he master of Paris, than the streets were swarming with masons." The shrewdness of Henri IV broke down the old superstition, of which Sully made himself the obstinate spokesman, that agriculture was the only source of wealth for France. The King persisted in encouraging the manufactures of silk and linen; in widening the circle of commercial interests; in teaching Frenchmen to achieve wealth and honour as architects, painters, sculptors and cabinet-makers. The prestige of the military nobles grew less and less, that of the *bourgeoisie* grew more and more, while between them a new class, refined, intelligent, a

The Hôtel de Rambouillet

little timid and supple in their professional adroitness, that *nouvelle aristocratie de robe*, of which M. Lavisse has spoken, came to the front and gave its tone to the surface of life.

The general trend of the best thought, at the beginning of the seventeenth century, was towards the polishing of society, left roughened and rusty by the long wars of religion. But the court of Henri IV was too coarse, and too little in sympathy with the mental aspirations of the age, to carry out this design, which needed other influences than those which could emanate from Marie de Médicis. Meanwhile, the great importance of the provincial centres had rapidly declined, and it was Paris that gave the tone to France. This then was the moment when a peculiarly Parisian centre was needed, independent of the court, yet in political sympathy with it, a centre of imagination and intelligence not too austere in its morals, not too pedantic in its judgments, to include the characteristic minds of the age, whatever their limitation or peculiarity; and yet definitely, unflinchingly and for a sufficient length of time, radiating politeness and authority. Such a Parisian centre must be aristocratic, yet liberal and intelligent; it must lay down rules of conduct, and contrive to get them obeyed; it must be recognized and haunted by the first men and women of the century; it must be actuated in equal proportions by the genius of discipline, and by that of easy grace and accomplished gallantry. In short, it must be what Providence astonishingly provided for French society at that moment of its sorest need, the unparalleled Hôtel de Rambouillet, with, as its prophetess and châtelaine, one of the most charming women who have ever occupied the pen of the memoir-maker.

In observing the history of the famous Chambre Bleue, it cannot but strike an English critic how far more articulate French opinion was than English in the seventeenth century. Although, as we shall presently see, documents have been slow in forthcoming, they existed, and still exist, in profusion. But while we can now study, almost from day to day, the intrigues, the amusements and

Aspects and Impressions

the enthusiasms of the group in the Rue Saint-Thomas, the record of a similar *salon* open in England at the same epoch is still shrouded in a darkness which is likely never to be penetrated. So far as we can venture to judge there must have been many points of likeness between the Marquise de Rambouillet and Lucy Countess of Bedford. The circle of the friends of each was illustrious. Donne was a greater poet-divine than Cospeau or Godeau; our national vanity may fairly set Daniel and Drayton against Voiture and Chapelain, while even Corneille is not shamed by being balanced by Ben Jonson. The coterie of the Countess of Bedford may probably have been less wealthy, less sparkling, more provincial than that of Madame de Rambouillet, but the melancholy thing is that we lack the opportunity of comparing them. Save for vague allusions in the poets, and for a dim tradition of politeness, we form no detailed impression of the feasts of wit at Twickenham, whereas about those in the Rue Saint-Thomas we know almost as much as heart can wish. In the communication of social impressions England stood much farther behind France in the seventeenth century than the individual genius of her writers accounts for. We have, however, one possible recompense : the field of irresponsible conjecture is infinitely wider in our island chronicle. In France, even the craziest of faddists could not hope for a hearing if he suggested that the tragedies of Pierre Corneille were secretly written by Richelieu in his lighter moments.

On the history of the Hôtel de Rambouillet the documents which survive are very numerous, and probably have not yet been exhaustively examined. The seventeenth century in France was awake to the importance of its own immortality, and set down the records of its social and literary glory with complacency. The memorials of the Hôtel de Rambouillet to be found scattered over the works of such contemporaries as Segrais, Pellisson and Conrart have long been known. The poems and correspondence of Voiture, of course, form a mine of treasure, which was first competently worked by Ubicini in his

The Hôtel de Rambouillet

edition of Voiture's works. It is now sifted to its last crumb
of gold by M. Émile Magne in the eloquent and learned
volumes which he has just published. There is also, and
most important of all, Tallemant des Réaux, of whom I
shall presently speak at greater length. M. Magne and M.
Collas, with Voiture and Chapelain respectively in their
particular thoughts, have turned over the priceless wealth
of MSS. in the *Archives nationales*. It is probable that
we now possess, thanks to the researches of these scholars,
as full an account of the Hôtel de Rambouillet as we are
likely to obtain. It may be pointed out that these exact
records, founded upon positive documents, show the
danger of such hypotheses as not a few previous
historians have rashly taken up. In the light of present
knowledge, it is necessary to use not merely Roederer
(1835), but even the more accurate Livet (1870), with
caution.

The Hôtel existed, as a centre of light and civility,
for nearly seventy years, and involved the whole careers
of two generations. Its history, which was developed by
circumstances, and somewhat modified in its course by
changes of taste, found no chronicler until it had existed
some twenty years. That preliminary period, from the
death of Henri IV to the arrival of Tallemant and Voiture,
is precisely the time about which we should like to know
most, and about which we are doomed to know least.
The violent close of the reign, in a last wild crime, had,
as we see from every species of evidence, brought with
it a longing for serenity and repose. The keynote of the
best society became a cultivation of simplicity, refinement,
and delicacy. This growth of a new spirit was identified
with the Marquis and Marquise of Rambouillet, but
exactly how at first we are at a loss to tell, and even
M. Magne is silent. A careful setting side by side of
scattered impressions may enable us, however, while
avoiding these hypotheses of which we have given warning, to form some idea of the foundation of the Hôtel and
its prestige.

Charles d'Angennes, Marquis of Rambouillet and

Aspects and Impressions

Pisani, who has given its title to the celebrated union of hearts, must not long detain us, for the excellent reason that not much is recorded about him. He was probably born about 1577, and he died in Paris in 1652, having become blind about twelve years earlier. His eyesight was very peculiar; perhaps he was colour-blind. On this subject he was sensitive, and tried to conceal his condition. On one occasion, when the Duc de Montausier, who was known to have recently ordered a gorgeous scarlet costume, appeared at the Hôtel de Rambouillet, his host called out "Ah! Monsieur, la belle escarlate!"—which was unlucky, because the Duc had happened to call in a black suit. Tallemant says that the Marquis "avait terriblement d'esprit, mais un peu frondeur." In this he doubtless resembled most of the wits of that age, who liked to let their antagonists feel that there were claws under the fur. In wit his wife, with her sweet consideration and delicate humorous tact, was immeasurably his superior; it was she, and not he, who gave the Hôtel its famous amenity. We must not measure this in all things by our standards. About 1625 there was quite an inundation of spiteful, and sometimes obscene, verse in France, and this has to be taken into consideration in dealing with the *salons*. The Hôtel de Rambouillet kept this in some check, but was amply aware of the entertainment to be got by clothing satire—what Agrippa d'Aubigné called *la malplaisante vérité*—in smooth and well-turned verse. The Marquis was himself a versifier, and he shared to the full his wife's respect for letters.

There is nothing, however, to show that this agreeable man would have been able, by his unaided talents, to make a mark upon the age he lived in. He was the satellite of an infinitely more refulgent luminary, his extraordinary wife. If there is such a thing as social genius, on the same lines as literary or artistic genius, this was undoubtedly possessed, in a very high degree, by Catherine de Vivonne, Marquise de Rambouillet. She was born at Rome in 1588; half an Italian, her mother was a Roman princess, Julia Savella; and when, long after-

The Hôtel de Rambouillet

wards, the Marquise had become not merely French, but almost the culture of France incarnate, she loved to dwell on her Italian parentage. Tallemant tells us that she always thought the Savelli the best family in the world; it was her faith. At the age of six, she became a naturalized French citizen, and in January, 1600, being in her twelfth year, she was married to Charles d'Angennes, who, his father being still alive, was then Vidame du Mans. Her own sober and stately father, the Marquis de Pisani, was just dead. He had left Catherine a conspicuous heiress. In later years, she spoke with characteristic humour of the way in which she was intimidated, poor child of twelve, by her husband's years, since he was twenty-three, and she said that she had never become quite used to feeling grown-up in his presence. But this was her whimsical way of talking, for there really existed between them the closest and most intimate affection. The Marquis and the Marquise were always in love with one another, throughout their extended married life of more than half a century; and in that age of light loves and cynical relationships, even baseless ill-nature never found any serious charge of frivolity to bring against this gracious lady.

It is true that it could not be difficult to show complaisance to Catherine de Rambouillet. She was never dull, never inattentive, never indiscreet. We hear that she had an extraordinary native gift for being present when she was wanted, and occupied elsewhere when her company would have been inconvenient. As years grew upon her, it seems as though this instinct for pleasing became a little too emphatic. Almost the only fault which any chronicler brings against her is that, towards the end, she was not critical enough, that she liked too many people, that her individuality melted into a general indulgence. But she was surrounded by petulant poets and snarling courtiers, and that this mild censure of her should be insinuated is, probably, but another tribute to her tact. She was like Milton's Lady; not indeed "chained up in alabaster," but serene, open-eyed and gay in the midst

Aspects and Impressions

of a monstrous rout of ambitions and vanities which often resembled "stabled wolves or tigers at their prey." One of her most striking characteristics obviously was her power of ruling a society from its centre without making her rule oppressive. All the anecdotes of her discipline in her *salon* show the coolness of her judgment and the velvet strength of her hand. She was capable of strong dislike, yet with an Italian faculty for concealing it. She hated Louis XIII to the inmost fibre of her being, for what seemed to her his despicable qualities, yet he never discovered it.

Those who regard Catherine de Rambouillet as one of the most engaging figures of Europe in the seventeenth century, must regret that, from an age where portrait-painting was so largely cultivated, no picture of her has come down to us. All we know is that she was beautiful and tall; the poets compared her to a pine tree. It was supposed that she never consented to sit to a painter, but M. Magne has discovered that there were portraits. Scudéry, he believes, possessed engravings from paintings by Van Mol and by du Cayer. The earlier of these, painted in 1645, represented her gazing at the dead body of her father. These works of art appear to be hopelessly lost. We are thrown back on the written "portraits," in the alembicated style of the middle of the century, which adorn a host of novels and poems. Of these the fullest is that introduced by Madeleine de Scudéry into the seventh volume of her huge romance, *Le Grand Cyrus*. M. Emile Magne, confronted with the "precious" terms of this description, and the vagueness of it, loses his temper with poor Mlle. de Scudéry, whom he calls *cette pécore*. It is true that the physical details which would interest us are omitted, but it is hardly true to say, that "il est impossible de rien démêler au griffonage [de Mlle. de Scudéry], sinon que Mme. de Rambouillet était belle." This is not quite just, and to avenge the great Madeleine for being called a *pécore*, I will quote, what M. Magne surprisingly omits, part of the character of Cléomire, the pseudonym of Mme. de Rambouillet in *Cyrus*:

The Hôtel de Rambouillet

She is tall and graceful. The delicacy of her complexion is beyond expression. The eyes of Cléomire are so admirably beautiful that no painter has ever been able to do justice to them. All her passions are in subjection to her good sense.

This might be more precise, but the touch about the eyes is helpful. Chapelain celebrated (in 1666, just after her death)

> Cet air, cette douceur, cette grâce, ce port,
> Ce chef d'œuvre admiré du Midi jusqu'au Nord;

And Tallemant, always the best reporter, speaks of the permanent beauty of her complexion, which she would never consent to touch artificially. The only concession to fashion which she made in old age was to rouge her lips, which had turned blue. Tallemant wished she would not do even this. When she was very old, her head shook with a sort of palsy; this was attributed to her having indulged too much in the eating of pounded ambergris, but perhaps a more obvious reason could be found for so natural an infirmity.

In an age so troubled and so turbulent as that of Henri IV, public attention was concentrated in wonderment on the serene beatitude of the Rambouillets. "So rest, for ever rest, O princely pair!" the admiring court might be conceived as saying to a couple so dignified, so calm and so unaffected in their attachment. "Tout le monde admire la magnifique entente, à travers leur vie limpide, du Marquis et de la Marquise." Their limpid life—that was the just description of a mode of conduct so rare in that age, and at that social elevation, as to be relatively unique. What existences the reverse of limpid, lives tortured and turbid and mud-stained, do memoir-writers of that time, the Segrais and the Tallemants, reveal on all sides of them! Both were gifted, and each was persuaded of the excellence of learning and literature, although in talents the wife considerably surpassed the husband. Madame de Rambouillet was versed in several literatures. She spoke Italian and Spanish, the two fashionable languages of the time, to perfection. She loved all beautiful objects, and not one of the fine arts failed to find eager appreciation from her. In order to enjoy the sources of poetic distinction, she taught herself Latin, that she might read Virgil in the original. But she soon relaxed these studies, which might easily have landed her in pedantry. She became the mother of seven children, to whose bringing-up she gave strict attention. She found that her health, although her constitution was good, needed care. Perhaps she gave way, a little, to an amiable Italian indolence; at all events, the strenuousness which her early years had threatened subsided into a watchful, hospitable, humorous and memorable hospitality. If there could be rank maintained in such matters, Madame de Rambouillet would probably take place as the most admirable hostess in history.

But, to entertain, a house was needed. The old Marquis de Pisani had bought, in 1599, a ramshackle dwelling, close to the Louvre, in the Rue Saint-Thomas, which became, at his death, the property of his daughter. In 1604 when, it is to be noted, she was only sixteen years of age, she pulled it down and built the famous Hôtel on the site.

Young as she was, it is certain that the Marquise was herself the architect of the Hôtel de Rambouillet. A professional architect had been called in to rebuild the house, but when he submitted his designs to her they dissatisfied her by their conventionality. Tallemant describes them—a saloon on one side, a bedroom on the other, a staircase in the middle, nothing could be more poor. Moreover, the courtyard was pinched in extent and irregular in shape. One evening, after she had been dreaming over the drawings, the young Marquise called out "Quick! some paper! I have thought of what I want!" She had been trained to use a pencil, and she immediately drew out an elevation, which the builders followed point by point. Her design was so bold, so original, and so handsome, that the house made a sensation in Paris. The Queen-Mother, when she built the

The Hôtel de Rambouillet

Luxembourg, sent her architects to study the Hôtel de Rambouillet before they started their plans.

In all this matter of the foundation of the Hôtel and the opening of the famous *salon,* M. Magne has made considerable discoveries, which should be distinguished from much in his charming books in which he has had no choice but to follow earlier published authorities. He has made excellent use of the *Inventaires* of 1652, 1666 and 1671, to which attention had, however, already been drawn by M. Charles Sauze. But a ground plan of the Hôtel de Rambouillet, from a contemporary map of Paris by Gomboust, is less known, and a reproduction of this is a singular aid to the reader of M. Magne's *Voiture.* We see that it stood actually next door to the famous Hôtel de Chevreuse, in comparison with which, in its sparkling newness, in its slated turrets and its charming combinations of pale stone and salmon-coloured brick, it seemed an expression of the new age in a triumphant defiance of the old. From both houses could be seen, just across the quiet Rue Saint-Thomas, and over a strip of waste ground, the massive contour of the Louvre; a great garden, on the west side, stretched away behind the house, down to the corner of the Rue de Richelieu.

M. Magne has discovered that M. and Mme. de Rambouillet took up their abode in their new house early in 1607; this fixes what has hitherto been quite vague, the commencement of the Hôtel de Rambouillet. But the Marquise was still only nineteen years of age, and it would be a mistake to suppose that, precocious as people were in those days, she began at once to exercise her celebrated hospitality, or to fill the rooms with tapestry, statues and men of wit. This came on gradually and naturally, without any violence of forethought. It has been suggested that the Marquise founded her *salon,* or, less pompously, began to gather congenial friends about her, in 1613. It is difficult to say on what documents this exact date is based. Her known aversion from Louis XIII, and her growing preference for receiving her friends at home over appearing in a crowd at court—both of them, doubtless, symptoms of her personal delicacy, which shrank from the suspicion of roughness—were probably emphasized after the murder of Concini in 1617, when the great nobles, who had defied the weak regency of Marie de Médicis, boldly swept back into Paris. Doubtless this was the time when Madame de Rambouillet began to practise a more cloistered virtue among the splendour and fragility of her treasures, and first intimated to noble and elegant friends, who were scandalized by the rowdiness of the Louvre, that here was an asylum where they might discuss poetry for hours on the velvet of her incrusted couches, or walk, in solemn ranks, among the parterres of her exquisite walled garden.

The character of pedantry and preciosity which the Hôtel afterwards incurred, is not to be traced in any of its original features. In its early years there was no atmosphere of "intellectual beatitude" about it. But that a certain intellectual standard was set up from the very first it is impossible to question. From the compliments of the earliest inmates of the Hôtel to the eulogistic epitaphs which were scattered on the hearse of the Marquise, all her devotees agree in celebrating her passionate love of literature. Clumsy phrases, rude expressions, the coarseness of a language still in process of purification, were a positive distress to her; and Tallemant has a droll anecdote about the agitation into which she was thrown by the use of so vulgar a word as "scurvy," *teigneux*, in an epigram which was being read to her. With these tendencies, she was peculiarly fitted to welcome to her intimacy the man who of all others was at that time most occupied with the task of correcting and clarifying the French language. An inevitable attraction must have drawn Malherbe to the doors of the Hôtel de Rambouillet.

It would be of interest, and even of some importance, if we could discover the date at which Malherbe began to frequent the Hôtel de Rambouillet, since there can be little doubt that it was to him that it owed its intellectual

The Hôtel de Rambouillet

direction. Unfortunately, this is not easy to do. The poet Racan, whose invaluable notes and anecdotes were adopted by Tallemant to form the body of the *historiette* on Malherbe, did not anticipate how grateful posterity would be for a few dates sprinkled here and there over his narrative. But the fact that Tallemant here took the line, so very unusual with him, of adopting somebody else's life of one of his heroes, can only be accounted for by the double supposition that Malherbe could not be omitted from his gallery, and yet had quitted the scene too early for Tallemant to know much about him at first hand. He must indeed have arrived at the Hôtel very soon after its formation, since he was sixty-two years of age when we suppose it to have begun, and in 1628 he died. The Duc de Broglie was probably right when he conjectured that Malherbe was practically the first, and as long as he lived the foremost, of the literary clan which met in the Chambre Bleue. Racan, who accompanied and may have introduced the elder poet to the Hôtel de Rambouillet, says that it was "sur les vieux jours de Malherbe" that the latter had the curious conversation about the proper heroic name, or poetic pseudonym, which ought to fix all future references to the Marquise, a conversation which led to his writing an eclogue in which he calls himself Mélibée and his disciple Arcan. I quote Tallemant, who is quoting Racan :

"The very day that he sketched out this eclogue, fearing that the name Arthénice [Catherine] if it were used of two persons [for Racan had addressed Catherine Chabot as Arthénice, in a pastoral] would make a confusion between those two persons, Malherbe passed the whole afternoon with Racan turning the name about. All they could make of it was Arthénice, Eracinte and Carintée. The first of those they considered the prettiest, but as Racan was using this also in a pastoral, Malherbe concluded by choosing Rodante."

Unfortunately Madame de Rambouillet, who had plenty of humour, declined the name of Rodante, which would better have adorned a mouse than a great lady, and

Aspects and Impressions

Malherbe threw his consideration for Racan to the winds. Madame de Rambouillet became for him and remained

> Celle pour qui je fis le beau nom d'Arthénice,

and he called her

> Cette jeune bergère à qui les destinées
> Sembloient avoir donné mes dernières années.

We gather that the sound judgment and the exquisite charm of Madame de Rambouillet attracted Malherbe away from the other *salons* which he affected, particularly from those of the Vicomtesse d'Aulchy and of Madame des Loges. It was the latter lady whose ears the grim poet soundly boxed in her own house on a celebrated occasion. He was a formidable guest as well as a tyrant in literature.

But the relations of Malherbe with Madame de Rambouillet during the last ten years of his life were kept on a level of unruffled dignity on the one side and on the other. It is evident that the Marquise was predisposed to accept *la Doctrine* which Malherbe, with so splendid a force and pride, was about to impose upon his countrymen. No man of letters has lived, in any country, who was more possessed than he by the necessity of watching over the purity of language, of cultivating in prose and verse a simple, lucid, and logical style, of removing from the surface of literature, by an arrogant discipline, all traces of obscurity, pomposity and looseness. He held the honour of the French language above all other obligations, and the stories of his sacrificing questions of personal interest, and even affection, to his passion for correct diction, for a noble manner of writing and speaking, are eloquent of the austere and dry genius of this masterful rather than charming poet, who, nevertheless, had so profound and so lasting an influence on French letters. Such a man as this, fanatically possessed by an abstract ambition, needs the sympathy of a wise and beneficent woman, and the old Malherbe, in the twilight of his days, found such an Egeria in Catherine de Rambouillet. It was in the Hôtel

The Hôtel de Rambouillet

that the famous discussions on the value, selection, and meaning of words, on nobility in eloquence, on purity and force in versification, first took place, and the heat from them radiated through France. The new era of style found its cradle in the Chambre Bleue.

But what was this Blue Room, this mysterious and azure grot in which the genius of French classic poetry went through its transformation? There was not much mystery about it. It was a room, deep in the magnificence of the Hôtel, where the Marquise was in the habit of receiving the familiar visits of her best friends. The novelty of it was its colour; all other *salons* in Paris being at that time painted red or drab. Out of the Blue Room there opened a more secret retreat, her *cabinet* or *alcove,* where she could withdraw from all companionship, and spend her time in reading or meditating. The furniture of the whole Hôtel de Rambouillet was on a scale of opulent splendour, but the rarity of the objects brought together was concentrated in the *cabinet,* which was, as M. Magne puts it, a sort of altar which the Marquise raised to herself. Every object in it was fragile, brilliant, and precious. In the days when Malherbe frequented the Hôtel, it is probable that no inner room existed. Tallemant gives us the very odd history of what led to its formation. The Marquise in her youth was active and ready to expose herself to the weather, but about 1623 she began to be threatened by an *incommodité,* which made her unable to bear exposure to heat. She had been in the habit of taking long walks in Paris, but one summer's day, when the sun suddenly came out while she was strolling at La Cour-la-Reine, on the Champs Elysées, she nearly fainted, and was threatened with erysipelas. The following winter, the first time that she drew up her chair to read by the fire, the same phenomenon came on. She was now divided between perishing with cold or suffering miseries of heat, and she therefore invented, taking the idea from the Spanish " alcove," a little supplementary room, where she could sit close to her friends, while they gathered round the hearth, and yet not be smitten by the flames. In

1656, in the great winter, we hear of her, now an elderly woman, lying on her bed, heaped over with furs, but not daring to have a fire in sight.

Her energy did not leave her because of this disability. The letter-writers of the period describe her extraordinary activity. She had a great love of pretty and elaborate practical jokes which were in the taste of the time. Hers, however, were distinguished by the fact that they were never indecent and never ill-natured. But when an idea occurred to Madame de Rambouillet, she rested not until the wild scheme was accomplished. Voiture and Tallemant are full of instances of her fertility. One instance out of many was the passion which she expended in making a cascade in the park at Rambouillet, to startle a party of guests. The water had to be brought up from the little tarn of Montorgueil, and the Marquise superintended every spade and every pipe. Carried on by her enthusiastic presence, a team of workmen laboured night and day to complete the prodigious plaything, conducting their ingenious hydraulics by the flare of torches. I could fill pages with the proofs of her gaiety, her ingenuity, the amazing freshness and vivacity of her mind, but the reader can turn to the original sources for them. It may be suggested that, while the various independent authorities really confirm the legend in its outline, when they tell the same story, it will generally be found that Tallemant tells it more naturally and more exactly than Segrais or Voiture. It is also to be remembered that it was Tallemant who observed longest and most closely, and brought least suspicion of vanity to bear on his relation. There is a phrase buried somewhere in the vast tissue of the *Historiettes* which deserves to be better known. Speaking incidentally of the Marquise de Rambouillet, Tallemant betrays that she was really the source of all his inspiration : "c'est d'elle que je tiens la plus grande et la meilleure partie de ce que j'ai escrit et que j'escriray dans ce livre." This gives his statements their peculiar authority with regard to that Blue Room, which he elsewhere calls "le rendez-vous de ce qu'il y avait de plus

The Hôtel de Rambouillet

galant à la Cour, et de plus joly parmy les beaux-esprits du siècle." He quite frequently introduces an anecdote with the words "J'ay ouy dire à Mme. de Rambouillet."

It would therefore be ungrateful to speak of the Hôtel de Rambouillet without paying a tribute to the strange quality of Tallemant des Réaux. French criticism, in applauding his industry, has hardly done justice to the talent, almost the genius, of this extraordinary man. With an unrivalled gift of observation, he combined that clear objective sense of the value of little things, which is so valuable in a memoir-writer, and he is the very prince of those biographers to whom nothing regarding the subjects of their art seems common or unclean. He has the keen eye for detail of his English contemporary, John Aubrey, and his *Historiettes* are really, in the sense of Aubrey, *Minutes of Lives*. But Tallemant has much more design in his work, and a broader sense of the relation of moral and intellectual values. Saint-Simon, who was a child when Tallemant died, has more passion, a more impetuous and broader sweep of style, and a more intelligent appreciation of the scene of life. It was not for Tallemant des Réaux to paint "des grands fresques historiques." He is as trivial and as picturesque as Boswell, as crude as Pepys, and, like them both, he is completely indifferent to what other people may find scandalous. He moved in the best society, and he was of it; but in his lifetime no one seems to have paid him much attention. Voiture was often in the centre of the stage at the Hôtel de Rambouillet, and what answered in those days to limelight followed him whenever he made one of his brilliant appearances; Tallemant was a shadowy super, hanging about in the wings, but he was always there.

He had the best right in the world to be there. Gédéon Tallemant was a close kinsman of the Marquis, whose sister, Marie de Rambouillet, had married the biographer's father, a Huguenot banker of Bordeaux, head of one of the best provincial families of the day. Gédéon was born at La Rochelle in 1619, and was therefore thirty years younger than his cousin's wife, the famous châtelaine of

the Hôtel de Rambouillet, whom he adored.[1] When he
came to Paris, about 1637, her coterie was already at its
height, but he was immediately admitted to it, and no
doubt began no less immediately to ask questions and to
take notes. He had every possible opportunity; his
brother and a cousin were members of the new French
Academy: his father was a Mæcenas to Corneille and
others: he himself married (in January, 1646) his cousin
Elizabeth de Rambouillet, a union which made him the
familiar of La Fontaine and La Sablière. In 1650 he
bought the château and estate of Plessis-Rideau, in
Touraine, and by letters-patent changed the name to Les
Réaux, which he then adopted as a surname. Here he
entertained his lifelong friends—the associates of the
Hôtel, and other men of high professional rank, Patru,
Ablancourt, the Père Rapin. He knew absolutely everybody; he was adorably indiscreet; and those who associated
with him perceived in him only a wonderful talker
(Maucroix says that he "racontait aussy bien qu'homme de
France "), and a lover of poetry who started writing an
Œdipe before Corneille. What few of them knew was that
this obliging friend and graceful companion was putting
down In an immense MS. all the anecdotes, all the
intrigues, all the tricks of manner, all the traits of
character, of the multitude of his polite acquaintances. He
has left more than 500 of his little highly finished portraits
of people he knew, and he knew everyone in that age and
place worth knowing.

It is doubtful at what particular time he wrote the
Historiettes. He was composing, or perhaps revising, part
of them in 1657, but some must be later, and many may be
earlier in date than that; it is probable that he ceased
writing in 1665. He has been accused of being a spiteful
chronicler of the vices of the great, and he has been
charged with a love of looseness. But his own description
is more just: "Je prétends dire le bien et le mal, sans
dissimuler la vérité." He writes with an air of humorous

[1] Much fresh light on his career was thrown by M. Émile Magne
in his *Joyeuse Jeunesse de Tallemant des Réaux,* 1921.

The Hôtel de Rambouillet

malice, pleased to draw the cloak off the limbs of hypocrisy, but not moved by any strong moral indignation. Like Pepys, he enjoyed giving a disinterested picture of the details of ordinary private life, but was rather more cynically amused by them than scandalized. He wrote, or at least intended to write, *Mémoires de la régence d'Anne d'Autriche*, but this has totally disappeared, and we need not regret it. Gédéon Tallemant is amply immortalized by the *Historiettes*, which fill ten closely printed volumes in the excellent edition of MM. Monmerqué and Paulin of Paris. They are like the work of some brilliant Dutch painter of sordid interiors. He is not always well inspired. He says nothing more adequate about Pascal than that he was "ce garçon qui inventa une machine admirable pour l'arithmétique," but Pascal was hardly of his world. In 1685 Tallemant became a Catholic, converted by the Père Rapin, and, having outlived all his friends, he died, probably in November, 1692, leaving a huge MS., the principal subject of which is an analysis of the society that met within the Hôtel de Rambouillet.

At his death that MS. vanished, "as rare things will." It turned up again in a library at Montigny-Lencoup in 1803. We may note, as a curious coincidence, that while the publication of Evelyn's *Diary* dates from 1818, and while the deciphering of Pepys began in 1819, it was in 1820, that Châteaugiron set to work at copying out the *Historiettes*, which were not published until 1835. Three of the most important MS. memoirs of the seventeenth century were thus independently examined for the first time at practically the same moment of the nineteenth. Each publication was an event in literary history.

No such concealment, no such late discovery, has marked the course of Voiture, whose letters and poems were published by his nephew Pinchesne in 1650, only two years after the poet's death. In this remarkable miscellany, which has been incessantly reprinted, and which forms one of the recognized lesser classics of France, we find ourselves breathing the very atmosphere of the Hôtel de Rambouillet. It is, indeed, amusing to reflect that, for fifteen years before her death, the Marquise and all her circle possessed, and shared with a wide public, this elaborate body of evidence as to their friendships, their tastes, and their amusements. In the *Œuvres* of Voiture, reprinted at least seventeen times during the lifetime of the Marquise, the world at large was admitted to the conversations of the Blue Room, and it eagerly responded to the invitation. There was something about the supple genius of Voiture, at once daring and discreet, apparently tearing every veil off an intimacy, and yet in fact wrapping it in an impenetrable gauze of mystery, which made him the ideal revealer to excite and baffle curiosity, so that though he tells so much, as he stands at the top of the stairs of the Hôtel and takes the town into his confidence, yet he leaves plenty of things untold, to be whispered into the ears of posterity by Tallemant and Conrart.

The father of Voiture was a shopkeeper who sold wine at the sign of the Chapeau de Roses at Amiens, and there his son Vincent was born in 1595. The author of *Alcidalis et Zélide,* was therefore the contemporary of Herrick and of George Herbert. If the last-mentioned had not rejected "the painted pleasures of a Court-life" for the retirements of a saint, he might have been the English Voiture, with his charming gifts and ingenious graces. The year 1626, which saw Herbert adopt the solemn vocation of a priest, is probably that in which Voiture, introduced by Chardebonne, took up his station for the rest of his life, as principal literary oracle and master of the gaieties in the Hôtel de Rambouillet. His father was honestly supplying wine to the Queen-Mother, Marie de Médicis, and there was no question in his son's case, as in that of some others, of doubtful or partial nobility. Vincent Voiture was frankly and openly a *bourgeois,* admitted into that strictly guarded aristocracy because of his abundant talents, his wit, his pleasantness, his delicious social qualities, and also because it was part of the scheme of the Marquise de Rambouillet to break down the boredom of the exclusive privilege of rank for its own sake.

The main principle of the Hôtel was a study of the art

The Hôtel de Rambouillet

of how to behave. The rules of *la bienséance* were strictly laid down there, after close discussion among persons of light and leading. There was a strong resistance made to the roughness of the country noble, to the awkwardness of the ordinary citizen, to the inky fingers of the pedant, to the slovenly petticoat, the disordered wig, the bespattered boot. The attention of both sexes was persistently called to these matters of behaviour and *tenue*, which had an importance at that date which we may easily, in our twentieth-century intolerance, ridicule and ignore. We see the comic side of this extreme solicitude about dress and ceremony, etiquette and behaviour, in such a book as Furetière's amusing *Roman Bourgeois* (1666), but we may see the seriousness, the stately value of it, in the tragedies of Corneille and the maxims of La Rochefoucauld. The school of *la politesse* became that in which every talent must graduate, however grave its after-labours were to be. Even the solemn Baillet, writing the life of no less dignified a person than Descartes, mentions that the philosopher passed, like all other well-bred lads, "aux promenades, au jeu et aux autres divertissements qui font l'occupation des personnes de qualité et des honnêtes gens du siècle." In this school, the elegant and supple Voiture, impregnated with the literature of *Amadis de Gaule*, and with the language of Spanish chivalry, intimidated by no hyperbole of compliment, capable alike of plunging into the deep waters and of swimming safe to shore, always on the verge of absurdity, always gliding down the agreeable side of it, persistent, subtle, entertaining, extravagant—in this school Voiture was the triumphant, the unmastered master. His best letters, his best sonnets, show him to have been able, at his most vibrating moments, to rise out of this element of billets-doux to better things. He is of all composers of society verse and prose the lightest and the swiftest, and we may say to those who sneer at so unique a talent what Madame de Sévigné said of them in her day : "Tant pis pour ceux qui ne l'entendent pas ! "

If one literary figure is more closely identified with the Hôtel de Rambouillet than Voiture, it must be Chapelain.

Aspects and Impressions

It is therefore curious that while M. Magne was preparing his picturesque volumes on the former, M. Collas should be independently writing the earliest biography of the latter. These coincidences are odd, but we are accustomed to them; they show that a subject is " in the air." When Chapelain made his first appearance at the Hôtel, perhaps in 1635, Voiture had long been installed there. They fell out at first sight, like dog and cat. When the author of the *Préface de l'Adone* stumbled over the precious floor, dressed like a scarecrow, in hunting boots and dirty linen, and made his clownish obeisance to the Marquise, she shrank a little from him, and Voiture broke into a scream of elfish laughter. Madame de Rambouillet never learned to care for Chapelain, and when he made clumsy love to Mlle. Paulet, "the lioness," the Blue Room shook with mirth. But when Mlle. Julie became a great personage, and especially as soon as the Duc de Montausier introduced the pure cultivation of pedantry into the Hôtel, the strong character of Chapelain asserted itself, while the death of Voiture left him unquestioned in authority. Grotesque as Chapelain was, he had a wonderful talent for adapting himself to circumstances, and his conversation, though massive and solemn, had charm, which even his enemies admitted to be extraordinary. Chapelain was never on those terms of petted intimacy with his host and hostess which the insinuating Voiture enjoyed, but he conquered a position of more genuine respect and esteem.

But to follow M. Collas and M. Magne into the later years of the Hôtel, when Mlle. de Rambouillet gave to the Blue Room a peculiar air of her own, would be impossible for us, with the limited space at our command. We must not go further than 1641, the year in which was produced the celebrated *Guirlande de Julie*. After this point, not merely does the character of the scene change, and its tone become less pleasing, or at least less sympathetic, but for the reviewer the abundance of trees makes the wood itself almost invisible. Here we may point to an example of the superabundance of French material, which may almost console us for the comparative dimness and bareness of the

The Hôtel de Rambouillet

contemporary English landscape. In dealing with this crowded age, M. Magne and M. Collas have shown a learned adroitness and the happy logic to which scholars of their race are trained. Of the two, M. Magne is the more vivacious, as befits the biographer of Voiture. M. Collas has more difficulty in reconciling us with the tedious and pedantic Chapelain, who, nevertheless, as the founder of modern criticism and the mainstay of the infant Académie Française, deserved to find a biographer at last. The worst of it is that while Voiture, dancing-master to the Muses if you will, and *petit-maître* in excelsis, is at least a brisk and highly diverting personality, poor Chapelain, the typical academician, the mediocre poet, the spider at the heart of the wide intellectual web of his time, is not man enough to awaken our vivid sympathies. Moreover, to conclude on a note of bathos, M. Collas has neglected to append an index to his vast compendium of facts.

We must therefore refrain from entering the labyrinths of the later *préciosité*, amusing as they are, and must continue to concentrate our attention on the clearness, the sweetness, the purity with which the founder of the Hôtel, the great Madame de Rambouillet, throughout her long life, created an atmosphere of sympathy and unity around her. As long as she was paramount there, and until the influence of her daughter and her daughter's husband, together with her own languor, pushed her a little into the second line, gaiety was in the ascendant at the famous Hôtel. It is needful to assure ourselves of this, because in the later days it became purely intellectual, and dry in its priggishness. M. Magne, it is true, attributes this change not so much to the pedantic Latinism of the Duc de Montausier, and the hair-splitting of the academicians, as to the decay produced by gaiety itself. In an ingenious passage he says:

The taste for badinage perverted in Voiture the taste for beauty. His genius glittered, quivered, frisked and palpitated, and the smile he wore was ever melting into irony. To depth he deliberately preferred an elegant futility. He was impregnated with the quality to which the age had given, in a noble sense, the name of gallantry. But, in reacting everywhere against vulgar roughness, the very excess of his effort landed him at last in preciosity.

It never had that deplorable effect upon Madame de Rambouillet herself, on whose charming figure, swaying like a young pine-tree of the forest, we must fix our attention, if we would see only what was best in that remarkable and so vividly French revival of civilization which took place under Louis XIII. Her purity of conduct was combined with no uncouth prudery. She refrained from judging others hardly, but she preserved, without a lapse, her own high standard of behaviour. She had a lively horror of scandal, and desired that those about her, if they could not contrive to be virtuous, should at least be discreet. It was detestable to her to hear the gallants of the court boasting of their conquests. She said, in her amusing way, that if she herself could ever have been persuaded to leave the path of propriety, she must have chosen for a paramour some unctuous and secret prelate, but that she had never discovered one whom she could trust. It was her temperament, both of heart and brain, which led her to rejoice in the new spirit of Malherbe, whose simple, firm and lucid verses responded, after a revel of romanticism, to her classic craving for harmony and dignity. In Racan's pastoral poems, she welcomed a recovered love of country pleasures, and the graceful convention of a shepherd. She liked private letters, hitherto so pompous, to be composed in such terms that one seemed to hear the writer's voice chatting at the chimney-corner. Richelieu, although M. Magne denies the legend of his *Discours sur l'Amour*, used to come to the Blue Room to have a good laugh with its delightful occupant, and everyone unbent in her sweet and easy presence. Tallemant has a story of no less dignified a personage than the Cardinal de La Valette romping with the Rambouillet children, and discovered by the Marquise hiding from them under a bed.

The close of the life of this marvellous woman was a sad one. She outlived all her early friends, even outlived

The Hôtel de Rambouillet

the prestigé of her own Blue Room. Six days after her death, Robinet composed a sort of funeral ode to her memory, closing with an epitaph, which, as it is little known, may be given here. It was written in January, 1666 :

> Ci gist la divine Arthénice,
> Qui fut l'illustre protectrice
> Des Arts que les neuf Sœurs inspirent aux humains.
> Rome luy donna la naissance;
> Elle vint rétablir en France
> La gloire des anciens Romains.
> Sa maison, des vertus le temple,
> Sert aux particuliers d'un merveilleux exemple,
> Et pourrait bien instruire encor les souverains.

This is not very good poetry, but it would be difficult to sum up more neatly the services of Madame de Rambouillet to France and to civilization.

MALHERBE AND THE CLASSICAL REACTION [1]

IN contemplating the chart of literary history we are confronted by phenomena which more or less closely resemble those marked on the geographical map. The surface is not uniform, but diversified by ups and downs, of the feature that we call taste or fashion. A special interest attaches to what may be described as the watersheds of literature, the periods which display these changes of direction in thought and language. I propose to bring before you briefly some characteristics of one of the most saliently marked of all these points of alteration, that which led irresistibly and imminently to the classical school, as it is called, in France, and from France ultimately to the whole of Europe. Before doing so, I must draw your attention to the fact that while most of us are led to give special heed to movements which tend, like the Romantic renaissance of poetry in England two centuries later, to the emancipation and even the revolution of literature, that of which I am about to speak was deliberately introduced in the interests of law and order, and was in all its features conservative, and, if you choose to call it so, retrogressive. It did not aim at enlarging the field of expression, but at enclosing it within rules, excluding from it eccentricities and licentious freaks, and rendering it subservient to a rigorous discipline. In this University of Oxford, where the practice of poetry is now conducted with so much ardour and with such audacity of experiment, you may or may not, as you please, see any parallel between the condition of France in 1595 and our

[1] Delivered before the University of Oxford as the Taylorian Lecture for 1920.

own condition to-day. My purpose is, with your leave, to describe the former without criticizing the latter.

The sixteenth century had been a period of great activity in the literature of France, where the interaction of two vast forces, the Renaissance and the Reformation, had introduced wholly new forms of expression into the language. Prose had started from its mediæval condition into full modernity in Calvin, and then in Montaigne. In poetry, with which we are concerned to-day, there had existed since 1550 the brilliant and feverish army of versifiers who accompanied Ronsard, "the Prince of Poets," and claimed with him to have created out of the rude elements of the Middle Ages a literary art which linked modern France directly with ancient Greece. While England was still languishing under the early Tudors, and Italy had grown weary of her burst of chivalrous epic, France gave the world the spectacle of a society palpitating with literary ambition. Ronsard's magnificent audacity had conquered for poetry, an art which had hitherto enjoyed little honour in France, the foremost position in the world of mental activity. Verse, which had been treated as a butterfly skipping from flower to flower, was now celebrated by the Pléiade as a temple, as a sunrise, as the apotheosis of the intellect. Immensely flattered by being suddenly lifted to the status of a priesthood, all the budding versifiers of France, who a generation earlier would have withered into insignificance, expanded into affluent and profuse blossom. By the year 1560 it was "roses, roses all the way," but the misfortune was that the flowers were foreign, had been transplanted from Greece and Rome and Italy, and were not really native to the soil of France.

During the next generation, under conditions with which we have no time to occupy us to-day, there was a steady, indeed an almost precipitous decline in the quality of French verse. If we turn to our own literature of half a century later, we see a parallel decline in the drama down from Shakespeare to Shirley and the later disciples of Ben Jonson. We all know how dis-

Malherbe and the Classical Reaction

concerting it is to pass from the sheer beauty of the great Elizabethans to the broken verse and the mixture of flatness and violence of the lesser poets of the Commonwealth. But in France the decadence had been still more striking, because of the extremely high line adopted by Ronsard and Du Bellay in their prose manifestos. The doctrine of the Pléiade had been as rigorous and lofty as a creed in literature could well be, and it rose to an altogether higher plane than was dreamed of by the English critics half a century later. No dignity, no assurance of high and pure poetic resolution could surpass the apparent aim of the manifestos of 1549. Frenchmen, it seemed, had nothing to do but follow these exalted precepts and to produce the most wonderful poetry which the world had seen since the days of Pindar and Sappho. We cannot to-day enter into the question why these high hopes were almost immediately shattered, except so far as to suggest that excellent principles are sometimes insufficient to produce satisfactory practice. We have to look abruptly this afternoon into the conditions of French poetry in the last years of the sixteenth century, and to realize that those conditions had brought French literature to a point where reform was useless and revolution was inevitable.

There was no slackening—and I ask your particular attention to this fact—there was no slackening in the popularity of the poetic art. There existed, in 1595, as great a crowd of versifiers as had been called forth fifty years earlier by the splendour of the Pléiade. A feature of poetic history which is worthy of our notice is that an extreme abundance of poetical composition is by no means necessarily connected with the wholesomeness and vigour of the art at that moment. There was a crowd of poets in France during the reign of Henri IV, but they were distinguished more by their exuberance and their eccentricity than by their genius. I shall, in a few moments, endeavour to give you an idea of their character. In the meantime, let us be content to remark that the exquisite ideals of the Pléiade had degenerated into extravagant conventionality, into which an attempt was made to infuse life by a spasmodic display of verbal fireworks. The charm of sobriety, of simplicity, was wholly disregarded, and the importance of logic and discipline in literature ignored and outraged. The earlier theory, a very dangerous one, had been that poetry was the language of the gods rather than of men, that it was *grandiloquentia,* an oracular inspiration. Being above mankind in its origin, it was not for mortal men to question its authority. It possessed a celestial freedom, it was emancipated from all rules save what it laid down for itself. Let us see what was the effect of this arrogance.

The scope of imaginative literature as practised by the Pléiade had been curiously narrow, so much so that it is difficult to distinguish the work of different hands except by the dexterity of the technique. The odes and pastorals of the lesser masters are just like those of Ronsard, except that Ronsard is very much more skilful. But by the close of the century there was a wide divergence between the various poets in their themes and their points of view. Two of them greatly excelled their contemporaries in eminence and popularity, and these two were as unlike each other in substance as it was easy for them to be. The elder of these two was Salluste du Bartas, a writer whose quartos are now allowed to gather dust on the shelves, and who, when he died in 1590, was, with the exception of Tasso, the most eminent European writer of verse. His influence on English poetry in the next generation was immense. Translations of his works by Joshua Sylvester and others had begun to appear before his death, and were extremely popular. Du Bartas possessed qualities of intellect and art which are by no means to be despised, but his taste was execrable. He wished to create a national religious poetry on a large scale, and he has been called the "Milton manqué de la France." Du Bartas is all relinquished to evangelical and moral exhortation, and his immense *Les Semaines,* besides being one of the longest, is the most unblushingly didactic encyclopædia of verse that was ever put forth as a poem. He had a very heavy hand, and he sowed with the

Malherbe and the Classical Reaction

whole sack. Our own Bishop Joseph Hall of Norwich, who called him "some French angel, girt with bays," described Du Bartas as—

> The glorious Sallust, moral, true, divine,
> Who, all inspirèd with a holy rage,
> Makes Heaven his subject, and the earth his stage.

In his own time his myriad admirers preferred him above "golden Homer and great Maro." His earnestness and his cleverness—among other things he was the first man after the Renaissance to see that the obsession of the heathen gods was ridiculous in a Christian literature—his abundance and his vehemence, made Du Bartas a very formidable figure in the path of any possible reform.

As an instance of the violence of fancy and gaudy extravagance of language which had become prevalent with the decline of the Pléiade, I will now present to you what I select as a favourable, not a ridiculous, example of the art of Du Bartas. He wishes to paraphrase the simple statement in Genesis that, on the fourth day, God set the stars in the firmament of heaven to give light upon the earth. This is how he does it, as translated by Joshua Sylvester :

> Even as a peacock, prickt with love's desire,
> To woo his mistress, strutting stately by her,
> Spreads round the rich pride of his pompous vail,
> His azure wings and starry-golden tail,
> With rattling pinions wheeling still about,
> The more to set his beauteous beauty out,—
> The Firmament, as feeling like above,
> Displays his pomp, pranceth about his love,
> Spreads his blue curtain, mixt with golden marks,
> Set with gilt spangles, sown with glistening sparks,
> Sprinkled with eyes, speckled with tapers bright,
> Powdered with stars streaming with glorious light,
> To inflame the Earth the more, with lover's grace
> To take the sweet fruit of his kind embrace.

Our first impression of such a passage as this is one of admiration of its colour and of its ingenuity. It is more than rich, it is sumptuous; the picture of the wheeling peacock is original and brilliantly observed. But there commendation must cease. What could be meaner or less appropriate than to compare the revolution of the starry firmament as it proceeded from its Creator's hands with the strut of a conceited bird in a poultry-yard? The works of Du Bartas are stuffed full with these strained and fantastic similes, his surface sparkles with the glitter of tinsel and pinchbeck. At every turn something majestic reminds him of an embroidery, of a false jewel, of something picturesque and mean. The planets, in their unison, are like the nails in a cart-wheel; when darkness comes on, heaven is playing at blind man's buff; the retreat of the armies of the King of Assyria reminds the poet of a gamekeeper drawing his ferret. He desires the snow to fall that it may "perriwig with wool the bald-pate woods." All is extravagant and false, all is offensive to the modesty of nature.

Du Bartas is stationed at the left wing of the army of poets. The right is held by Philippe Desportes, whose name has recently been made familiar to us by Sir Sidney Lee's investigations into the extraordinary way in which his works were pillaged in his lifetime by our Elizabethan sonneteers. Even Shakespeare seems to have read, and possibly imitated, Desportes's *Amours de Diane*. The producer in vast quantities of a kind of work which is exactly in the fashion of the moment is sure of a wide popular welcome, and the cleverness of Desportes was to see that after the death of Ronsard French taste went back on the severity of Du Bellay's classicism, and returned to the daintiness and artificial symmetry of the Petrarchists. It has been said that to the Italians of the sixteenth century Petrarch had become what Homer was to the Greeks and Virgil to the Latins. He was the unquestioned leader, the unchallenged exemplar. This infatuation, which spread through Europe, is of importance to us in our inquiry to-day, for Petrarch was really the worm, the crested and luminous worm, at the root of sixteenth-century poetry. It was extremely easy

Malherbe and the Classical Reaction

to imitate the amorous conceits of the Italian imitators of Petrarch, and of these imitators in France by far the most abundant, skilful, and unwearying was Philippe Desportes, to whom Petrarch's ingenious elocution appeared, as it appeared to all the critics of Europe, "pure beauty itself." By the close of the century it was no longer the greater Italians, such as Francesco Molza, who represented at its height the victorious heresy of Petrarchism, it was a Frenchman, of whom our own great lyrist, Lodge, in his *Margarite of America* in 1596, wrote: "few men are able to second the sweet conceits of Philippe Desportes, whose poetical writings are ordinarily in everybody's hand." Desportes exercised over the whole of Europe an authority which surpassed that of Tennyson over the British Empire at the height of his reputation.

Here, then, was another and still more formidable lion couched at the gate of poetry to resist all possible reform. The career of Desportes had been one of unbroken prosperity. He had become, without an effort, the wealthiest and the most influential person of letters of his time. His courtly elegance had enabled him to be all things to all men, and although a priest of unblemished character, he had attended one Valois king after another without betraying his inward feelings by a single moral grimace. He had found no difficulty in celebrating the virtues of Henri III, and the anecdote about him that is best known is that he had been rewarded with an abbey for the homage of a single sonnet. He had exaggerated all the tricks of his predecessors with a certain sweetness and brilliance of his own, which had fascinated the polite world. The best that can be said of Desportes is that he was an artificer of excellent skill, who manufactured metrical jewellery by rearranging certain commonplaces, such as that teeth are pearls, that lips are roses, that cheeks are lilies, that hair is a golden network. But I will give you his own statement of his aim, not attempting to paraphrase his remarkable language. Desportes gives the following account of his ambition:

Aspects and Impressions

I desire to build a temple to my chaste goddess. My eye shall be the lamp, and the immortal flame which ceaselessly consumes me shall serve as candle. My body shall be the altar, and my sighs the vows, and I will intone the service in thousands and thousands of verses.

What a ridiculous confusion of imagery! Here we have a man whose body is an altar, and whose eye—one of whose eyes—is a lamp, and whose passion is the candle in that lamp, and whose mouth and throat are detached from his body, and are performing miracles in the vicinity. This is to take Desportes at his worst, and it is only fair to admit that the reader who winnows the vast floor of his work will find some grains of pure gold left. But the mass of these sonnets and odes and madrigals is extraordinarily insipid and cold, the similes are forced and grotesque, and everywhere pedantry takes the place of passion. When there is beauty it is artificial and affected, it is an Alexandrine beauty, it is the colour of the dying dolphin.

Such was the poetry which occupied the taste of France at the close of the sixteenth century, and whether its form was brief and amorous, as in the sonnets of Desportes, or long-winded and hortatory, as in the sacred epics of Du Bartas, it was uniformly exaggerated, lifeless, and incorrect. In all its expressions it was characterized by an abuse of language, and indeed, in the hands of the poets of the late Valois kings, the French tongue was hurrying down to ruin. One curious vice consisted in the fabrication of new phrases and freshly coined composite words. Of these latter, some one has counted no fewer than 300 in the writings of Du Bartas alone, and Professor Paul Morillot has observed that the licence which the poets of that age indulged in has been the cause of subsequent poverty in that direction, French having received and rejected such a glut of new and useless words as to have lost all appetite for additions of vocabulary. Another vice of the period was the ceaseless cultivation, in season and out of season, of a sort of antithetical wit. The sincerity of Nature was offended at every turn by the monstrous cleverness of the writer, who evidently was thinking far more about himself than about his subject. Here is an example:

> Weep on, mine eyes, weep much, ye have seen much,
> And now in water let your penance be,
> Since 'twas in fire that you committed sin,

and so on, with wearisome iteration of the hyperbole. We were to suffer from the same disease fifty years later, when a great English poet, capable of far nobler things, was to call the eyes of St. Mary Magdalene

> Two walking baths, two weeping motions,
> Portable and compendious oceans.

An excellent grammarian, M. Ferdinand Brunot, has remarked that at the end of the sixteenth century a lawless individualism—and in this term he sums up all the component parts of literature, style, grammar, treatment, and tone—had set in; that everybody had become a law to himself; and that the French language was suffering from the incessant disturbance caused by "the fantastic individuality of writers" both in prose and verse.

This chaotic state of things, which threatened French literature with anarchy and French logic with bankruptcy, was brought to a standstill and successfully confronted by the energy and determination of a single person. I recollect no other instance in the history of literature in which one individual has contrived to stem the whole flood of national taste. Of course, an instinct of French lucidity and reasonableness must have been ready to respond to the doctrine of the new critic, yet it is none the less certain that through the early years of the struggle there remains no evidence of his having been supported by any associate opinion. I dare say you recollect a famous Japanese print which represents a young lady standing on the edge of a cliff, and gazing calmly out to sea while she restrains the action of a great plunging horse by simply holding one of her feet down upon the reins. In the same way the runaway Pegasus of France was held, and was reduced to discipline, by the almost unparalleled resolution of a solitary man. This was François Malherbe, whose name, but perhaps very little else, will be familiar to you. I hope to show you that this poet, by the clearness of his vision and his rough independence, brought about a revolution in literature which was unparalleled. He cut a clear stroke, as with a hatchet, between the sixteenth century and all that came after it down to the romantic revival at the beginning of the nineteenth century, and he did this by sheer force of character. Malherbe was not a great poet, but he was a great man, and he is worthy of our close consideration.

François Malherbe was a Norman; there is a hint of the family having come from Suffolk, in which case the name may have been Mallerby, but we need not dwell on that. His parents were Calvinists, and he was born at Caen in 1555. This was, you observe, between the births of Spenser and Shakespeare; and Rabelais was just dead. Cervantes was eight years old, Lope de Vega was to be born seven years later. We ought to notice these dates: they give us a sense of what was preparing in Europe, and what was passing away; a great period of transition was about to expand. Until he was thirty years of age Malherbe appears to have taken no interest whatever in poetry; he was a soldier, a military secretary, a man of business. Then he went to live in Provence, where he read the Italian verse fashionable in his day, and began to imitate it. The kindest and most enthusiastic of his later disciples told Tallemant that Malherbe's early poems were "pitiful." We can judge for ourselves, since at the age of thirty-two he published a paraphrase, or rather a series of selections from Tansillo's *Lagrime di San Pietro*. The bad poets of the age were lachrymose to the last degree. Nothing but the honour of addressing you to-day would have induced me to read these "Tears of St. Peter." I have done so, and have even amused myself by paraphrasing some of them, but these I will not

Malherbe and the Classical Reaction

inflict upon you. It is sufficient to assure you that up
to the age of forty the verses of Malherbe were not merely,
as Racan put it, pitiful, but marred by all the ridiculous
faults of the age. After all, I must give you a single
example. This is translated literally from "The Tears
of St. Peter":

Aurora, in one hand, forth from her portals led,
Holds out a vase of flowers, all languishing and dead;
And with the other hand empties a jar of tears;
While through a shadowy veil, woven of mist and storm,
That hides her golden hair, she shows in mortal form
All that a soul can feel of cruel pains and fears.

At what moment Malherbe observed that this was a
detestable way of writing, and conceived the project of a
great reversal of opinion, we do not know. His early life,
and just that part of it on which we should like light to
be thrown, remains impenetrably obscure. But we do
know that when he arrived in Paris he had formulated
his doctrine and laid out his plan of campaign.
At Aix-en-Provence he had been admitted to the
meetings of a literary society, the chief ornament
of which was the celebrated orator and moralist
Du Vair, who ought perhaps to be considered as in some
directions the master of Malherbe. The ideas of Du Vair
have been traced in some of Malherbe's verses, and the
poet afterwards said, in his dictatorial way, "There is no
better writer in our language than M. Du Vair." It was
probably the dignity of the orator's attitude and the
severity of his taste in rhetoric which encouraged the poet
to adopt a similar lucidity and strenuousness in verse.
The two men, who were almost exactly of the same age,
may perhaps be most safely looked upon as parallel re-
formers, the one of French verse, the other of French
prose.

Few things would be more interesting to us, in our
present mood, than to know how Malherbe, arriving in
Paris at the mature age of fifty, set about his revolution.

Aspects and Impressions

He found the polite world tired of frigid conceits and extravagant sentimentality, above all tired of the licence of the poets and the tricks which they were taking with the French language. There was undoubtedly a longing for order and regularity, such as invariably follows a period of revolutionary lawlessness, but no one was giving this sentiment a voice. What was wanted after such a glut of ornament and exuberance was an arbiter and tyrant of taste who should bring poetry rigidly into line with decency, plainness, and common sense, qualities which had long been thought unnecessary to, and even ridiculously incompatible with, literature of a high order. All this we may divine, but what is very difficult to understand is the mode in which Malherbe became the recognized tyrant of taste. It was not by the production, and still less by the publication, of quantities of verse composed in accordance with his own new doctrine. Malherbe had hesitated long in the retirement of the country, waiting to be summoned to Court. Somehow, although he had published no book and can scarcely have been known to more than a handful of persons, he had a few powerful friends, and among them, strange to say, three poets whose work was characteristic of everything which it was to be Malherbe's mission to destroy. These were the Cardinal Du Perron, Bertaut, and Vauquelin de la Fresnaye. They formed the van of the poetical army of the moment, and it is a very curious thing that these three remarkable writers, each of whom remained faithful to the tradition of Ronsard, should have welcomed with open arms the rebel who was to cover Ronsard with ridicule. With a divine simplicity, they opened the wicket and let the wolf in among the sheep. They urged the King to invite Malherbe to Court, and, when His Majesty delayed, Malherbe very characteristically did not wait for a summons. He came to Paris of his own accord in 1605, was presented to Henri IV, and composed in September of that year the long ode called a "Prayer for the King on his going to Limoges." This is the earliest expression of classical verse in the French language.

Malherbe and the Classical Reaction

In those days the intelligent favour of the King did more for a reputation than a dozen glowing reviews in the chief newspapers will do to-day. We must give credit to Henri IV for the promptitude with which he perceived that the cold new poetry, which must have sounded very strangely on his ears accustomed to the lute of Desportes and the trumpet of Du Bartas, was exactly what was wanted in France. He himself had laboured to bring back to this country, distracted as it had been in its late political disorders, the virtues of law, logic, and discipline. He recognized in this grim, middle-aged Norman gentleman the same desires, but directed to the unity and order of literature. A recent French historian has pointed out that "the very nature of Malherbe's talent, its haughty, solemn, and majestic tone, rendered him peculiarly fitted to become the official and, as it were, the impersonal singer of the King's great exploits, and to engrave in letters of brass, as on a triumphal monument, the expression of public gratitude and admiration." Malherbe, as has been said, was appointed "the official poet of the Bourbon dynasty."

The precious correspondence with his Provençal friend Peiresc, which Malherbe kept up from 1606 till his death in 1628, a correspondence which was still unknown a hundred years ago, throws a good deal of light upon the final years of the poet, and in particular on the favour with which he was entertained at Court. There are more than 200 of these letters, which nevertheless, like most such collections of that age, succeed in concealing from us the very facts which we are most anxious to hear about. Thus, while Malherbe expatiates to Peiresc about queens and princes, he tells us nothing, or next to nothing, about the literary life in which we know that he made so disconcerting a figure. But that most enchanting of gossips, Tallemant des Réaux, has preserved for us an anecdote of a highly illuminating nature. We have seen that the supremacy in French poetry had been held for many years by Philippe Desportes, who was now approaching the close of a long life of sumptuous success. It could not be a matter of indifference to the last and most magnificent of

Aspects and Impressions

the Ronsardists that an upstart, till now unheard of, should suddenly be welcomed at Court. He desired his nephew, Mathurin Régnier—himself a man of genius, but not in our picture to-day—he desired Régnier to bring this M. de Malherbe to dinner. They arrived, but were late, and dinner stood already on the table. The old Desportes received Malherbe with all the politeness conceivable, and said that he wished to give him a copy of the new edition of his *Psalms,* in which he had made many corrections and additions. Such a compliment from the acknowledged head of French poetry was extreme, but Malherbe had already made up his mind to bring down the reputation of Desportes with a crash, as Samson destroyed the gates of Dagon in Gaza. Desportes was starting to go upstairs to fetch the book, when Malherbe in rough country fashion (*rustiquement*) told him he had seen it already, that it was not worth while to let his soup grow cold, for it was likely to be better than his *Psalms* were. Upon this they sat down to dinner at once, but Malherbe said nothing more, and when dinner was done he went away, leaving the host heart-broken and young Régnier furious. This must have been very soon after Malherbe's arrival in Paris, for Desportes died in 1606.

All that has been recorded of the manners and conversation of Malherbe tends to explain this story. He could be courtly and even magnificent, and he had a bluff kind of concentrated politeness, when he chose to exercise it, which was much appreciated by the royal family. He was a tall, handsome man, with keen eyes, authoritative and even domineering, generally silent in society, but ready to break in with a brusque contradiction of what somebody else was saying. He was a scorner of human frailty, believing himself to be above the reach of all emotional weakness. The violent force, which burned arrogantly in his spirit, comes out in everything which is preserved about him, in his verses, in his letters, in the anecdotes of friends and enemies. His retorts were like those of Dr. Samuel Johnson, but without the healing balsam of Johnson's tenderness. There was nothing

Malherbe and the Classical Reaction

tender about Malherbe, and we may admit that he could not have carried out his work if there had been. His intellectual conscience was implacable; he allowed nothing in the world to come between him and his inexorable doctrine. When he learned that the Vicomtesse d'Auchy (Charlotte des Ursins), the "Caliste" of his own verses, had been encouraging a poet of the old school, he went to her house, pushed into her bedroom, and slapped her face as she lay upon her bed.

Tallemant tells us that "meditation and art made a poet" of Malherbe, *non nascitur sed fit*. At no time did he learn to write with ease, and after so many years spent in the passionate cultivation of the Muse, his poetical writings are contained in as narrow a compass as those of Gray, who confessed that his "works" were so small that they might be mistaken for those of a pismire. Malherbe had long pauses during which he seemed to do nothing at all except meditate and lay down the law. Balzac, who was one of those young men in whose company he delighted, declares that whenever Malherbe had written a thousand verses he rested for ten years. All this was part of a studied frugality. The Ronsardists and their followers had been lavish in everything; they had poured out floods of slack verse, loose in construction, faulty in grammar. If a slight difficulty presented itself to them, they evaded it, they leaped over it. Having no reverence for the French language, they invented hideous and reckless words, they stretched or curtailed syllables, in order to fit the scansion. There is recorded a saying of Malherbe which is infinitely characteristic. When he was asked what, in fact, was his object in all he was doing, he replied that he proposed "to rescue French poetry from the hands of the little monsters who were dishonouring it." The glorious Desportes, the sublime Du Bartas, the rest of the glittering and fashionable Petrarchists of Paris, what were they in the eyes of this implacable despot of the new intellectual order? They were simply "little monsters" who were "dishonouring" what he worshipped with a fanatic zeal, the language of France.

Aspects and Impressions

When we turn to his own poetry, we see what there was in it which fascinated the opening seventeenth century. After all the tortures and the spasms, the quietude of it was delicious. If you go to Malherbe now, you must learn to put aside all your romantic preoccupations. His verse is very largely concerned with negations: it is *not* ornamented, it is not preposterous, it is not pedantic. It swept away all the insincere imagery and all the violent oddities of the earlier school. For example, Bertaut had written, wishing to explain his tears:

> By the hydraulic of mine eyes
> The humid vapours of my grief are drawn
> Through vacuums of my sighs.

Desportes had talked of a lover who was "intoxicated by the delectation of the concert of the divine harmony" of his mistress. All this preciousness, all this affectation of the use of scientific terms in describing simple emotions, was the object of Malherbe's ruthless disdain. Ronsard had said, "The more words we have in our language, the more perfect it will be." Malherbe replied, "No, certainly not, if they are useless and grotesque words, dragged by the hair of their heads out of Greek and Latin, an outrage on the purity of French grammar." He advised his disciples to eject the monstrous creations of the neo-Hellenes, and to go down to the quays of Paris and listen to the dock-labourers. They used genuine French words which ought to be redeemed from vulgar use, and brought back to literary service.

The existing poems of Malherbe, written at intervals during the last twenty years of his life, are largely pieces of circumstance. They are odes on public events, such as the retaking of Marseilles, the official journeys of the King, the regency of the Queen Mother, and the alliance between France and Spain. They are elegies on the deaths of private persons, a subject on which Malherbe expatiates with the utmost dignity and solemnity. They are sonnets, very unlike the glittering rosy gimcracks of the preceding generation, but stiff with stately compliment

Malherbe and the Classical Reaction

and colourless art. There is no exact English analogue to the poetry of Malherbe, because in the seventeenth century whenever English verse, except in the hands of Milton, aimed at an effect of rhetorical majesty, its stream became clouded. We may observe the case of Cowley, who, I think, had certainly read Malherbe and was influenced by him, in spite of the diametrical views they nourished with regard to the merit of Pindar. Cowley, at his rare and occasional best, has the same serious music, the same clear roll of uplifted enthusiasm, the same absolute assurance as Malherbe. He has the same felicity in his sudden and effective openings. But there is too frequently confusion, artifice, and negligence in Cowley. In Malherbe all is perfectly translucent, nothing turbid is allowed to confuse the vision, no abuse of wit is left to dazzle the attention or trip up steadily advancing progress of thought. It is not easy to give an impression in English of the movement of this clear and untrammelled advance. But here are a couple of stanzas from the 1611 Ode to the Queen Regent on occasion of the King's Mediterranean expedition :

> Ah! may beneath thy son's proud arm down fall
>   The bastions of the Memphian wall,
> And from Marseilles to Tyre itself extend
>   His empire without end.

> My wishes, p'rhaps, are wild; but—by your leave—
>   What cannot ardent prayer achieve?
> And if the gods reward your service so
>   They'll pay but what they owe.

By general consent the crown of Malherbe's poetic genius is the famous "Consolation to Monsieur Du Périer on the death of his daughter." It contains the best-known line of Malherbe—

> Et, Rose, elle a vécu ce que vivent les roses,

about which I would merely say that it is one of those accidental romantic verses which occur here and there in all the great classical poets. There are several in Pope, where they are no more characteristic of his general style than is this of Malherbe's. So far from being the chief line in the poem, it is, in spite of its beauty, the least important to us in our present inquiry. The "Consolation" consists of twenty-one stanzas, written long after the sad event of the death of the young lady, whose name, by the way, was not Rose, but Marguerite. The advice which the poet gives to the stricken father is stoical and Roman. Weary yourself no more with these useless and prolonged lamentations; but henceforth be wise, and love a shadow as a shadow, and extinguish the memory of extinguished ashes. The instances of Priam and Alcides may seem to have little in them to cheer Du Périer, but we must remember that antiquity was held a more sacred authority three hundred years ago than it is now. Malherbe, with great decorum, recalls to Du Périer the fact that he himself has lost two beloved children. The poor man under his thatched roof is subject to the laws of death, nor can the guard on watch at the gates of the Louvre protect our kings against it. To complain of the inevitable sacrifice, and to lose patience with Providence, is to lack wisdom. The only philosophy which can bring repose to a heart bereaved is implicit submission to the will of God.

All this may not seem very original, but it is exquisitely phrased, and it is sensible, dignified, and wholesome. There is in it a complete absence of the ornament and circumstance of death which had taken so preposterous a place in the abundant elegiac poetry of the sixteenth century. We are familiar with the grotesque and sumptuous appeals to the *macabre* which we meet with in Raleigh, in Donne, in Quarles, all the dismal trappings of the tomb and embroideries of the winding-sheet. They are wholly set aside by Malherbe, whose sonnet on the death of his son is worthy of special study. This young man, who was the pride of the poet's life, was killed in a duel, or, as the father vociferously insisted, murdered by a treacherous ruffian. Malherbe made the courts ring with

Malherbe and the Classical Reaction

his appeals, but he also composed a sonnet, which is a typical example of his work. It is not what we should call "poetical," but in clearness, in force, in full capacity to express exactly what the author had in mind to say, it is perfect. We seem to hear the very cry of the fierce old man shrieking for revenge on the slayer of his son. The sonnet was composed some time after the event, for the whole art of Malherbe was the opposite of improvisation. One amusing instance of his deliberate method is to be found in the history of his ode to console President Nicolas de Verdun on the death of his wife. Malherbe composed his poem so slowly, that while he was writing it the President widower not merely married a second time, but died. The poet, with consummate gravity, persisted in his task, and was able to present the widow with the consolation which her late husband should have received after the death of her predecessor.

During thirty years of growing celebrity, Malherbe fought for his doctrine. He had but slowly become a convert to his own laws, but when once they were clearly set out in his brain, he followed them scrupulously, and he insisted that the world should obey them too. It seems a strange thing that it was the young men who followed him first, and with most enthusiasm, until the fashionable ladies of Paris began to compete with one another in support of the classical doctrine, and in repudiation of their old favourite Desportes, whose fame came down clattering in a single night, like Beckford's tower at Font-hill. Malherbe brought poetry into line with the Court and the Church, in a decent formality. Largely, as is always the case in the history of literature, the question was one more of language than of substance. Take, for example, the "Stanzas to Alcandre on the Return of Oranthe to Fontainebleau," and you will find them as preposterous in sentiment, as pretentious and affected in conception, as any sonnet of Desportes, perhaps more so, but their diction is perfectly simple and graceful, and they are composed in faultless modern French. Long before Molière was born Malherbe was in the habit of reading his

verses to an old servant, and if there was a single
phrase which gave her difficulty, he would scrupulously
revise it.

He was supported by a sublime conviction of his own
value. It was a commonplace in all the poetical literature
of the sixteenth century to claim immortality. Desportes
had told his mistress that she would live for ever like the
Phoenix, in the flame of his sonnets. We all remember
Shakespeare's boast that "not marble, nor the gilded
monuments of princes shall outlive this powerful rhyme."
But no one was ever more certain of leaving behind him
a lasting monument than Malherbe. He said, addressing
the King :

> All pour their praise on you, but not with equal hand,
> For while a common work survives one year or two,
> What Malherbe writes is stamped with immortality.

The self-gratulation at the close of the noble "Île de
Ré" ode is quite disconcerting. In this case, also, he
reminds the King that

> The great Amphion, he whose voice was nonpareil,
> Amazed the universe by fanes it lifted high ;
> Yet he with all his art has builded not so well
> As by my verse have I.

His boast, extravagant as it sounds, was partly justified.
Not in his own verse, but in that which his doctrine
encouraged others to write—and not in verse only, but
in prose, and in the very arrangement and attitude of
the French intellect—Malherbe's influence was wide-
spreading, was potent, and will never be wholly super-
seded. He found French, as a literary language, confused,
chaotic, no longer in the stream of sound tradition. He
cleared out the channel, he dredged away the mud and
cut down the weeds; and he brought the pure water back
to its proper course. Let us not suppose that he did this
completely, or that his authority was not challenged. It

Malherbe and the Classical Reaction

was, and Malherbe did not live to see the victory of his ideas. He did not survive long enough to found the Académie, or to welcome Vaugelas, the great grammarian who would have been the solace of his old age. There were still many men of talent, such as Pélisson and Agrippa d'Aubigné, who resisted his doctrine. But he had made his great appeal for order and regularity; he had wound his slug-horn in the forest. He had poured his ideas into the fertile brain of Richelieu; he had started the momentous discussions of the Hôtel Rambouillet. He had taught a new generation to describe objects in general terms, to express natural ideas with simplicity, to select with scrupulous care such words as were purely French and no others, to eschew hiatus and inversion and to purify rhyme, to read the ancients with sympathetic attention but not to pillage them. His own limitations were marked. He seems to have had no sense whatever for external nature; while he overvalued a mathematical exactitude of balance in versification and a grandiose severity in rhetoric.

But we are not attempting this afternoon to define the French Classic School, but merely to comprehend how and when it came into being. It preceded our own Classic School by the fifty years which divide Malherbe from Dryden, who, in like manner, but with far less originality, freed poetry from distortion, prolixity, and artifice. When Malherbe died no one could guess how prodigious would be the effect of his teaching. Indeed, at that moment, October 6, 1628, there might even seem to be a certain retrogression to the old methods, a certain neglect of the new doctrine, which seemed to have been faintly taken up. But, looking back, we now see that at the moment of Malherbe's death, Corneille was on the point of appearing, while there were children in the nurseries who were to be La Fontaine, Pascal, Molière, Mme. de Sévigné, Bossuet. Boileau and Racine were not even born, for Malherbe sowed early and the harvest came late.

The ruling passion accompanied this resolute reformer

Aspects and Impressions

to the very close of his career. His faithful disciple, Racan, his Boswell, has drawn for us the last scene :

One hour before he died, Mr. de Malherbe woke with a start out of a deep slumber, to rebuke his hostess, who was also his nurse, for using an expression which he did not consider to be correct French. When his confessor ventured to chide him, he replied that he could not help it, and that he wished to preserve up to the moment of his death the purity of the French language.

THE FOUNDATION OF THE FRENCH ACADEMY

FOR three centuries past there have been frequent discussions as to the possibility of founding an Academy of Letters in England, but it was not until June, 1910, that a modest and partial experiment in this direction was successfully made. After long deliberations between two accredited bodies, the Royal Society of Literature and the Society of Authors, thirty-three persons were nominated to form, within the corporation of the former, an Academic Committee which should attempt to exercise something resembling the functions of the Académie Française. Lord Morley was elected President, and now, without claiming any excessive publicity, this Academic Committee, founded for the protection and encouragement of a pure English style in prose and verse, has occupied a position in letters which gives every evidence of persisting and increasing. It was assailed, as was natural and right, by satire and by caricature, but it has survived the attacks which were directed against it, and there can be little doubt that, with good luck, it may become a prominent feature of our intellectual and social system. Already, although so young, it has received that consecration of death which makes it a part of history. No fewer than eight, that is to say nearly a quarter, of its original members have passed away, and among them those delicate humanists Butcher and Verrall, a poet so philosophical as Alfred Lyall, critics of such fine temper as Andrew Lang and Edward Dowden. Like the Académie Française, the Academic Committee has its *parti des ducs*, and it mourns the loss of an exquisite amateur, George Wyndham. These men leave to their

Aspects and Impressions

successors the memory of lives devoted to the purest literature.[1]

This, then, seems a not inappropriate moment for considering more closely in detail than has commonly been done, the circumstances attending the most successful experiment that the world has seen to create and sustain a public body whose duty it should be to guard the purity of a national language and to insure the permanence of its best literary forms. It will not be necessary here to do more than remind our readers that the Académie Française was not the earliest corporation in Europe, or even in France, which was formed for the purpose of carrying out these difficult and perilous designs. It was simply the most successful and the most durable. As early as about the year 1490, an Academy was founded in Florence in the deepest piety of the Renaissance. Its motives were pathetically Greek. The gardens of the Medicis were to represent Academe; Arno was to be its Cephisus; in the great Plotinist, Marsiglio Ficino, it was to find its incomparable leader, its visible Plato. By the sixteenth century, Italy was full of imitations; there were the Intronati at Siena, the Della Crusca at Florence, the Otiosi at Bologna, the Humoristi and the Fantastici in Rome. In France itself, in 1570, the poets of the Pléiade instituted, under Charles IX, their Académie de Musique et de Poésie, which became in due course the Académie du Palais, and died inglorious during the Civil Wars. Later there was founded, in Savoy, that Académie Florimontane, which flourished for a little while under St. François de Sales. It was in imitation of those vague and ephemeral institutions that, supported by the powerful patronage of Richelieu, the great corporation which still exercises so lively an influence in France came, in the fulness of the seventeenth century, into permanent existence. It is too seldom realized out of what accidental conjunction of circumstances it arose, and how humble and unfavourable were the auspices which attended its birth.

[1] Since this was written the Academic Committee has lost Henry James, Lady Ritchie and Austin Dobson.

146

The Foundation of the French Academy

The French Academy came into the world so silently, and was long so inconspicuous, that it is difficult to point to its exact source. But there is no doubt that its inception was due to the hospitable temper and the intellectual curiosity of a young man whose name deserves well of the world. He was not a great writer, nor even a great scholar, but he possessed to an extraordinary degree the gift of literary solidarity. In the year 1629, Valentin Conrart, who was twenty-six years of age, was living in a convenient and agreeable house at the corner of the Rue Saint Martin and the Rue des Vielles-Etuves. About this time his relative, probably his cousin, Antoine Godeau, two years younger than Conrart, came up to Paris from Dreux to seek his fortune. It is thought that he lodged with his cousin; at all events Conrart looked after him in his universally obliging way. Godeau confessed that he wrote verses, and he showed them to Conrart, who adored poetry, and who burned to spread an appreciation of it. He thought his kinsman's verses good, and he invited a few of his literary friends to come and listen to them. No doubt he asked them to dinner, for he had a famous cook; and after dinner the company settled down to listen. The poet was excessively short and preposterously ugly, but he was subtle and agreeable, and he already possessed to a conspicuous degree the art of pleasing.

When the future bishop of Grasse and Vence had recited his poems, which were love-pieces and doubtless of a light description—for he afterwards begged them back from Conrart and burned them—the conversation became general, and the evening passed so pleasantly that the company was unanimous that these instructive and entertaining meetings must be repeated. There were eight of these friends gathered together, all authors or men intimately occupied with literature. They were agreed in determining to keep up their discussions, and first of all it was proposed that they should meet successively in each other's houses. But no one of them was rich, and Conrart's house was far the most comfortably situated; he was anxious to be the perpetual host, and the rest were glad to give way to him. They decided to meet once every week to discuss literature and language in Conrart's house at the corner of the Rue Saint Martin. The names of the eight friends are not equally celebrated in the history of French literature; most of them, indeed, are not celebrated at all; but I must record them here, before I proceed, because of the leading part they took at the inception of the Académie. They were Chapelain, Conrart, Godeau, Gombauld, Philippe Habert, Habert de Cerisy, Sérisay, and Malleville. We must try to form some impression of each of them, though most are but fugitive and phantasmal figures.

Of Valentin Conrart a tolerably clear image can be formed by collating what the memoir-writers have recorded of him. It was much noted that he was no scholar; like Shakespeare he had little Latin and less Greek; indeed it was roundly asserted that he had none of either. But he studied much Italian and Spanish, and he had a fine library exclusively of modern literature. He wrote a great deal in prose and verse, but mainly for his private pleasure; he kept a prudent silence about his works, which were understood to be mediocre. He was always an invalid; already, in his youth, he began to be a sufferer from the gout, which was to torture him for thirty years. But pain did not affect his temper, nor his extraordinary gregariousness. He lived for the small enjoyments of others. He was the confidant of everybody, the healer of all quarrels and disputes. As time went on, and Conrart became absorbed in the duties of perpetual Secretary to the Académie, his qualities may have become exaggerated. His enemies began to say that he was too indulgent, too easy-going with offenders. The super-subtle declared that he had become infatuated with his own friendliness, and that he went through Paris murmuring " Ah! ma belle amitié! " He was a great depositary of secrets, and liked nothing so much as to run about—or rather, poor man! to hobble about—pouring oil upon troubled waters. Tallemant des Réaux, who hated him, says that Conrart had an unpleasant wife, whose face was like a gingerbread nut, but we need not believe all that Tallemant des Reaux says.

Conrart, however, with all his serviceable friendliness, could not have done much without Chapelain, who was really the founder of the Académie. Jean Chapelain was not merely an active man of letters, he was the man of letters pure and simple. He had, in that age of intellectual curiosity, a passion for literature not surpassed, if equalled, by a single contemporary. M. Lanson has shown, what scarcely needed showing, that Chapelain was no artist, but if he was a bad poet, he was intensely interested in the technique of poetry. He has been called the founder of French criticism; he had pertinacity, courage, and a passionate love for the French language. Perhaps he was the inventor of the law of the Three Unities in drama. His influence in French thought lasted until the days of Boileau. In 1629 Chapelain was thirty-five years of age, old enough and dogmatic enough to impress his will and his opinions on his younger companions. Because he was a detestable epic and a ridiculous lyric poet, because we cannot be drawn by wild horses to read the *Pucelle* or the *Ode à Richelieu*, we must not overlook the fact that Chapelain was one of the great intellectual forces of his time, although when the meetings began he had scarcely printed anything except the much-discussed *Préface de l'Adone* (1623). Ceremonious and yet rough, a courtier and yet a sort of astute Diogenes, hating all luxury and ruining himself to buy rare books, a stormy petrel in every literary tempest, Chapelain presents to us the shrewd and violent figure of a captain who steered the youthful Académie through its vicissitudes into safe anchorage.

Among all these young men, there was one old man, and he too, like Chapelain, was an authentic man of letters. This was Jean Ogier, Sieur de Gombauld, who was not less than sixty years of age already. He had been born youngest son in the fourth marriage of a redoubtable Huguenot of Xaintogne, and he came to Paris towards the end of the reign of Henry IV, with a mass of strange MSS. He was very poor, very proud, extravagant and eccentric

K 149

to the last degree. He managed to appear at Court, and there must have been something striking about him, since his fortune began by Marie de Medicis noticing him at the coronation of Louis XIII. It was said that she saw in him a striking likeness to a man of whom she had been very fond years before in Florence. After the ceremony, the Queen-Mother sent for Gombauld, and he was attached to her Court, where he was called "le Beau Ténébreux," but he remained very shy and helpless. He nourished a frenzied passion for her Majesty, yet was incapable of speech or movement in her presence; during his brief splendour at Court, he wrote the most famous of his works, the romance of *Endymion* (1624), in which the Queen-Mother appeared as that leading character, "La Lune." There are delightful stories of the *gaucherie* and pathetic simplicity of this old poet, who was a very fine country gentleman, always carefully dressed, holding his tall, spare figure well upright, and with quantities of real hair pushing out his wig on all sides. Gombauld, in spite of "La Lune," could never feel at his ease in the presence of fine ladies, and sighed for a farmer's daughter. After the death of Richelieu, all the pensions were struck off, and Gombauld grew very poor and wrinkled. He was touched with the mania of persecution, and became rather a terror to his fellow-Academicians, one of whom called him "the most ceremonious and the most mysterious of men." He grew to be very unhappy, but like Tithonus could not die, and he was "a white-haired shadow roaming like a dream" in the world of Molière and Racine. He died, at the age of ninety-six, in 1666, having been born in the lifetime of Ronsard, and out-living the birth of Massillon.

The other four members of the original group have not left so deep a mark on the history of literature. Jacques de Sérisay was accustomed to literary coteries, for he had been a constant attendant on Montaigne's adopted daughter, that enthusiastic and grotesque old maid, Mlle. Marie de Gournay, who loved to collect the wits around her "shadow" and her cat, Donzelle. Sérisay cannot have

The Foundation of the French Academy

been a man of letters of much force, since his works, to the end of time, consisted of half a tragedy, which he could never finish.   Later on he contrived to read this fragment aloud to Richelieu, who yielded to fatigue before the end of the exercise.   This vague person was known as "le délicat Sérisay."   Then, there was Claude de Malleville, who had just come back from attending Bassompierre in England.   He was a man of considerable originality of character, and afterwards a power in the Académie.   He liked the pleasant informality of the meetings at Conrart's house, and objected to their being turned into official sessions.   We shall see that he stood alone, a little later, in stout opposition to the proposals of the Cardinal.   Malleville was a little wisp of a man, with black locks and dim dark eyes.   He translated vaguely and amorously from the Italian, and had a great deal to do with the composition of the *Guirlande de Julie*.   Except for some Ovidian Epistles, which he is said to have published as early as 1620, Malleville's own poems were posthumous.   M. Magne says that Malleville was "un faiseur de bibus" (a term of contempt almost beyond the range of translation) "qui frétillait autour des jupes"; but that is because he opposed Boisrobert.   Shadows they were, and shadows they pursued.

Most shadowy of all are to us now the two Haberts.   Germain Habert, the youngest of the original Académiciens, wrote a very affected poem on the metamorphosis of the eyes of Phillis into stars.   As he grew older he neglected Phillis to devote himself to good works. Ménage, who was his friend, says he was "un des plus beaux esprits de son temps."   But where are the evidences of his wit?   His brother, Philippe Habert, is the last of the original coterie and the faintest phantom of them all. He was a soldier in the artillery, and he was killed, in 1637, at the siege of Emery, crushed under a wall that had been accidentally blown up by gunpowder.   Just before this melancholy event, Philippe Habert had prophetically published his poem called *Le Temple de la Mort*, which was very much admired, but is now not easily accessible.

Aspects and Impressions

He was a cold and solemn young man, reserved in manner, but held to be both brave and friendly.

Such were the eight companions who met, week by week, all innocent and unconscious, to discuss in familiar intercourse every species of subject—business, the news of the day, the movement of letters. If any one of them had written something, as frequently happened, he would read it aloud, and ask for criticism, which would be frankly given. Often their discussions would end in a stroll through the streets, or in a meal prepared by Conrart's really estimable *chef*. It was a delightful time, and, in after years, when the Académie was celebrated and powerful, the original members looked back wistfully at this happy period of almost pastoral quietude. Pellisson, interviewing the survivors in a later generation, says that "ils parlent encore aujourd'hui de ce premier âge de l'Académie, comme d'un âge d'or, durant lequel avec toute l'innocence et toute la liberté des premiers siècles, sans bruit et sans pompe, et sans autres lois que celles de l'amitié, ils goûtaient ensemble tout ce que la société des esprits et la vie raisonnable ont de plus doux et de plus charmant."

It is curious and interesting to find that this "little clan," as Keats would call it, contrived to preserve its unity and its privacy for several years. The friends met, as we have seen, with remarkable frequency, yet they did not quarrel, nor grow bored, nor break up through the action of any outward accident. It is, surely, even in much quieter centuries than ours, unusual that a party of this kind should continue to exist, suspended as in a vacuum, not dwindling nor increasing, and unknown to the world outside. In those Valois times, such a collection of persons would be in danger of being accused of political plotting, and so the visitors to Conrart were pledged to an absolute silence. This pledge was first broken by Malleville, who told Nicolas Faret, apparently in 1632. Faret was a young provincial lawyer, lately arrived in Paris from the town of Bourg-en-Bresse. He was still very poor, but ingenious and active; he was a

The Foundation of the French Academy

disciple of the great grammarian, Vaugelas, and later the intimate of Molière. He was a jolly man, with chestnut hair and rubicund face; his figure grew massive as the years went by. Faret was consumed with curiosity, and when he had once wormed the secret of the meetings out of Malleville, he gave the latter no peace until he consented to introduce him. Faret had just published a book of some merit and considerable popularity, *L'Honnête Homme*, a breviary of how a gentleman should behave, a sort of courtier's *vade mecum;* and he brought an early copy of this with him as a credential. Faret was an active, boisterous person, boon companion of the more gifted poet Saint-Amant. He had no sooner secured a footing in Conrart's house than he made himself very useful to the body, for he was by far the most business-like of the group. It was Faret who, in 1634, drew up the original scheme for the foundation of the Académie. He did not add much to the glory of the corporation, when once it was formed, for the other members complained that he did not attend the meetings unless there was some practical business on hand, and that then he was apt to be drunk. Faret, who was attached to Henry of Lorraine, the comte d'Harcourt, and served as his go-between with Richelieu, was not a very shining Académicien, but he had his temporary value.

Faret's chief merit was that he brought to the meetings a man of letters who was destined to take a very prominent place, for the time being, both in the French Academy and in literary life—namely, Jean Desmarets de Saint-Sorlin. He was an indefatigable writer, and a man exactly suited to be useful to a group of literary persons, because he had experience of the world, great enthusiasm for the craft of letters, and a wide and humorous outlook on life. Chapelain, glancing back many years later, defined Desmarets as "un des esprits les plus faciles de ce temps," and that is just what he was, an inexhaustible and rapid producer of prose and verse in the spirit and fashion of the age. He was much valued by Richelieu, who forced him, against his will, to collaborate in the composition of

153

tragedies. Desmarets had no dramatic inspiration, but he was able to satisfy the Cardinal. At the time of which we are speaking, probably in 1633, Desmarets was brought to Conrart's house by Faret and received a courteous welcome. It was characteristic of him that, instantly entering into the spirit of the company, he pulled out of his pocket the proof-sheets of his new prose romance *Ariane,* and asked leave to submit them to discussion.

Desmarets was rich and influential, and he had the true Academic spirit. He became a prominent public character, and Controller-General of the King's Army, but he never lost his close hold upon the Académie, of which he was elected the first Chancellor. In the moment of transition, the dark hour before the dawn, he was eminently useful, for when, in 1633, Conrart married, and it was no longer convenient to meet in his house, Desmarets transferred the whole cluster of bees to a new hive, the sumptuous Hôtel Pellevé, which he had just rebuilt at the corner of the Rue du Roi de Sicile and of the Rue Tison. Then, and not till then, did they begin seriously to think of founding an Academy. Desmarets's numerous writings have stood the test of time very ill. His epic of *Clovis* was ridiculed by Boileau, and perhaps the only work of his which can be read to-day without boredom is his comedy of *Les Visionnaires* (1635), a merry piece of literary criticism, in which the various coteries of that day, and the famous salons, are satirized. Nevertheless, it is not beyond the range of possibility that, in these days of revival, somebody may be found to resuscitate Desmarets de Saint-Sorlin.

In that entertaining volume, *Le Plaisant Abbé de Boisrobert,* the great rival of Desmarets has already found an eloquent resuscitator, M. Magne. François de Metel de Boisrobert is an unedifying figure of a scapegrace priest, whose giggling face is seen peeping round most doors in the scandalous memoirs of the time. No one was more contemptuously insulted, no one more bitterly ridiculed, than Richelieu's supple jackal, the author of *Anaxandre*

The Foundation of the French Academy

et Orazie and of *Pyrandre*. These heroic works of faded imagination are read no longer, nor the *Recueil de Lettres Nouvelles* nor *Le Sacrifice des Muses*. On the other hand, the sarcasms of the epigrammatists and the scandalous tales of contemporaries continue to invest the memory of Boisrobert with a nasty odour. M. Magne, who brings a marvellous erudition to the task, has bravely endeavoured to redeem a talent and a character so deeply compromised. We cannot join in the whole of his whitewashing, but we may admit that he has proved the "plaisant abbé" to be neither the dunce nor the blackguard that legend had painted him. Moreover, it is quite certain that he exercised a most useful energy in the foundation of the French Academy.

When the indiscretion of Faret brought Desmarets to the literary meetings in Conrart's house, it had the inevitable result of exciting the jealous curiosity of Boisrobert. He was the great rival of Desmarets in the affection and confidence of Richelieu, and we may be certain that when "le plaisant abbé" found out that Desmarets was attending secret and mysterious assemblies, he plainly intimated to Faret that he also must be taken into the secret or else he would report the plot to the Cardinal. Accordingly, some time in 1633, Boisrobert too was brought to Conrart's house, and instantly conceived a great scheme for his own honour and the glory of French literature. He clung, through every storm, to the robes of Richelieu, who had originally disliked him, but who proved in the long run powerless to resist the devotion and the entertainment which Boisrobert provided. The poet took no snub; on one occasion when Richelieu had rudely ignored him, he flung himself on his knees, crying "You let the dogs eat the crumbs which fall from your table. Am I not a dog?" The Cardinal admitted that he was, and thenceforth Boisrobert occupied an intimate place in Richelieu's household, sometimes as a retriever, more often as a poodle. It is impossible to deny that Boisrobert was a poltroon, but in his lifelong devotion to the Académie he really behaved extremely well. The secret,

155

no doubt, was that with the minimum of regard for purity of conduct, the "plaisant abbé" combined a genuine solicitude for the purity of language.

It was Boisrobert who first conceived the idea that an Academy of Letters might be useful to Richelieu and Richelieu indispensable to an Academy of Letters. For this scheme he deserves great credit, and we gather that it was first to the Cardinal and not first to Conrart's friends that he spoke. It seems probable that the latter had already begun to suggest among themselves that their relation might be permanent. There is a letter dated as early as December, 1632, in which Godeau, writing to Chapelain, seems to speak of the Académie as already a recognized thing. If we may suppose that Louis Giry, the Hellenist, who was not an original member, but whose name is mentioned as that of one of Conrart's friends, was already a visitor, the body now consisted of twelve persons, with all of whom I have endeavoured to make my readers acquainted. It was after one of the meetings in 1633 that, as Pellisson tells us, having observed what kind of books had been examined, and that the conversation had not been a commerce of compliment and flattery, where each person gave praise that in his turn he might receive it, but that faults of style, and even very small ones, had been seized upon boldly and frankly for discussion, Boisrobert was "fulfilled with joy and admiration." It crossed his mind that this was the very toy to enliven the petulant leisure of his Cardinal. When that scheme occurred to "le plaisant abbé" the Académie Française practically started into being.

No small part of the success of the policy of Richelieu came from the brilliant intuition which he had of the importance of regulating intellectual effort. He did not ignore the Press, as had so stupidly been done before his day, but he had no idea of leaving it to follow its own devices. In 1626 he had used a very remarkable expression; he had said "Les faiseurs de livres serviraient grandement le roi et ceux qui sont auprès de lui, s'ils ne se mêlaient de parler de leurs actions ni en bien ni en

The Foundation of the French Academy

mal." Literature was to be encouraged and protected, on the understanding that it would attend to its own affairs, and not disturb the King's government with *libelles* which were none of its concern. Richelieu's genuine enthusiasm for scholarship and poetry is not to be questioned, but with it all he was pre-eminently an ambitious statesman. Public policy was the business of his life, literature his enchanting relaxation and entertainment. But he wished to be master in the temple of the Muses, no less than in the King's palace, and he would only protect the authorship of the day on the terms of being recognized as its absolute tyrant. He was to be the Miltiades of letters, but once acknowledge his authority, and he became literature's "best and truest friend." His lightning intelligence had perceived, in 1631, the importance of journalism, and he had protected the earliest of French newspapers, the *Gazette,* on the understanding that it proceeded from his own official cabinet. It was his scheme to break the prestige of the nobility, and in carrying out his plans, he was glad of the support of the intellectual classes. He was aided, of course, by the development of public feeling in this direction.

There can be little doubt that it was by Boisrobert rather than by Desmarets that the Cardinal was originally informed of the literary meetings in the house of Conrart. His curiosity was vividly awakened. Knots of persons meeting privately and with regularity were the objects of his lively suspicion, and there is some reason to suppose that his first impulse was to break up the company and forbid the meetings. But Boisrobert, who held his ear, reassured him.

He did not fail [says our earliest authority] to give a favourable report of the little assembly in whose deliberations he had taken a part, and of the persons who composed it; and the Cardinal, whose temper was naturally attuned to great designs, and who loved the French language to infatuation, being himself an excellent writer, after having praised the scheme, asked M. Boisrobert whether these persons would not like to become a corporation, and to meet regularly, and under public authority.

He desired Boisrobert to put this proposition before the next meeting, as from himself.

It appears that at first the idea was not received with enthusiasm. The friends were simple men of letters, not ambitious of power, and timid in the face of such formidable patronage. But the Cardinal consulted Chapelain, and won him over to his views. There can be no doubt that Desmarets and Faret supported a plan from which they could reap nothing but personal advantage. When the ground was ready and the hour was ripe, Boisrobert came down to a meeting, with a definite proposal from the Cardinal, who offered to these gentlemen his protection for their Society, the public compliment of Letters Patent, and also—this was so like the vehement *bonhomie* of Richelieu—a promise of personal affection "en toutes rencontres" for each of them individually. The friends were, in fact, to be attached in permanence to his personal household.

The meeting at which Boisrobert made this startling announcement was one of which it would be interesting indeed to have a detailed report. Unfortunately, this is wanting. But we know that the friends were smitten with timidity and dismay. Scarcely any one of them but expressed his vexation, and regretted that the Cardinal had done them this most unwelcome honour, that he had come down from his majestic heights to "troubler la douceur et la familiarité de leurs conférences." We can imagine the agitation and the anxiety, the babble of voices which had never before been raised above the tone of scholarly amenity. Those who were pledged to support the scheme doubtless held their peace until the storm had subsided, and until Sérisay and Malleville, who were the most intractable opponents, had done their worst in denunciation of it. Then the voices of the supporters were heard, and some-one, doubtless the honey-tongued Boisrobert, suggested that as Sérisay was master of the household to the Duc

The Foundation of the French Academy

de la Rochefoucauld, and Malleville secretary to the Maréchal de Bassompierre, it would, unjustly but most inevitably, be believed that they were incited by the enmity which their respective patrons were supposed (but how unfairly!) to nourish against the Cardinal. This impressed the company, and Sérisay withdrew his opposition, but Malleville continued to be intractable. It was important, however, that the reply of the infant Academy to the Cardinal should be cordial, and that it should be unanimous.

Chapelain, who had held his arguments in reserve, now came forward with that mixture of tact and force which was his great quality. He was certainly the most eminent man of letters in the assembly, and the others supposed him to be more independent than he really was. As a matter of fact, he had succumbed to the fascination of the Cardinal, who, to put it vulgarly, had Chapelain safe in his pocket. With a great show of impartiality, the poet put before his friends the sensible view that, no doubt, it would have been more agreeable to continue in private their confidential gatherings, but that it was no longer a question of what was agreeable. They had—he would not insist on pointing out how—lost all chance of keeping themselves to themselves. The secret was out, and they had attracted the attention of the most formidable of men, one who was in the habit of being implicitly obeyed, and who was not accustomed to meet with resistance; that this all-powerful statesman would not forgive the insult of their refusing his proffer of protection, and that he would find a way to chastise each individual member. But certainly, the first thing he would be sure to do would be to disperse their assembly and destroy a society which all of them had already begun to hope would be immortal. Nothing more was heard of Malleville's "minority report"; the infant Academy surrendered unanimously. Before the company dispersed, M. de Boisrobert was desired to convey to Monsieur le Cardinal the very humble thanks of the assembly for the honour he designed to show them, and to assure him that, though none of them had ever dreamed of such distinction, they were all of them resolved to carry out the wishes of his Eminence.

Richelieu always responded to this sort of attitude. He expressed to "le plaisant abbé" his great satisfaction, and no doubt they laughed together in private over the oddities of Conrart's guests, for such was their habit, and such the influence of Boisrobert over his master. A doctor once facetiously recommended, when the Cardinal was ill, "two drams of Boisrobert after every meal." But in public, and in fact, Richelieu took the most lively interest in the scheme. One is inclined to believe, that, by a flash of prophetic imagination, this great man saw what a place the Académie Française would take in the French order of things during three coming centuries at least. He urged the friends to meet without delay, now no longer at Conrart's, but in Desmarets's palatial hôtel, "et à penser sérieusement à l'établissement de l'Académie." All this was early in 1634, probably in February.

The first direction which the Cardinal deigned to give to the embarrassed and slightly terrified friends was that they should add to their number, or in his own words that "ces Messieurs grossirent leur Compagnie de plusieurs personnes considérables pour leur mérite." This appears to have been begun at the official sitting of March 20, 1634, and that may be considered as the date of the formation of the Académie. Existing members sat round the table, no doubt, and names were suggested and voted for. It would be a somewhat rough-and-ready choice, and the critical attitude would not be precisely that which would meet with approval at the Institut to-day. But the errors of choice have been abundantly exaggerated by those who have written loosely on this subject. Before the end of 1634 they had added, it seems, twenty-three names to their original list of eleven (or twelve), so that the Académie now consisted of about thirty-five men. Among these, it is perfectly true that there existed many obscurities and some obvious nonentities. But, besides those whom we have already described, the names now appeared of Balzac, Maynard, Gomberville, Saint-Amant, Racan, Vaugelas,

The Foundation of the French Academy

and Voiture. All these were writers extremely eminent in the literature of their own age, and not one of them but is interesting and distinguished still. Not to have included them in a French Academy would have been a grave and obvious errror.

Some of the accusations brought against the infant Academy are absurd. It has been vilified for omitting to make Molière and Pascal original members; the latter was eleven years of age at the time and the former twelve! Descartes was, of course, already one of the intellectual glories of France, but he was a wanderer over the face of Europe, and still only known as a writer in Latin. Arnauld d'Antilly was elected, but refused to take his place. Like Pascal, Brébeuf was still a schoolboy. Pierre Corneille, who was very little known in 1634, and not a resident in Paris, was elected later, and so was Lamothe le Vayer. Charles Sorel, the author of *Francion* and *Le Berger Extravagant*, who was historiographer of France and a satirist of merit, was not invited to join, it is true; but his caustic pen had spared no one, and he was essentially "unclubable." Scarron in 1634 was only a wild young buck about town. There remains unexplained —and I confess there seems to me to remain alone—the strange omission of Rotrou, a tragic poet of high distinction who never formed part of the French Academy. Since 1632 he had been the friend of Chapelain, and the Cardinal was devoted to him. That Rotrou's duties as a magistrate forced him to reside at Dreux is the only reason which I can think of to account for his absence from the list of 1634. If there was one other representative man of letters eligible, and yet omitted from that list, my memory is at fault.

Among those who were invited there was one whose support was absolutely essential to the youthful society. It may be said, without exaggeration, that the Académie Française could not have survived contemporary ridicule if it had failed to secure the co-operation of Jean Louis Guez de Balzac. In 1634 Balzac was thirty-seven years of age and by far the most prominent man of letters in

Aspects and Impressions

France. The first volume of his famous *Lettres*—which were not letters in our sense, but chatty and yet elaborate essays on things in general—had appeared in 1624, and had created what the Abbé d'Olivet described as "a general revolution among persons of culture." Balzac immediately took his place as the official leader and divinity of what were afterwards known as the Précieuses; but he was a great deal more than that: he was the enchanting artist of a new French prose. "Le grand Epistolier de France" was to French prose all, and more than all, that Malherbe (who died in 1628) was to French verse. Brunetière has dwelt on Balzac's great service to letters, in the studied cultivation of harmony and lucidity, order and movement. His *Lettres* ushered in a new epoch in the production of prose, far more sudden and obvious than was brought about half a century later, in English, by the *Essays* of Sir William Temple, but similar to that in character. The most agreeable present any man of fashion could make to his mistress, says Ménage, was a copy of Balzac's book, and yet the gravest of scholars was not too learned to imitate its cadences.

The objects which the infant French Academy set before itself were the encouragement of grace and nobility of style in all persons employing the French language, and, as a corollary to this, the persistent effort to raise that language, in all particulars, until it should become an instrument for expression as delicate, as forcible and as comprehensive as Latin and Greek had been in their palmiest hours. But these were the very objects which Balzac had first, and most imperiously, impressed upon his readers, and there was a sense in which it could be said that the new body was merely emphasizing and extending, giving legislative authority to, ideas which were the property of Balzac. It was therefore obvious that whosoever was made an original member, the "grand Epistolier" should not be missing. This was obvious to the wise Boisrobert, of whom Balzac himself amusingly said that he was "circomspectissime" in the smallest actions of his life. As early as March 13, 1634, and therefore in all probability

The Foundation of the French Academy

before anyone else was approached, Boisrobert took care that Balzac was invited to join the new Académie.

But it was one thing to whistle to Balzac, and quite another for him to come at the call. His character was not an agreeable one; he was excessively proud, painfully shy, quivering with self-consciousness, ever ready to take offence. Tallemant des Réaux, putting the universal opinion into an epigram, said that if ever there was an *animal gloriæ* it was Balzac. He was a finished hypochondriac, with his finger ever on his own pulse; before he was thirty he described himself as more battered than a ship that has sailed three times to the Indies. He was a hermit, hating society, and scarcely ever leaving that garden of amber and musk within the walls of his castle of Balzac which hung above the mingling waters of the Charente and the Touvre. But Balzac, whose character and temperament had many points of likeness to those of Pope, knew the value of friendship, though he was capable of amazing disloyalty under the pressure of vanity. Conrart, Boisrobert, Chapelain, and even perhaps the magnificent Cardinal himself—for there is talk of a pension—brought simultaneous pressure to bear, and Balzac consented to let his name appear in the list of original members of the Académie. This did not induce in him much zeal for the works or deeds of his nominal colleagues, upon whom, from his far-away garden-terraces, he looked down with great contempt. Still, the Académie Française was in existence, for Balzac was of the number.

Among the other original members, Voiture and Gomberville, the author of *Polexandre,* have never lost their little place in the crowded history of French literature. Saint-Amant and Maynard, who sank out of sight for a long time, are now regarded with more honour than ever before since their death. Honorat de Beuil, Marquis de Racan, is one of the minor classics of his country. A dreamy, blundering man, innocent and vague, his whole outlook upon life was that of a pastoral poet. He had "no common sense," we are told, but walked in a cloud conducting an imaginary flock and murmuring his beautiful Virgilian verses. Racan took the Academy more seriously than any other member; he never missed a sitting. But he could not be depended on. Once, the Academy met to listen to an address by the Marquis de Racan, who entered, holding one torn sheet of paper in his hand. "Gentlemen," he said, "I was bringing you my oration, but my great greyhound has chewed it up. Here it is! Make what you can of it, for I don't know it by heart, and I have no copy." The story of how old Mlle. de Gournay was gulled by successive impostors who pretended to be Racan, and then at length spurned the real poet, as an obvious idiot, is too long to be told here in detail. At the close of his life, Racan had allowed himself to retain no friends except his fellow academicians, so completely had he become absorbed in the Académie.

These illustrious names, however, are not sufficient to prevent the eye which runs down the list of original members from being startled by the obscurity of at least half the names. It must be remembered that in 1635 it was no envied distinction or disputed honour to form part of this new and untried corporation. The labours of the academicians were disinterested, for the Académie was not yet endowed, and there was little or no reward offered, besides the favour of the Cardinal, for the zealous labours of scholarship. Moreover, it was necessary to silence opposition and disarm ridicule. The general feeling of the public, as reflected in the action of parliament, was hostile. Louis XIII himself, although he had passed the Letters Patent, was far from favourable to his Minister's literary project, as we learn from a letter of Chapelain. But Richelieu was passionately bent on its success, and we see from Tallemant that whenever the Académie made a step in advance, the Cardinal was at no pains to conceal his lively satisfaction. But there were more seats than eminent men of letters to fill them, and consequently almost anyone who would consent or could be inveigled was elected. Scarron says the only thing that some of the original Immortals were fit for was to snuff candles or to sweep the floor. There was a class of academicians who were styled "the children of the pity of Boisrobert," because the "plaisant abbé," in filling up the *fauteuils,* was merciful to needy men of letters without talent, and fetched them in so that they might eat a piece of bread. They were buoyed up with the hope that Richelieu would bring in an age of gold for scribblers.

But another element must not be forgotten. There was a great temptation to turn poachers into gamekeepers, and a certain number of the original members of the Académie Française were wits whose bitterness Richelieu himself, or Chapelain, or Boisrobert, dreaded. Maynard was one of these, but perhaps the most curious example was a man called Bautru. He was no writer, for one scurrilous piece in the *Cabinet Satirique* represents his complete works. But he was a savage practical joker, whose tongue was universally dreaded. His wit seems to have been ready. He was a "libertine " in the sense of that day, and openly irreligious. One day, he was caught taking his hat off to a crucifix as he passed in the street. "Ah ! then," said his friends, "you are on better terms with God than we supposed? " "On bowing terms; we don't speak," Bautru replied. In 1642, he called our Charles I "a calf led from market to market; and presently they will take him to the shambles," he prophetically added. His was an evil tongue with a sharp edge to it, which it was safest to have inside the Académie, and there were others of the same sort among the false celebrities, *les passe-volans* or dummies, whose presence in the original list is at first so disconcerting.

In order to give dignity and discipline to their assemblies, the Academicians now created three offices, those of Director, Chancellor, and Perpetual Secretary; these were held by Sérisay, Desmarets, and Conrart respectively. They appointed the famous printer, Jean Camusat, their librarian and typographer, meeting sometimes at his house for easier correction of the press. On the 20th of March, 1634, they settled on their all-important name, and thenceforth were to the world "l'Académie françoise." Two days later, in a very long letter, they detailed to the

Aspects and Impressions

Cardinal the objects and functions of their body, not failing to begin with the request that he would permit them to publish his own tragedies and pastorals. This document is very interesting to-day. In it the new Academy proposes to cleanse the French language from all the ordure which it has contracted from vulgar and ignorant usage; to establish the exact sense of words; seriously to examine the subject and treatment of prose, the style of the whole, the harmony of periods, the propriety in the use of words. Moreover, the Academicians undertook to examine the books of one another with a meticulous attention to faults of style and grammar. This "Projet," which was drafted by Faret, was submitted to Richelieu, and printed in an edition of thirty copies, in May, 1634.

In this first manifesto, which was kept extremely secret, nothing was said about the plan of a Dictionary. But Chapelain's heart had been set upon that from the first, and he did not forget to bring it forward. He insisted, in season and out of season, on the necessity of labouring in unison "for the purity of our language and for its capacity to develop the loftiest eloquence." On the 27th of March he brought forward his idea of a Dictionary. Balzac supported him by letter, Vaugelas offered his invaluable grammatical services, and at last the Academy so far accepted the idea as to instruct Chapelain and Vaugelas to report on the subject. But this was not until 1637, so that we must realize that the French Academy had existed three years before it finally settled down to the work with which its early existence is most popularly identified. But for the persistency of Chapelain this might never have been commenced.

On the other hand, the Academicians were very busily engaged over their statutes, which were drawn up by one of the latest of the original members, Hay du Chastelet, a learned lawyer of high repute. They were passed and accepted by the Cardinal, before the close of 1634. It was, very properly, Conrart himself who drafted the Letters Patent, a very long and dignified document, which Louis XIII signed in Paris on the 29th of January, 1635. But

The Foundation of the French Academy

now came the first difficulty which beset the primrose path of the young Académie. It was not enough for the King to sign the Letters Patent; they had to be *vérifiées* by Parliament; and this was not done until the 10th of July, 1637. There has been much discussion as to the cause of this delay, which was intensely irksome to the Cardinal and threatened the existence of the infant association. It was early thought that the Parliament suspected Richelieu of having a design in creating the Académie which was much more directly political than appeared on the surface. If so, the placid and modest demeanour of the Academicians ultimately disarmed hostility, and they obtained their Letters Patent.

At this point we must draw our inquiry to a close, since the foundation of the Académie Française was completed by this action on the part of the Parliament. It will be seen that eight years had gone by since the first meetings of selected men of letters had taken place in Conrart's house, and that many tedious formalities had to be completed before the body was in a position even to begin its work. The humble nature of the origin of the Académie Française, the surprising and painful adventures of its youth, and the glories of its subsequent existence, should make us indulgent to the slow growth of any similar institution. Rome is not the only corporation which was not built in a day.

ROUSSEAU IN ENGLAND IN THE NINETEENTH CENTURY

BURKE, in his *Reflections on the Revolution in France* (1790), although he called Rousseau an "eccentric observer of human nature," had not attempted to deny his penetration. He wrote of him, already without sympathy, as one who for the sake of playing upon that love of the marvellous which is inherent in man, desired extraordinary situations, "giving rise to new and unlooked-for strokes in politics and morals." But he gave the Genevese philosopher credit for nothing worse than levity; he had raised up political and social paradoxes in the spirit in which a story-teller, eager to arouse the attention of an idle audience, evokes giants and fairies to satisfy the credulity of his hearers. And Burke has the indulgence to admit that, "I believe, were Rousseau alive, and in one of his lucid intervals, he would be shocked at the fanatical frenzy of his scholars, who . . . are servile imitators; and even in their incredulity discover an implicit faith."

But when events had rapidly developed, and Burke came to write the flaming sentences of his great *Letter to a Member of the National Assembly* (1791), the importance of Rousseau's influence in bringing about the events which Burke so passionately deplored had greatly widened and deepened. He saw that the very blood of Rousseau had been transfused into the veins of the National Assembly of France. "Him they study," he wrote, "him they meditate; him they turn over in all the time they can spare from the laborious mischief of the day, or the debauches of the night. Rousseau is their canon of holy writ; in his life he is their canon of *Polyclitus;* he is their standard figure of perfection." Burke felt obliged to denounce, with his unparalleled wealth of picturesque eloquence, the fatal character of the fascination exercised by the author of the *Lettres de la Montagne* and the *Confessions*.

To Burke, thus brought face to face with what he believed to be the very Ragnarok of the gods, the ruin of all which made life in Europe worth living, it now became a religious duty to expose the malefic character of the charming, exquisite pleadings of the revolutionary of Geneva. He declared that the virtue propounded by Rousseau was not virtue at all, but "a selfish, flattering, seductive, ostentatious vice." This was a theory new to Englishmen, a theory which had, of course, in faltering accents, been here and there suggested by opponents, but never before deliberately and logically asserted by a great master of English oratory. Burke spoke, not merely with the immense prestige of his position, but as one who had been subjected to the personal charm of Rousseau, and who had studied him in his lifetime, not merely without prejudice, but with sympathy and admiration. His grave censure of the philosopher came with unction from the lips of one who was known to have been in communication with him, during his first visit to London, almost from day to day.[1] Burke spoke with authority to a large section of the public when he stated that he had gradually become persuaded that Rousseau "entertained no principle either to guide his heart, or to guide his understanding, but *vanity*." He did not deny the charm of Rousseau's writing, or pretend to depreciate his incomparable talents, but he pronounced him to be deranged and eccentric, and to have gloried in the illumination of the obscure and vulgar vices. He described the *Confessions*, over which the English world had bowed in transports of emotional adulation, as the record of "a life that, with wild defiance, he flings in the face of his Creator." Violence carried Burke so far as to describe

[1] By far the best account of Rousseau's visit to England is contained in *Le Séjour de J. J. Rousseau en Angleterre* (1766-1767), published from original documents by M. Louis J. Courtois (A. Jullian, Genève, 1911).

Rousseau in England in the 19th Century

Rousseau as a man, by his own account, without a single virtue. There can be no question that this diatribe, prominently brought forward by the first of English orators, in a work which was read by every educated man in Great Britain, sapped the reputation of Rousseau amongst our countrymen, and led to the gradual decline of his fame in England all down the nineteenth century.

The attack on Rousseau, contained in many fulminating pages of the *Letter to a Member of the National Assembly,* is extravagant and unjust. We read it now with a certain indignation, tempered by a mild amusement. It should have been injured by its absurd denunciation of Frenchmen and of the French nation, in whom Burke saw little but a furious congeries of dancing-masters, fiddlers, and *valets-de-chambre.* But there were already in England, in the reaction of terror brought about by the French Revolution, many who were delighted to accept this grotesque perversion of the truth, and Burke, with all his powers of speech, all his knowledge of his countrymen, knew how to play upon the alarms and the ignorances of the English. He had, at all events, the dangerous gift of unqualified statement, and when he solemnly declared, as if by reluctant conviction, that "the writings of Rousseau lead directly to shameful evil " both in theory and practice, there were thousands only too ready to accept the warning.

We may observe, too, that Burke was the earliest English critic of weight who suggested that the exquisite literary art of Rousseau had its limitations. His remarks are worthy of being quoted at length, since they contain the germ of the English attitude through the whole of the nineteenth century :—

I have often wondered how he comes to be so much more admired and followed on the Continent than he is here. Perhaps a secret charm in the language may have its share in this extraordinary difference. We certainly perceive, and to a degree we feel, in this writer, a style glowing, animated, enthusiastic; at the same time that we find it lax, diffuse, and not in the best taste of composition; all the members of the piece being pretty equally laboured and expended, without any due selection or subordination of parts. He is generally too much on the stretch, and his manner has little variety. We cannot rest upon any of his works, though they contain observations which occasionally discover a considerable insight into human nature.

The attacks of Burke upon their idol were not accepted tamely by the Whigs, or by the Radical wing of their party, which included most of the intellectual men of the time. It was recognized that Burke spoke with excessive violence, and that his emotion was largely provoked by political apprehensions which were not shared by the more enlightened of his countrymen. It was easily pointed out that the great orator's objection to Rousseau was founded on a predilection for aristocracy, a dread of innovation, an abhorrence for abstract politics, rather than on a serious and philosophical consideration of Rousseau's contributions to literature. There were many indignant replies to his denunciation, the most effective being those contained in Sir James Mackintosh's famous *Vindiciæ Gallicæ*. Mackintosh, with less eloquence but far more knowledge, denied the responsibility of Rousseau for the excesses of the Revolution, and suggested that Burke had not made himself acquainted with the *Contrat Social*. Rousseau was vindicated as one of the immortal band of sages "who unshackled and emancipated the human mind," and he was assured a place in eternal glory, by the side of Locke and Franklin.

All that was generous, all that was enthusiastic in English opinion, was still marshalled on the side of Rousseau, but Burke's measured attack, so universally considered, was the gradual cause of an ever-increasing defection. For the time being, however, this was confined to the more timid and the less intelligent part of the community. Burke had assailed in Rousseau the politician and the moralist, but although it was evident that he was out of sympathy with the imaginative writer, his diatribe did little at first to weaken the spell of the sentimental and

Rousseau in England in the 19th Century

literary writings. There was no sign, in 1800, that the *Nouvelle Héloïse* had lost its magic for English readers, though it may be doubted whether these were so numerous as they had been twenty years earlier. The famous romance had been the direct precursor of the school of romantic-sentimental novels in England, but it would take us too far back to consider in any detail its influence on Holcroft, whose *Hugh Trevor* dates from 1797; on Bage, in such romances as *Hermsprong* (1796); on Mrs. Inchbold, in *Nature and Art* (1796); and on Charlotte Smith. But it must be remembered that these popular novelists lived well on into the nineteenth century, and that their romances were still widely read, and by advanced thinkers warmly accepted, long after our period begins. Moreover, in William Godwin (1756-1836), once known as "the immortal Godwin," we have the most pronounced type in English literature of the novelist started and supported by a devotion to the principles of Rousseau. *Caleb Williams* (1794) is still a minor English classic, and *Fleetwood* (1804) is an example of a Rousseau novel actually written within the confines of our century. But with these names the list of the novelists directly inspired by the *Nouvelle Héloïse*, and in a much lesser degree by *Emile*, practically ceases, and the advent of Walter Scott gave them their *coup de grâce*.

The excessive admiration of Englishmen for the imaginative writings of Rousseau was already on the wane, or rather it was beginning to be old-fashioned. That very remarkable work, *The Diary of a Lover of Literature*, by Thomas Green (1769-1825), gives us a valuable insight into the critical opinions of the opening years of the nineteenth century. It was published in 1810, but it reflects the feeling of a slightly earlier time. It represents the views of an independent and transitional thinker, remote from all the literary cliques, who read extensively in his hermitage at Ipswich, and it mirrors the mind of the average educated Englishman between 1795 and 1805. We discover that there were persons of cultivation in England at that time who did not hesitate deliberately to pronounce that Rousseau was, "without exception, the greatest genius and the finest writer that ever lived." This opinion the judicious Green is by no means able to endorse; but he makes a very curious confession which throws a strong light on the best English opinion in 1800. The Lover of Literature says that Rousseau is a character "who has by turns transported me with the most violent and opposite emotions of delight and disgust, admiration and contempt, indignation and pity." He points out, with great acumen, the peculiar conditions of Rousseau's "distempered sensibility," and says that his wrath against evildoing burns "in consuming fire." Green's analysis of Rousseau's genius is very ingenious and glowing, but he sees spots in the sun, and thus, at the immediate opening of the new century, we meet with high critical commendation, but also with the faint beginnings of reproof.

It is necessary to note that the earliest objections made to Rousseau's influence by Englishmen were political. They were not directed against the *Nouvelle Héloïse*, nor *Emile*, nor the *Confessions*, but against the *Contrat Social*. The name of Rousseau was used, in connexion with this work, to justify the horrors of the French Revolution, the *jacqueries*, the September massacres. Serious English people, whom Burke had originally awakened to suspicion, became more and more persuaded that it was the doctrine of Rousseau which had conducted Louis XVI to the scaffold. The book itself was never much read in England, but it formed part of a tradition. It was understood to have consecrated the violent acts of the Revolution, and English people began to shrink from a name so tainted with blood. This view found a striking exponent in the opening number of the *Edinburgh Review*, where Jeffrey, reviewing Monnier's *Influence attribuée aux Philosophes*, warned his readers with earnest unction against "the presumptuous and audacious maxims" of Rousseau, which had a natural tendency to do harm. The arguments of the *Contrat Social* were exposed by the Whig critic as unsettling the foundations of political duty, and as teaching the citizens of every established Government that they were enslaved, and had the power of being free. Whatever influence Rousseau still had, and in 1802 it was already waning, the *Edinburgh Review* solemnly declared to be "unquestionably pernicious."

By English politicians of the Tory type, Rousseau was now regarded with growing suspicion. They looked back to first causes, and found him at the end of the vista. They blamed him all the more because they still lay under the spell of his style and his sentiment. He was beginning to be regarded with more disapproval than other and more definitely revolutionary philosophers, than Condorcet, for instance, as being more presumptuous and less logical, more "improvident," to use the expression of an early English critic. There was no considerable desire in England for the subversion of monarchy, and it was only in countries where there was a wish to believe that kings were toppling from their thrones that the political writings of the arch-firebrand could expect to find a welcome. All such speculation had been pleasant enough before the great revolution set in in France, but England, thrilled for a moment by Quixotic hopes, had turned into another path, where Rousseau had not led her, nor could ever be her companion. He appeared as a demagogue and a disturber of the public peace, as an apostle of change and crisis and unrest. In England everyone, or almost everyone, craved a respite from such ideas, and his prestige began to sink. Let us note, then, that beyond question the earliest objection to Rousseau came from the political side.

The personal character of the Genevese philosopher was still little known. It was revealed, in certain unfavourable aspects, by several collections of memoirs, which now began to be published. Those of Marmontel, in 1805, were widely read in England, and were recommended to a large circle of readers by Jeffrey in a famous essay. The anecdotes, so amusing and often so piquant, appeared to the Scotch critic and to his British audience more discreditable than Marmontel, who belonged to an earlier and looser generation, had intended them to seem. From 1805 began to arise in England the conception of a Rousseau full of cruel vanity, implacable, calumnious, and wholly wanting in that frankness and bluff candour upon which John Bull delights to pride himself. But the splendour of his writings was still uncontested. In 1809, the *Edinburgh Review* said of the *Contrat Social* that "it contains some deep observations, and many brilliant and elevated thoughts, along with a good deal, we admit, of impracticable and very questionable theory." The *Confessions* was not much read, but the precise Jeffrey did not hesitate to recommend it, in 1806, as in some respects the most interesting of books, and in 1807 Capel Lofft declared, "If I had five millions of years to live upon the earth, I would read Rousseau daily with increasing delight."

It would take us too far to consider how the sentimental Pantisocracy of the youthful Lake Poets coincided with the direct influence of Rousseau. That movement, moreover, belongs to the eighteenth, not the nineteenth century, since it was all over by 1794. But so far as it was an outcome of the teaching of Rousseau, the reaction which followed it was not favourable to the prestige of works which now came to seem almost hateful to the Lake Poets. Wordsworth branched away irrevocably, and his account of the Saturnian Reign in *The Excursion* (finished in 1805) would have given little satisfaction to Rousseau. Southey was early, and permanently, disgusted with himself for having supposed that the millennium would be ushered in from Geneva. But perhaps the best example of the revulsion of opinion which followed the juvenile raptures of the Lake Poets is to be found in the pages of *The Friend* (1809-10), where Coleridge derides

Rousseau, the dreamer of love-sick tales, and the spinner of speculative cobwebs; shy of light as the mole, but quick-eared, too, for every whisper of the public opinion; the teacher of stoic pride in his principles, yet the victim of morbid vanity in his feelings and conduct.

Yet this was premature, as an expression of general critical disapprobation. In November, 1809, the high

Rousseau in England in the 19th Century

Tory organ, the *Quarterly Review*,[1] spoke, without a shade of disapproval, of "the tremendous fidelity " of the picture of life in the *Confessions*.   In 1812, the same severe periodical, then forming the most dreaded tribunal of British intellectual taste, devoted several pages to an examination of the moral character of Rousseau, and the result was by no means unfavourable.   The writer was John Herman Merivale (1779-1844), who declared that "Rousseau's system of morality is as little practicable as would be a system of politics invented by one who had always lived in a state of savage independence," and suggested, but without bitterness, that portions of the *Nouvelle Héloïse* betrayed "a certain lack of just moral taste and feeling."   The *Confessions* are described in faltering terms which suggest that Merivale had not read them with any attention.   On the whole, we find, up to this point, no difference between the views of Englishmen and of similarly placed Frenchmen.   Even Shelley, in his *Proposals for an Association* (1812), blames the tendency of some of Rousseau's political writings in exactly the conventional Continental tone.

But a brief and limited, though splendid revival was now approaching, the last which the reputation of Rousseau was to enjoy in England. We must note the sphere within which this esoteric celebration of his genius was confined; it was not an explosion of national enthusiasm, but the defiant glorification of a power which had already begun to decline; it was not a general expression of approval, but the effort of a group of revolutionaries. It was roused, no doubt, by the attitude of the official critics who were affecting to think that the influence of Rousseau was exploded.   The *Quarterly* had said in 1813, "As it is probable that we may not soon be again in the company of this extraordinary man, we would willingly take leave of him in good humour," and though it was quite unable to keep up this attitude of dignified dismissal, and returned

---

[1] The writer, as I am courteously informed by the present editor of the *Quarterly Review,* was James Pillans (1778-1864), the Scottish educational reformer, the " paltry Pillans " of Byron's satire in *English Bards and Scottish Reviewers*.

to the attack in April, 1814, nevertheless that was the tone adopted towards Rousseau, as of a man played out, and rapidly being forgotten.

The publication of the voluminous *Correspondence* of Grimm, which was much read in England, led Englishmen to review the subject of the character and writings of Rousseau, and in the remarks which contemporaries made in 1813 and 1814 we may trace a rapid cooling of their enthusiasm. The scorn of all French habits of thought and conduct, which immediately succeeded the anxious and wearisome period of the Napoleonic wars, makes itself particularly felt in the English attitude towards Rousseau, who was regarded as the source from which all the revolutionary sorrows of Europe had directly proceeded. The *Quarterly Review* for April, 1814, pronounced a judgment upon Rousseau, of which a portion must be quoted here, since it may be considered as the original indictment, the document which served to start the unfavourable opinion which now became more and more that which sober and conservative Englishmen were to adopt during the next fifty years. The opening lines give a new warning, which was to gain more and more in emphasis, while the end repeats praise which was conventional in 1814, but was already fading, and was soon to disappear.

It says:—

A writer who professes to instruct mankind is bound to deliver precepts of morality. But it is by inflaming the passions, and by blotting out the line which separates virtue from vice, that Rousseau undertakes to teach young ladies to be chaste, and young men to respect the rights of hospitality. His heroine, indeed, in conformity to his own example, is always prating about virtue, even at the time when she deviates most essentially from its precepts; but to dogmatize is not to be innocent. Yet, with all its defects, there are numerous passages in this celebrated work which astonish by their eloquence. Language, perhaps, never painted the conflicts of love in colours more animated and captivating than in the letter written by St. Preux when wandering among the rocks of Meillerie.

Rousseau in England in the 19th Century

Unfortunately, the name of this critic is un-known.

But the charm was not to be broken without a violent effort being made to restore to Rousseau his earlier supremacy. It came from the group of brilliant Radical writers, who had not accepted the Toryism of the ruling classes, to whom the discredited principles of the Revolution were more dear than they had ever been, and who pinned their attractive and enthusiastic æsthetic reforms to the voluptuous ecstasy of the *Nouvelle Héloïse* and the chimerical sentiment of *Emile*. Already, in *The Round Table* (1814), Hazlitt had recommended the *Confessions* as the "most valuable" of all Rousseau's writings; he was presently in his *Liber Amoris* (1823) to produce the work which of all important books of the English nineteenth century was to reproduce most closely the manner of the Genevese master. Two years later, having made a very careful examination of the works, Hazlitt published his essay *On the Character of Rousseau*, which was not sur-passed, or approached, as a study of the great writer until the appearance of Lord Morley's monograph, nearly sixty years afterwards.

Hazlitt exposes the baneful effect of Burke's attacks, while acknowledging that from his own, the Tory point of view, Burke was justified in taking the line that he did. It is perfectly true that "the genius of Rousseau levelled the towers of the Bastille with the dust," but Hazlitt, an intellectual revolutionary, exults in the admission. Hazlitt allows, nevertheless, that the exaggerated hopes founded upon such books as the *Contrat Social* have been followed by inevitable disappointment. It was, however, not the fault of Rousseau, but of his sanguine and absurd disciples, that Europe, or particularly England, has "lost confidence in social man." Ecstatic admirers of his in-spired visions had expected the advent of Rousseau to .bring in a millennium, and in the disappointment founded on the excesses of the French Revolution they had turned, with ingratitude, upon the pure and Utopian dreamer who had drawn things as they should be, not as it was humanly possible that they ever could be. The writings of Rousseau, he declares, are looked up to with admiration by friends and foes alike as possessing "the true revolutionary leaven," but it needs political foresight and a rare capacity of imagination to perceive that this operates, through temporary upheaval and distraction, to produce an ultimate harmony and a beneficent beauty. In the course of his writings, Hazlitt frequently quotes Rousseau, and always with admiration. He is the most illuminating and the most thoughtful of all his early English critics.

In the summer of 1816 the two young poets of the day who displayed the most extraordinary genius in England, or perhaps in Europe, made acquaintance with one another for the first time, and instantly determined to travel together. They met in Switzerland, intoxicated with the unfamiliar beauty around them, and Byron took the Villa Diodati, close to Geneva, where he and Shelley steeped themselves in the *Nouvelle Héloïse* under the shadow of Mont Blanc. In June they started together round the lake on a journey, which turned into a pilgrimage. In Shelley's *Letters* may be read the enthusiastic account of the poets' visit to Meillerie. Shelley refrained from gathering acacia and roses from Gibbon's garden at Lausanne, "fearing to outrage the greater and more sacred name of Rousseau, the contemplation of whose imperishable creations had left no vacancy in his heart for mortal things." As they sauntered along the shores of the enchanted Leman, the friends "read Julie all day." They lived, with the characters of the great romance, in an endless melancholy transport. Byron's enthusiasm took the form of the famous stanzas in "Childe Harold III," beginning:

Here the self-torturing sophist, wild Rousseau.

It is a remarkable instance of the complete decline of the prestige of Rousseau in England that Byron's editor of 1899 is astonished that Byron and Shelley "should not only worship at the shrine of Rousseau, but take delight in reverently tracing the footsteps of St. Preux and Julie." He is so completely disconcerted that he can only exclaim, "But to each age its own humour!" The age of 1899 was certainly not in the humour for Rousseau, but it was almost to go beyond the boundaries of reason to denounce, as this editor did, in the face of Byron's raptures, "the unspeakable philanderings" of Rousseau. Such was not the poet's judgment when, in a trance of pleasure, he visited all the scenes of the *Nouvelle Héloïse*. To Byron the long-drawn loves of St. Preux and of Julie seemed "most passionate, yet not impure," and he vivaciously proclaimed their creator as the one prophet of Ideal Beauty. The five or six stanzas mentioned above are so well-known as to be positively hackneyed. We no longer set on them any very high poetical value; we see that none of them are good as verses, and that some of them are bad. But the whole passage retains its full interest for us. It is a perfectly logical statement of the author's unbounded admiration for Rousseau, and in particular for the "burning page, distempered though it seems," upon which are celebrated the devouring loves of Julie and St. Preux.

Further on, in the same poem, Byron rose to far purer heights of style. The invocation to Clarens, in the texture of which the result of his recent intercourse with Shelley may be plainly perceived, is probably the most impassioned tribute ever paid by one great writer to the literature of another.

All things are here of *him*; from the black pines,
    Which are his shade on high, and the loud roar
Of torrents, where he listeneth, to the vines
    Which slope his green path downward to the shore,
    Where the bow'd waters meet him, and adore,
Kissing his feet with murmurs, and the wood,
    The covert of old trees, with trunks all hoar,
But light leaves, young as joy, stands where it stood,
Offering to him, and his, a populous solitude.

Aspects and Impressions

A populous solitude of bees and birds,
  And fairy-form'd and many-colour'd things,
Who worship him with thoughts more sweet than words,
  And innocently open their glad wings,
  Fearless and full of life.

This was a challenge, addressed by the most powerful poet of the day, and couched in idolatrous language, which it was not possible that those in England who were opposed to the influence of Rousseau could fail to take up. Nor did Byron pause here. Writing from Diodati, July, 1816, his famous *Sonnet to Lake Leman,* Rousseau's was the first illustrious name he mentioned in the brief roll of "Heirs of Immortality." Enthusiasm for the *Nouvelle Héloïse* led directly to the composition of *The Prisoner of Chillon.* Byron discussed and repudiated, with Stendhal in 1817, his mother's old dream that he closely resembled Rousseau. All that prevented his embracing this notion, and insisting on being considered an *avatar* of the philosopher, was his perception of something turbid in the character of Rousseau, hostile to the fiery ideal of 1816. The English poet preferred to be thought to resemble "an alabaster vase lighted up within." But all his life the memory of Jean Jacques continued to haunt him; he recollected the *ranz des vaches* when he was writing *The Two Foscari* (1821) and *la pervenche* in the fourteenth canto of *Don Juan* (December, 1823). When Byron died at Missolonghi the latest and the most passionate of Rousseau's English admirers passed away with him.

The rapture of the sentimental poets was not allowed to pass unrebuffed. In October, 1816, no less an authority on romance, no less sane and typical, and yet moderate and sound exponent of English feeling than Sir Walter Scott took up his parable against the sentimentality of the disciples of Rousseau. In reviewing "Childe Harold III" in the *Quarterly,* Walter Scott takes Byron severely to task for his exaggerated praise of Rousseau. He says of himself that he is "almost ashamed to avow the truth—he had never been able to feel the interest or discover the merit of the *Nouvelle Héloïse*. . . . The dulness of the story is the last apology for its exquisite immorality." It is impossible to overestimate the importance of this utterance of Walter Scott, who was at that very moment bringing forth the amazing series of his own novels, which were to destroy the taste of his countrymen for all such works of the imagination as Rousseau had produced. Scott is no less condemnatory of the political influence of the philosopher. Deeply blaming the French Revolution, he styles Rousseau "a primary apostle" of it. "On the silliness of Rousseau," on the subject of political equality, "it is at this time of day, thank God! useless to expatiate." This was a counter-blast, indeed, to the melodious trumpetings of Byron and Shelley.

To a reputation already much reduced, the publication, in 1818, of the *Mémoires et Conversations* of Madame d'Epinay was a serious blow. These were very much discussed in England, and Jeffrey called the special attention of his readers to the lady's revelations of Rousseau's "eccentricity, insanity, and vice." This produced a painful effect. It was urged by English critics that Jean Jacques, who had been held up as a portent of almost divine moral beauty, seemed, on the contrary, to have claimed, "as the reward of genius and fine writing, an exemption from all moral duties." Jeffrey called indignant attention to the "most rooted and disgusting selfishness" of Rousseau, and quoted with approval the *boutade* of Diderot, "Cet homme est un forcené." The publication of Madame de Staël's *Œuvres Inédites,* brought out by Madame Necker Saussure in 1820, further lowered the English estimate of the "selfish and ungrateful" Rousseau. He was still praised for his "warmth of imagination," but told that he was vastly inferior to Madame de Staël in style. The *Edinburgh Review* now proclaimed, as a painful discovery, that Rousseau's affection for mankind was entirely theoretical, and "had no living objects in this world," and blushed at the "very scandalous and improper" facts about his private life which were now more and more frequently being revealed.

The publication of Simondi's *Voyage en Suisse* (1822), which was widely read in England, continued the work of denigration. Simondi spoke with contempt and even with bitterness, of the character of Rousseau. His English critics pointed out that, although a republican, Simondi rose above political prejudice. He called the *Confessions* the most admirable, but at the same time the most vile of all the productions of genius. Jeffrey, once again, was eloquent in the denunciation of Rousseau's personal character, which there seemed to be no one left in England to defend. This was about the time that special attention began to be drawn to Rousseau's exposure of his natural children, which had long been known, but which now began to excite English disgust. Moreover, the loose way in which Rousseau treated fact and logic irritated the newer school of English and Scotch politicians much more than it had their predecessors, and the invectives of Burke were revived and confirmed. There were still some private, though few public, admirers of Rousseau in England. Carlyle was too original not to perceive the value of the Genevan philosopher's historical attitude, and not to feel a genuine sympathy for his character. But we find him quoting (in 1823) the habits of "John James," as he chose to call him, not adversely but a little slightingly.

Almost the latest eulogist of Rousseau, before Morley, was the veteran Republican poet Walter Savage Landor, whose admirable *Malesherbes and Rousseau* appeared, almost unnoticed, in the third series of the *Imaginary Conversations* (1828). This interesting composition was certainly not written when Landor reviewed his unpublished writings in 1824; we may probably date it 1826. It was a belated expression of the enthusiasm of a preceding generation, in full sympathy with the attitude of Hazlitt and Byron. It attracted no attention, for England was by this time wholly out of touch with the old preference of the impulse of the individual in opposition to the

needs of the State. There was in England a growing
cultivation of science, and by its side a growing suspicion
of rhetoric, and both of these discouraged what was superficially lax in the views and in the expression of Rousseau.
The *Discourse on the Origin of Inequality,* which had
delighted an earlier generation of English Liberals, was
now re-examined, and was rejected with impatience as
"dangerous moonshine," supported by illogical and even
ridiculous arguments. Moreover, the study of anthro-
pology was advancing out of the state of infancy, and was
occupying serious minds in England, who were ex-
asperated by Rousseau's fantastic theory of the purity of
savage society, and a Golden Age of primal innocence.
Moreover, as Morley long afterwards pointed out, from
about the year 1825, there was a rapid increase in England
of the superficial cultivation of letters, and particularly
of scientific investigation. At the same time, the temper
of the English nation repelled, with anger, the notion that
a Swiss philosopher, of discredited personal character,
could be allowed to denounce the science and literature of
Europe.

Thus from every point of view, the hold which
Rousseau had held on English admiration was giving
way. His influence was like a snow man in the sun; it
melted and dripped from every limb, from all parts of its
structure. But probably what did more than anything
else to exclude Rousseau from English sympathy, and to
drive his works out of popular attention, was the sterner
code of conduct which came in, as a reaction to the swinish
coarseness of the late Georgian period. We must pay
some brief attention to a moral and religious phenomenon
which was probably more than any other fatal to the
prestige of Rousseau.

The great feature of the new Evangelical movement was
an insistence on points of conduct which had, indeed,
always been acknowledged in the English Church as
theoretically important, but which were now exalted into
a lively pre-eminence. There was suddenly seen, throughout the country, a marvellous increase in religious zeal, in

the urging of penitence, contrition and unworldliness upon young minds, in the activity which made practical and operative what had hitherto been largely nominal. There was a very wide awakening of the sense of sin, and a quickening, even a morbid and excessive quickening, of the Christian instinct to put off "the old man, which is corrupt according to the deceitful lusts, and to put on the new man, which, after God, is created in righteousness and true holiness." This conviction of sin and humble acceptance of righteousness was to be accompanied by a cultivation of all the contrite and retired and decent aptitudes of conduct, so that not only should no wrong be done to the soul of others, but no offence given. These were the objects which occupied the active and holy minds of the early Evangelists, and of none of them more practically, in relation to the studies and the reading of the young, than of the great leader of the movement, Charles Simeon (1756-1836).

We have forgotten, to a great extent, the amazing influence which the preaching and the practice of these leading Evangelicals exercised in England between 1820 and 1840. It is certain that the young scholars of Cambridge who surrounded Simeon from 1810 onwards were much more numerous and no less active than those who surrounded Newman and Pusey at Oxford about 1835; while in each case the disciples trained in the school of enthusiasm were soon dispersed, to spread the flame of zeal throughout the length and breadth of the Three Kingdoms. In the preface of his famous *Helps to Composition*, a work of epoch-making character, Simeon boldly proposed three tests to be applied to any species of literature. When confronted by a book, the reader should ask, "Does it uniformly tend to humble the Sinner, to exalt the Saviour, to promote holiness?" A work that lost sight of any one of these three points was to be condemned without mercy. The simplicity and freshness of the Evangelicals, their ridicule of what was called "the dignity of the pulpit," their active, breathless zeal in urging what they thought a purer faith upon all classes of society, gave

Rousseau in England in the 19th Century

them a remarkable power over generous and juvenile natures. They were wealthy, they were powerful, they stormed the high places of society, and it may without exaggeration be said that for the time being they changed the whole character of the surface of English social life.

The work of the Evangelicals, in emphasizing the strong reaction against the coarseness of the Georgian era, has been greatly forgotten in England, and on the Continent has never been in the least understood. It is responsible, to deal solely with what interests us in our present inquiry, for the prudery and "hypocrisy" of which European criticism so universally accuses our Victorian literature and habits of thought. It is perhaps useless to contend against a charge so generally brought against English ideas, and this is not the place to attempt it. But, so far as Rousseau is concerned, it is necessary to point out that to a generation which revolted against lasciviousness in speech, and which believed that an indecent looseness in art and literature was a sin against God, the charm of the *Nouvelle Héloïse* and of the *Confessions* could not be apparent. It is of no service to talk about "hypocrisy"; English readers simply disliked books of that sort, and there must be an end of it.

A single example may serve to show how rapid the change had been. Sir James Edward Smith (1759-1828) was an eminent botanist, who travelled widely and wrote many letters. In 1832 his *Memoirs and Correspondence* were published, a lively work which was much read. But Smith, living at the close of the eighteenth century, had been an ardent admirer of Rousseau, and this appeared glaringly in his letters. Reviewers in 1832 had to find excuses for his "charitable eye" and to attribute his partiality to Rousseau's being a botanist. There was quite a flutter, almost a scandal. One critic plainly said that Sir J. E. Smith's "character would not have suffered if he had made some abatement from his extravagant eulogy" of Rousseau. The *Edinburgh Review* was very severe, and regretted that the worthy botanist had not realized that "religious toleration does not imply the toleration of immorality," and that "licentiousness of speculation is as hostile to civil liberty as licentiousness of conduct." A critic of the same period roundly says that "the vices and opinions of Rousseau are of so malignant an aspect that the virtues which accompany them serve only to render them more loathsome."

Thus Rousseau, who in 1800 was regarded in England, even by his enemies, as the most enchanting of writers, had by 1835 sunken to be regarded as despicable, not to be quoted by decent people, not to be read even in secret. He was seldom mentioned, save to be reviled. The career of Rousseau does not come within the scope of Hallam as a critic, yet that historian was unable, in the second volume of his *Literature of Europe* (1838), to resist a sneer at the *Contrat Social,* while he describes Rousseau's arguments as an "insinuation" and a "calumny." We find so grave and dignified an historian as Burton using his *Life of Hume* (1846) as a means of placing Rousseau in the most odious light possible, and without a word of sympathy. To the younger Herman Merivale, in 1850, the influence of Rousseau seemed "simply mischievous," but he rejoiced to think that his fame was "a by-gone fashion." Having, in October, 1853, been led to express an ambiguous comment on the *Confessions,* Mrs. Jameison, then the leading English art critic, hastened to excuse herself by explaining that "of course, we speak without reference to the immorality which deforms that work." It would be easy to multiply such expressions, but difficult, indeed, in the middle of the century, to find a responsible word published by an English writer in praise of Rousseau.

After this, till John Morley's monograph, there is very little to be recorded. Rousseau passed out of sight and out of mind, and was known only to those few who went to foreign sources of inspiration in that age of hard British insularity. But we have lately learned that there were two great authors who, in the seclusion of their own libraries, were now subjecting themselves to the fascination of the Genevan. On February 9th, 1849, George Eliot wrote thus privately to a friend:

Rousseau in England in the 19th Century

It would signify nothing to me if a very wise person were to stun me with proofs that Rousseau's views of life, religion, and government are miserably erroneous—that he was guilty of some of the worst *bassesses* that have degraded civilized man. I might admit all this : and it would not be the less true that Rousseau's genius has sent that electric thrill through my intellectual and moral frame which has wakened me to new perceptions. . . . The rushing mighty wind of his imagination has so quickened my faculties that I have been able to shape more definitely for myself ideas which had previously dwelt as dim *Ahnungen* in my soul; the fire of his genius has so fused together old thoughts and prejudices, that I have been ready to make new combinations.

Even more remarkable is the evidence which Edward Cook, in his *Life of Ruskin* (1911) has produced with regard to the attitude of that illustrious writer. It was in 1849, just when George Eliot was finding her spirit quickened by the inspiration of Rousseau, that John Ruskin, at the age of thirty, made a pilgrimage to Les Charmettes. The political revolt which coloured all his later years was now beginning to move in him, and for the first time he felt affinities existing between his own nature and that of Rousseau. This consciousness increased upon him. In 1862 he wrote, "I know of no man whom I more entirely resemble than Rousseau. If I were asked whom of all men of any name in past time I thought myself to be grouped with, I should answer unhesitatingly—Rousseau. I judge by the *Nouvelle Héloïse*, the *Confessions*, the writings of Politics and the life in the Ile St. Pierre." In 1866 Ruskin added, "The intense resemblance between me and Rousseau increases upon my mind more and more." Finally, in *Preterita* (1886) he openly acknowledged his life-long debt to Rousseau. We may therefore set down the impact of Rousseau upon Ruskin as marking the main influence of the Genevese writer's genius upon English literature in the nineteenth century, but this was sympathetic, subterraneous, and, in a sense, secret. Without Rousseau, indeed, there never would have been Ruskin, yet we are only now beginning to recognize the fact.

Aspects and Impressions

Of the overt cult of Rousseau, even of careful and detailed examination of his works, there was none until Mr. (now Viscount) Morley published his brilliant monograph in 1873. This famous book, so remarkable for its gravity and justice, its tempered enthusiasm, its absence of prejudice, the harmony and illumination of its parts, is the one exception to the public neglect of Jean Jacques by nineteenth-century Englishmen. It removed the reproach of our insular ignorance; it rose at once to the highest level of Continental literature on the subject. The monograph of Morley has become a classic. Incessantly reprinted, it has remained the text-book of English students of Rousseau. It is needless in this place to draw attention to its eminent qualities, or to the fact that it contained, and continues to contain, *lacunæ* which the eminent writer has not attempted to fill up by the light of later research. In particular, it is impossible not to regret that Lord Morley was unacquainted with the documents, so learnedly edited and lucidly arranged by Mr. L. J. Courtois, on the events of Rousseau's sojourn in England. But Lord Morley, immersed in the duties of a statesman, seems long ago to have lost all interest in the subject which he illuminated so brilliantly nearly fifty years ago.

The wide publicity given to Morley's book did not, strangely enough, lead to any great revival of the study of Rousseau in Great Britain. English readers were content to accept the statements and the views of Morley without any special attempt to examine or continue them. There was no outburst of Rousseau study in England in consequence of the volumes of 1873. English translations of his works continued to be few and poor, and over the *Nouvelle Héloïse* and the *Confessions* there still hung a cloud of reproach. They were held to be immoral, and dull in their immorality. During the last decade of the century, however, a certain quickening of interest began to show itself in a variety of ways. A Rousseauiste, who excelled all other disciples in the vehemence of her admiration, was revealed in 1895 by the *Studies in the France of Voltaire and Rousseau* of Mrs. Frederika Macdonald.

Rousseau in England in the 19th Century

These, however, were at first but little noticed, and the labours of this lady, culminating in her violent and excessive, but learned and original *New Criticism of J. J. Rousseau* (1906) and *The Humane Philosophy* (1908) belong to the twentieth century. It is to be hoped that the essays of Mrs. Macdonald may stimulate a new body of workers to remove the stigma which has lain on England for a hundred years of being dry with cynical neglect of Rousseau while all the rest of the threshing-floor of Europe was wet with the dews of vivifying criticism.

THE CENTENARY OF LECONTE DE LISLE

MANY English lovers of French poetry would have been sorry, though none could have been surprised, if public opinion in France had been too much agitated by the stupendous events of the War to spare a thought for one of the greatest of modern poets on the occasion of his hundredth birthday. But it was not so; on the eighteenth of October, 1918, when the fighting had approached its culminating point, and when all the fortunes of the world seemed hanging in the balance, the serenity of French criticism found room, between the bulletins of battle, for a word of reminder that the author of *Poèmes Antiques* and *Poèmes Barbares* was born a century before in the tropic island of La Réunion. The recognition was not very copious, nor was it universally diffused, but in no circumstances would it have been either the one or the other. Leconte de Lisle has never been, and will never be, a "popular" writer. He appeals to a select group, a limited circle, which neither expands nor contracts. His fame has never been excessive, and it will never disappear. It is modest, reserved, and durable.

He was commonly described as a Creole. His father, an army surgeon—exiled by the service to what used to be called the Ile Bourbon—was a pure Breton. Charles Marie René Leconte de Lisle, after several excursions to India, which left strong traces on his poetry, arrived still young in France, and ultimately settled in Paris. Thus he lived for half a century, in great simplicity and uniformity, surrounded by adoring friends, but little known to the public. In middle life he became a librarian at the Luxembourg; as old age was approaching, he found himself elected to succeed Victor Hugo at the French

Aspects and Impressions

Academy. If he was not exactly poor, his means were strictly moderate; and the most unpleasant event of his whole life was the discovery, at the fall of the Empire, that, although his opinions were republican, he had been receiving a pension from the government of Napoleon III. Nothing could be more ridiculous than the outcry then raised against him; for he was a poet hidden in the light of thought, and no politician. It was an honour to any government, and no shame to the austerest poet, that modest public help should enable a man like Leconte de Lisle to exist without anxiety. There can hardly be said to have been any other event in this dignified and blameless career.

There is a danger—but there is also a fascination—in the instinct which leads us, when we observe literature broadly, to find relations or parallelisms between independent and diverse personalities. In the most striking examples, however, where there has been no actual influence at work, these parallelisms are apt to be very misleading. Where it is impossible not to observe elements of likeness, as between Byron and Musset, we may take them to be actual, and no matters of chance. But the similarity, in certain aspects, between Alfred de Vigny and Thomas Hardy, between André Chénier and Keats, between Crabbe and Verhaeren, must be accidental, and is founded on a comparison between very limited portions of the work of each. Nevertheless, for purposes of illumination, it is sometimes useful—on what we may call the Lamarckian system—to see where the orbits of certain eminent writers of distinctive originality approach nearest to one another.

It is admitted that Leconte de Lisle is pre-eminently gifted among the poets of France in certain clearly defined directions. His poems, which are marked by a concinnity of method which sometimes degenerates into monotony, are distinguished above all others by their haughty concentration of effort, by their purity of outline, and by their extreme precision in the use of definite imagery. They aim, with unflinching consistency, at a realization of

194

The Centenary of Leconte de Lisle

beauty so abstract that the forms by which it is interpreted
to the imagination are almost wholly sculpturesque. Is
there an English poet of whom, at his best, the same
language might be used? There is one, and only one,
and that is Walter Savage Landor. It cannot but be
stimulating to the reader to put side by side, let us say,
the opening lines of *The Hamadryad* and of *Khirón,* or
the dialogue of *Niobé* and that of *Thrasymedes and Eunoë,*
and to see how closely related is the manner in which the
English and the French poet approach their themes. The
spirit of pagan beauty broods over *Hypatie et Cyrille* as
it does over the mingled prose and verse of *Pericles and
Aspasia,* and with the same religious *desiderium.* We
shall not find another revelation of the cupuscular
magnificence of the farthermost antiquity so striking as
Landor's *Gebir,* unless we seek it in the *Kaïn* of Leconte
de Lisle.

But we should not drive this parallel too far. If the
breadth and majesty of vision which draw these two poets
together are notable, not less so are their divergencies.
Landor, who so often appears to be on the point of utter-
ing something magical which never gets past his lips,
is one of the most unequal of writers. He ascends and
descends, with disconcerting abruptness, from an exquisite inspiration to the darkest level of hardness.
Leconte de Lisle, on the other hand, is the victim of no
vicissitudes of style : he floats in the empyrean, borne up
apparently without an effort at a uniform height, like his
own Condor :

Il dort dans l'air glacé, les ailes toutes grandes.

Many readers — particularly those on whom the
romantic heresy has laid its hands with the greatest
violence—resent this Olympian imperturbability; and the
charge has been frequently brought, and is still occasionally repeated, that Leconte de Lisle is lacking in
sensibility, that he dares to be "impassible" in an age
when every heart is worn, palpitating, on the sleeve of

the impulsive lyrist. He was accused, as the idle world always loves to accuse the visionary, of isolating himself from his kind with a muttered *odi profanum vulgus et arceo*. Such an opinion is founded on the aspect of reserve which his vast legendary pictures suggest, and on the impersonal and severely objective attitude which he adopts with regard to history and nature. His poems breathe a disdain of life and of the resilience of human appetite (*La Mort de Valmiki*), a love of solitude (*Le Désert*), a determination to gaze on spectacles of horror without betraying nervous emotion (*Le Massacre de Mona*), which seem superhuman and almost inhuman. He was accused, in his dramas—which were perhaps the most wilful, the least spontaneous part of his work—of affecting a Greek frightfulness which outran the early Greeks themselves. Francisque Sarcey said that Leconte de Lisle, in his tragedy of *Les Erinnyes,* scratched the face of Æschylus, as though he did not find it bloody enough already.

The subjects which Leconte de Lisle prefers are never of a sort to promote sentimentality or even sensibility. He writes of Druids moaning along the edge of hyperborean cliffs, of elephants marching in set column across hot brown stretches of sand, of the black panther crouched among the scarlet cactus-blossoms, of the polar bear lamenting among the rocks, of the Syrian sages whose beards drip with myrrh as they sit in council under the fig-tree of Naboth. He writes of humming-birds and of tigers, of Malay pirates and of the sapphire cup of Bhagavat, of immortal Zeus danced round by the young Oceanides, and of Brahma seeking the origin of things in the cascades of the Sacred River. These are not themes which lend themselves to personal effusion, or on which the poet can be expected to embroider any confessions of his egotism. If Leconte de Lisle chooses to be thus remote from common human interests—that is to say, from the emotions of our vulgar life to-day—his is the responsibility, and it is one which he has fully recognized. But that his genius was not wholly marmoreal, nor of an icy

The Centenary of Leconte de Lisle

impassibility, the careful study of his works will amply assure us.

It is strange that even very careful critics have been led to overlook the personal note in the poems of Leconte de Lisle : probably because the wail of self-pity is so piercing in most modern verse that it deadens the ear to the discreet murmur of the stoic poet's confession. Hence even Anatole France has been led to declare that the author of *Poèmes Barbares* has determined to be as obstinately absent from his work as God is from creation; and that he has never breathed a word about himself, his secret wishes, or his personal ideals. But what is such a passage as the following if not a revelation of the soul of the poet in its innermost veracity?

> *O jeunesse sacrée, irréparable joie,*
> *Félicité perdue, où l'âme en pleurs se noie!*
> *O lumière, ô fraîcheur des monts calmes et bleus,*
> *Des coteaux et des bois feuillages onduleux,*
> *Aubes d'un jour divin, chants des mers fortunées,*
> *Florissante vigueur de mes belles années . . .*
> *Vous vivez, vous chantez, vous palpitez encor,*
> *Saintes réalités, dans vos horizons d'or!*
> *Mais, ô nature, ô ciel, flots sacrés, monts sublimes,*
> *Bois dont les vents amis font murmurer les cimes,*
> *Formes de l'idéal, magnifiques aux yeux,*
> *Vous avez disparu de mon cœur oublieux!*
> *Et voici que, lassé de voluptés amères,*
> *Haletant du désir de mes mille chimères,*
> *Hélas! j'ai désappris les hymnes d'autrefois,*
> *Et que mes dieux trahis n'entendent plus ma voix.*

This is a note more often heard, perhaps, in English than in French poetry. It is the lament of Wordsworth for the "visionary gleam" that has fled, for "the glory and the dream" that fade into the light of common day.

Leconte de Lisle is unsparing with the results of his erudition, and this probably confirms the popular notion of his remoteness. Here, however, returning for a moment to Landor, we may observe that he is never so close-packed and never so cryptic as the author of *Chrysaor* and *Gunlaug*. What Leconte de Lisle has to tell us about mysterious Oriental sages and mythical Scandinavian heroes may be unfamiliar to the reader, but is never rendered obscure by his mode of narration. Nothing could be less within our ordinary range of experience than the adventure of *Le Barde de Temrah,* who arrives at dawn from a palace of the Finns, in a chariot drawn by two white buffaloes; but Leconte de Lisle recounts it voluminously, in clear, loud language which leaves no sense of doubt on the listener's mind as to what exactly happened.

His Indian studies became less precise in the *Poèmes Barbares* than they had been in the early *Poèmes Antiques;* perhaps under the stress of greater knowledge. But he had been from early youth personally acquainted with the Indian landscapes which he describes. With the ancient Sanscrit literature, I suppose he had mainly an acquaintance through translations, of which those by Burnouf may have inspired him most. Whether, if he had lived to read Professor Jacobi's proof that Valmiki was a historical character, and the author in its original form of the earliest and greatest epic of India, the *Ramayana,* Leconte de Lisle would have been annoyed to remember that he had treated Valmiki as a mythical person, symbolically devoured by white ants, it is impossible to say. Probably not, for he only chose these ancient instances to illustrate from the contemplative serenity of Brahmanism his own calm devotion to the eternal principle of beauty.

> *Bhagavat! Bhagavat! Essence des Essences,*
> *Source de la beauté, fleuve des Renaissances,*
> *Lumière qui fait vivre et mourir à la fois.*

Probably no other European poet has interpreted with so much exactitude, because with so intense a sympathy, the cosmogony and mythology of the Puranas, with their mystic genealogies of gods and kings.

The Centenary of Leconte de Lisle

The harmony and sonorous fullness of the verse of
Leconte de Lisle were noted from the first, even by those
who had least sympathy with the subjects of it.   He
achieved the extreme—we may almost say the excessive
—purity of his language by a tireless study of the Greeks
and of the great French poets of the seventeenth century,
with whom he had a remarkable sympathy at a time when
they were generally in disfavour.   His passion for the art
of Racine may be compared with the close attention which
Keats gave to the versification of Dryden.   He greatly
venerated the genius of Victor Hugo, who was perhaps
the only contemporary poet of France who exercised any
influence over the style of Leconte de Lisle.   It is difficult
to define in what that influence consisted; the two men had
essentially as little resemblance as Reims Cathedral has
to the Parthenon, Victor Hugo being as extravagantly
Gothic as Leconte de Lisle was Attic.   But the younger
poet was undoubtedly fascinated by the tumultuous
cadences of his more various, and, we must admit, more
prodigious predecessor.   They agreed, moreover, in ap-
pealing to the ear rather than to the eye.   Verlaine has
described Leconte de Lisle's insistence on the vocal harmonies of verse, and he adds : "When he recited his own
poems, a lofty emotion seemed to vibrate through his
whole noble figure, and his auditors were drawn to him
by an irresistible sympathy."   It must have been a wonderful experience to hear him, for instance, chant the iron
terze rime of *Le Jugement de Konor,* or the voluptuous
languor of *Nourmahal.*

Much has been said about the sculpturesque character
of Leconte de Lisle's poems.   But a comparison of them
to friezes of figures carved out of white marble scarcely
does justice to their colour, though it may indicate the
stability of their form.   It would be more accurate to
compare them to the shapes covered with thin ivory and
ornamented with gold and jewels, in which the Greeks,
and even Pheidias himself, delighted.   The *Poèmes
Antiques* are, in fact, chryselephantine.   But Leconte
de Lisle was a painter also, and perhaps the chief difference

to be observed between the early compositions and the
Poèmes Barbares consists in the pictorial abundance of
the latter. His descriptions have the character of broadly-
brushed cartoons of scenes which are usually exotic, as
of some Puvis de Chavannes who had made a leisurely
voyage in Orient seas. Leconte de Lisle floods his canvas
with light, and his favourite colours are white and golden
yellow; even his fiercest tragedies are luminous. India
he sees not as prosaic travellers have seen it, but in a
blaze of dazzling splendour :

> *Tes fleuves sont pareils aux pythons lumineux*
> *Qui sur les palmiers verts enroulent leurs beaux nœuds;*
> *Ils glissent au détour de tes belles collines*
> *En guirlandes d'argent, d'azur, de perles fines.*

It is natural that a nature so eminently in harmony with
the visual world, and so pagan in all its instincts, should be
indifferent or even hostile to Christianity. His stoic
genius, solidly based on the faiths of India and of Hellas,
finds the virtues of humility and of tender resignation
contemptible. In the very remarkable dialogue, *Hypatie
et Cyrille,* Leconte de Lisle defines, with the voice of the
Neoplatonist, his own conception of religious truth. It is
one in which *Le vil Galiléen* has neither part nor lot. We
have to recognize in his temper a complete disdain of all
the consolations of the Christian faith, or rather an
inability to conceive in what they consist, and no
phenomenon in literature is more curious than that, after a
single generation, French poetry should have returned to
the aggressive piety which strikes an English reader as so
incomprehensible in M. Francis Jammes and in M. Paul
Claudel. But poetry has many mansions.

The person of Leconte de Lisle is described to us as
characteristic of his work. He was very handsome, with
a haughty carriage of the head on a neck "as pure and as
solid as a column of marble." A monocle, which never
left his right eye, gave a modern touch to an aspect which
might else have been too rigorously antique. A droll

The Centenary of Leconte de Lisle

little pseudo-anecdote, set by Théodore de Banville in his
inimitable amalgam of wit and fancy, illuminates the effect
which Leconte de Lisle produced upon his contemporaries.
I take it from that delicious volume, too little remembered
to-day, the *Camées Parisiens*, of 1873 :

> Leconte de Lisle was walking with Æschylus one day, in
> the ideal fatherland of tragedy, when, while he was conversing
> with the old hero of Salamis and of Platea, he suddenly
> observed that his companion was so bald that a tortoise might
> easily mistake his skull for a polished rock. Not wishing,
> therefore, to humiliate the titanic genius, and yet not able
> without regret to give up an ornament the indispensable
> beauty of which was obvious, he made up his mind to be
> totally bald in front, while retaining on the back of his head
> the silken and curly wealth of an Apollonian *chevelure*.

It was perhaps in the course of these walks with
Æschylus that Leconte de Lisle formed the habit of spelling Clytemnestre "Klytaimnestra." The austerities of his
orthography attracted a great deal of attention, and
cannot be said to have succeeded in remoulding French
or spelling. People continue to write "Cain," although
the poet insisted on "Kaïn," and even, in his sternest
moments, on "Qaïn." He believed that his text gained
picturesqueness, and even exactitude of impression, by
those curious archaisms. They are, at least, characteristic
of the movement of his mind, and the reader who is
offended by them must have come to the reading with a
determination to be displeased. His vocabulary is more
difficult; and sometimes, it must be confessed, more questionable. He uses, without explanation or introduction,
the most extraordinary terms. Ancient Roman emperors
are said to have shown their largess by putting real pearls
into the dishes which they set before their guests. This
was generous; but the guest who broke his tooth upon a
gift must have wished that the pearl had been more con-
ventionally bestowed upon him. So the reader of Leconte
de Lisle may be excused if he resents the sudden appari-

tion of such strange words as "bobres," "bigaylles," and "pennbaz" in the text of this charming poet.

In spite of these eccentricities, which are in fact quite superficial, and in spite of a suspicion of pedantry which occasionally holds the reader's attention at arm's length, there is no French poet of our day more worthy of the attention of a serious English student. Leconte de Lisle cultivated the art of poetry with the most strenuous dignity and impersonality. He had a great reverence for the French language, and not a little of the zeal of the classic writers of the seventeenth century who aimed at the technical perfection of literature. He is lucid and direct almost beyond parallel. In England, among those who approach French literature with more enthusiasm than judgment, there is a tendency to plunge at once into what is fashionable for the moment on the Boulevard Saint Michel. We have seen British girls and boys affecting to appreciate Verlaine, and even Mallarmé, without having the smallest acquaintance with Racine or Alfred de Vigny. It is pure *snobisme* to pretend to admire *Prose pour Des Esseintes* when you are unable to construe Montaigne. For all such foreign folly, the rigorous versification, the pure and lucid language, and the luminous fancy of Leconte de Lisle may be recommended as a medicine.

TWO FRENCH CRITICS

EMILE FAGUET—REMY DE GOURMONT

THE importance of literary criticism in the higher education of a race has been recognized in no country in the world except France. Elsewhere there have arisen critics of less, or more, or even of extreme merit, but nowhere else has there been a systematic training in literature which has embraced a whole generation, and has been intimately combined with ethics. The line of action which Matthew Arnold vainly and pathetically urged on the Anglo-Saxon world has been unobtrusively but most effectively taken by France for now more than half a century. When the acrid and ridiculous controversy between the Classical and the Romantic schools died down, criticism in France became at once more reasonable and more exact. The fatuous formula which has infected all races, and is not yet extirpated in this country—the "I do not like you, Dr. Fell, the reason why I cannot tell "—passed into desuetude. It was implicitly recognized that it is your duty, if you express a view, to be able to "tell " on what principles it is founded. In fact, if we concentrate our attention on the progress of French professional criticism, we see it becoming steadily more philosophical and less empirical.

But about 1875, after the period of Taine and Renan, and, in a quite other field, after that of Gautier and Paul de Saint Victor, we find criticism in Paris rapidly tending in two important directions, becoming on the one hand more and more exact, almost scientific, on the other daringly personal and impressionist. Ferdinand Brunetière, who was a man of extraordinary force of character, gave a colour to the whole scheme of literary instruction throughout France. He resisted the idea that literature was merely an entertainment or a pastime. He asserted that it was the crown and apex of a virile education, and he declared its aim to be the maintenance and progress of morality. With Brunetière everything was a question of morals. He was a strong man, and a fighting man; he enjoyed disputation and snuffed the breath of battle. He advanced the impersonality of literature and stamped on the pride of authors. In the year 1900, an observer glancing round professorial circles had to admit that the influence of Brunetière had become paramount. His arbitrary theory of the *évolution des genres,* founded on Herbert Spencer and Darwin, and applied to the study of literature, pervaded the schools.

But the vehement tradition of Brunetière was undermined from the first by his two greatest rivals, Anatole France and Jules Lemaître, whose character was the exact opposite of his. They were "impressionist" critics, occupied with their own personal adventures among books, and not actively concerned with ethics. Their influence, especially that of Lemaître, since Anatole France retired from criticism before the close of the century, tempered what was rigid and insensitive in the too-vehement dogmatism of Brunetière, but they did not form a camp distinct from his. The sodality of the French Academy kept them together in a certain happy harmony, in spite of their contrast of character. Brunetière died in 1906, Lemaître in 1914; the effect of the one upon education, of the other upon social culture, had been immense, but it had not advanced since 1900. With the new century, new forces had come into prominence, and of the two most important of these we speak to-day.

It was the fate of France to lose, within a few months, the two most prominent critics of the period succeeding that of which I have just spoken. The death of Emile Faguet and of Remy de Gourmont marks another stage in the progress of criticism, and closes another chapter in its history. That their methods and modes of

Two French Critics

life were excessively different; that their efforts, if not hostile, were persistently opposed; that one was the most professorial of professors, the other the freest of free lances; that each, in a word, desired to be what the other was not; adds a piquancy to the task of considering them side by side. The first thing we perceive, in such a parallel, is the superficial contrast; the second is the innate similitude, so developed that these spirits in opposition are found in reality to represent, in a sort of inimical unison, the whole attitude towards literature of the generation in which they flourished. Their almost simultaneous disappearance leaves the field clear for other procedures under their guidance. In the extremely copious published writings of these two eminent men the name of each of them will scarcely be found. They worked, in their intense and fervid spheres, out of sight of one another. But, now both are dead, it is interesting to see how close to each other they were in their essential attitude, and how typical their activity is of the period between 1895 and 1915.

If anyone should rashly engage to write the life of Emile Faguet, he would find himself limited to the task of composing what the critic himself, in speaking of Montaigne, calls "the memoirs of a man who never had any occupation but thinking." Through the whole of a life which approached the term of threescore years and ten, Faguet was absorbed, more perhaps than any other man of his time, in the contemplation of the printed page. He said of himself, "I have never stopped reading, except to write, nor writing, except to read." In any other country but France, this preoccupation would have led to dreariness and pedantry, if not to a permanent and sterile isolation. But in France purely literary criticism, the examination and constant re-examination of the classics of the nation, takes an honoured and a vivid place in the education of the young. The literary teaching of the schools is one of the moral and intellectual forces of the France of to-day, and Faguet, who was the very type, and almost the exaggeration, of that tendency in teaching, was preserved from pedantry by the immense sympathy which surrounded him. His capacity for comprehending books, and for making others comprehend them, found response from a grateful and thirsty multitude of students.

Emile Faguet was born, on the 17th of December, 1847, at La Roche-sur-Yon, in Vendée, where his father was professor at the local lycée. M. Victor Faguet, who had received a prize for a translation of Sophocles into verse, nourished high academic ambitions for his son. From the noiseless annals of the future critic's childhood a single anecdote has been preserved, namely that, when he was a schoolboy, he solemnly promised his father that he would become a member of the French Academy. All his energy was centred towards that aim. He passed through the regular course which attends young men who study for the professoriate in France, and at last he became a professor himself at Bordeaux, and then in Paris. But in that career, as Dr. Johnson sententiously observed, "Unnumber'd suppliants croud Preferment's Gate," and at thirty-five Emile Faguet was still quite undistinguished. He saw his juniors, and in particular Lemaître and Brunetière, speed far in front of him, but he showed neither impatience nor ill-temper. Gradually he became a writer, but it was not until 1885 that his *Les Grands Maîtres du XVIe Siècle* attracted the attention of the public. He began to be famous at the age of forty, when his *Etudes Littéraires sur le XIXe Siècle*, clear, well arranged, amusing and informing, proved to French readers that here was a provider of substantial literature, always intelligent, never tiresome, who was exactly to their taste. From that time forth the remaining thirty years of Faguet's life extended themselves in a ceaseless cheerful industry of lecturing, writing, and interpreting, which bore fruit in a whole library of published books, perhaps surpassing in bulk what is known as the "output" of any other mortal man.

Though ever more concerned with ideas than with persons, Faguet did not disdain, in happy, brief, and salient lines, to sketch the authors who had written the books he

Two French Critics

analysed. Let us attempt a portrait of himself as he appeared in the later years of his life. No one ever less achieved the conventional type of academician. His person was little known in society, for he scarcely ever dined out. He had so long been a provincial professor that he never threw off a country look. In sober fact, Emile Faguet, with his brusque, stiff movements, his rough brush of a black moustache, and his conscientious walk, looked more like a non-commissioned officer in mufti than an ornament of the Institut. He was active in the streets, stumping along with an umbrella always pressed under his arm; on his round head there posed for ever a kind of ancient billycock hat. He had a supreme disdain for dress, and for the newspapers which made jokes about his clothing. He lived in a little stuffy apartment in the Rue Monge—on the fifth storey, if I remember right. He was an old bachelor, and the visitor, cordially welcomed to his rooms, was struck by the chaos of books—chairs, tables, the floor itself being covered with volumes, drowned in printed matter. Just space enough swept out to hold the author's paper and ink was the only oasis in the desert of books. I remember that, at the height of his fame and prosperity, there was no artificial light in his rooms. That army of his publications was marshalled by the sole aid of a couple of candles. Everything about him, but especially the frank dark eyes lifted in his ingenuous face, breathed an air of unaffected probity and simplicity, and of a kind of softly hurrying sense that life was so short, and there were so many books to read and to write, that there could be no time left for nonsense.

His image will long recur to the inner vision of his friends, as he went marching to his lecture or to his newspaper-office, nonchalant and easy, with his hands in his pockets, his elbow squeezing that enormous umbrella to his side. In the evening he would go, inelegantly dressed, in the same loosely martial way, to the theatre, for which he had an inordinate affection. He was not a "first-nighter," but dropped in to see a new piece whenever he wanted copy for his *feuilleton*. His lectures, it is reported,

Aspects and Impressions

were familiar and conversational, with frequent repetition and copious quotation, the whole poured out as a man tells a story which he intimately knows, with an inexhaustible flow of thoughts and facts. Sometimes he was so vivacious as to be a little paradoxical, and led a laugh against himself. He stood before his students, formidable only in his erudition, easy of approach, austere and gay. His congested rooms in the Rue Monge were open to any young inquirer, but it was observed that Faguet never asked what the name of his visitor was, but how old he was. The younger the student, the less dogmatic was the professor, but the more familiar, abundant, sympathetic. It was noticeable in all his relations, with young and old alike, that Faguet's one aim invariably seemed to be honestly to make his interlocutor comprehend the matter in hand.

Some recollections of the outer presence of Emile Faguet should not be without value to us in fixing the character of his inner life, the spirit which pervaded his profuse and honest labour. No one in the history of literature has been more distinguished for intellectual probity; and no one has cared less for appearances, or for the glorification of his own character and cleverness. His value as a critic consists primarily in his capacity for thoroughly understanding what each author under consideration meant by this or that expression of his art. Faguet does not allow himself to be stung into eloquence by the touch of a master-mind, as Lemaître does, nor does he fly off from his subject on the wings of an imperative suggestion, like Anatole France, but he sticks close to the matter in hand, so close that he reaches comprehension by becoming absorbed in it. There is no writer on literature who has ever crept so completely into the skin of each old author as Faguet has done. He makes the dry bones live; he resuscitates the dead, and revives in them all that was essential in their original life, all that was really vital in them, even if it be ultimately to condemn the taste or the tendency exhibited. The first object with him is to vivify; to analyse and dissect come next.

Two French Critics

He was open to all impressions, and he was particularly admirable in his periodical surveys of the four great centuries of French verse and prose, because of his unflagging open-mindedness. He saw the living thread of literary history, running, a pulsating stream, from Rabelais to Flaubert. He had followed it so often, up and down, this way and that, that no curve of it, no backwater was unfamiliar to him. Lassitude is as unknown to Faguet as it was to Shelley's "Skylark." His curiosity is always awake; no shadow of satiety ever comes near him. He was a Titan in his way, but never a "weary Titan"; he never felt "the orb of his fate," though it embraced so much, to be "too vast." The more elaborate or complex an author was, the more actively and ingeniously Faguet penetrated his work, smoothing out the complexities, throwing light into every dark corner. But it is very proper to notice that even where he devotes himself with what seems the most absorbing care to the investigation of a particular mind, he is always essentially detached from it, always ready to quit one tenement of genius and adapt himself with alacrity to another, like a soldier-crab, whose tender extremity will fit itself to any shell-habitation.

In one of his criticisms of Montesquieu—and on no French classic has he been more constantly felicitous—Faguet speaks of the faculty possessed by that prince of intelligence of wandering among souls, and of studying their spiritual experience "comme un anatomiste étudie le jeu des organes." The author of the *Esprit des Lois* took wide views and surveyed a vast expanse of society, but he was equally apt to map out a square inch of mossy rock at his feet. "Il a du reste beaucoup écrit, *comme en marge de ses grands livres.*" These words remind us of a section of Emile Faguet's writings which is peculiarly stimulating and useful. It is illustrated to great perfection in what is perhaps the most fascinating specimen of his vast and various production, the volume called *En lisant les Beaux Vieux Livres*, which he published so lately as 1911. This was followed by *En lisant Corneille* in 1913 and *En lisant Molière* in 1914. If the war had not intervened and if his own health had not failed him, it is probable that Faguet would have extended and developed this section of his work, which exhibited the ripest fruit of his subtle and vigorous criticism.

The method which he adopted in these treatises was to take a portion of a well-known book or a short poem, and read it with his imaginary audience exactly as though they, and he, had never met with it before. In *En lisant les Beaux Vieux Livres* he takes a score of such passages, and analyses them without pedantry, eagerly, curiously, cordially. He explains what the author meant, shows how he has succeeded in expressing his meaning, points out the ingenuities of thought and the felicities of language, and in short exhibits the piece of hackneyed prose or verse as though it had just been discovered. The process may sound perfunctory and pedagogic, but, conducted as Faguet conducts them, these little excursions are not less delightful than original. He takes things that everybody knows—such as Montaigne on Friendship, or Bossuet on the Romans, or a couple of La Bruyère's portraits; he takes a long poem, like Alfred de Vigny's *La Maison du Berger,* or a short lyric, like Victor Hugo's *Le Semeur;* he takes the character of Sévère in *Polyeucte* or a landscape out of the memoirs of Chateaubriand, and he illuminates these familiar things until the reader not merely sees in them what he never saw before, but has gained a method of reading by which he will in future extract infinite new pleasures from re-reading old familiar books.

In this system of analysis by conversation consists the chief originality of Faguet's criticism. The idea of it was not entirely new; so long ago as the seventeenth century Descartes said that "la lecture est une conversation continue avec les plus honnêtes gens des siècles passés." But it had not been planned on a practical basis until Faguet sketched out these enchanting books of his, in which we seem to see him seated, smiling, at a table, the volume open before him, expounding it to an eager circle of in-

Two French Critics

telligent young people. In these conversations, Faguet had not the weight of Brunetière or the sparkle of Lemaître; he was simpler than the one and soberer than the other. He achieved the dream of the teacher when he discovered how to write books which please and are useful at the same time. He avoided, by a whole continent, the vapid dreariness of the usual English manual, which looks upon the rose of Sharon and the lily of the valley as fit only to be pressed between sheets of blotting-paper in a *hortus siccus*. Faguet is always in earnest, although he sometimes indulges in immense humour and vivacity, not of the Parisian variety, but highly exhilarating. When he suddenly confesses to us that Balzac had "the temperament of an artist and the soul of a commercial traveller," or when he sums up an entirely grave summary of Pindare-Le Brun by telling us that "c'était un homme de beaucoup d'esprit, d'un caractère très méprisable, et excellent ouvrier de vers," it is no schoolmaster that speaks to pupils, but a friend who takes his intimates into his confidence.

It has been the habit to depreciate the style of Faguet, which indeed does not set out to be exquisite, and cannot compare with those of several of his great predecessors. He has been charged, in his zeal for the matter of literature, with a neglect of its form. It is true that his phrases are apt to be curt; he gives little attention to the conduct of a sentence, further than to define in it his precise intention. But his criticism has a great purity of design, which is in itself an element of style. It sets forth to accomplish a certain purpose and it carries out this aim with the utmost economy of means. No writer less than Faguet, to use a vulgar expression, "slops about all over the shop." He has at least this negative beauty of writing, and he adds to it another, the gift of discussing great authors in a tone that is in sympathy with their peculiarities. An instance of this, among a hundred, may be cited from his *Dix-huitième Siècle;* summing up what he has to impress upon us about Marivaux, he defines that author in these terms: "C'est un précieux qui est assez rare et qu'on s'interdit de condamner au moment même qu'on le désapprouve, parce qu'on n'est pas sans en jouir dans le moment même qu'on en souffre." It would hardly be possible to put more of critical value into so few words, but moreover it is said as Marivaux himself might say it.

Faguet had his prejudices, as every honest man may have. He adored the seventeenth and he loved the nineteenth centuries, but he had almost an aversion from the eighteenth. He put Buffon first among the writers of that age, and Montesquieu next; so loyal a spirit as Faguet's could not but be cordially attracted by Vauvenargues. But the lack of poetry, and, as he asserted, the lack of philosophy of the Encyclopædists annoyed him, and for their greatest name, for Voltaire, he had a positive hatred. Faguet found it difficult to be just to Diderot, and difficult to tolerate Rousseau, but to love Voltaire he made no effort whatever; he acknowledged that feat to be impossible. He did not fear to contradict himself, and about Rousseau his opinion grew steadily more favourable, until, in 1913, he positively published five independent volumes on this one writer alone. But Faguet could never persuade himself to approach Voltaire with any face but a wry one. Yet, even here, his antipathy is scarcely to be perceived on the surface. Faguet always leaves the judgment of his reader independent. He puts the facts before him; his own irony marks the line of thought which he suggests; but he is careful never to attempt to bully the reader into acceptance. Brunetière is apt to be vociferous in persuasion; Faguet never raises his voice.

In 1899, being called upon to sum up the qualities of the leading French critics from 1850 onwards, Faguet found himself confronted with his own name and work. It was characteristic of his candour and simplicity that he did not shrink from the task of describing himself, and that he undertook it without false modesty or affectation. When he comes to describe Emile Faguet he is as detached, as calmly analytic, as he is when he speaks of Théophile Gautier or M. René Doumic. He defines the

Two French Critics

qualities, acknowledges the limitations, and hints at the
faults of his subject. I do not know a case in all literary
history where a writer has spoken of himself in terms
more severely judicial. He closes this remarkable little
study with words which we may quote here for their
curious personal interest no less than as an example of
Faguet's style :

> Laborieux, du reste, assez méthodique, consciencieux, en
> poussant la conscience jusqu'à être peu bienveillant, ou en ne
> sachant pas pousser le scrupule consciencieux jusqu'à la
> bienveillance, il a pu rendre et il a rendu des services appré-
> ciables aux étudiants en littérature, qui étaient le public qu'il
> a toujours visé. Sans abandonner la critique, qu'il est à croire
> qu'il aimera toujours, il s'est un peu tourné depuis quelques
> années du côté des études sociologiques, où c'est à d'autres
> qu'à nous qu'il appartient d'apprécier ses efforts.

In this connexion a phrase of the great critic may be
recalled. When the war broke out in 1914, someone who
knew Faguet's absorbing love of books sympathized with
him on the blow to literature. He responded, in a tone
of reproof, "L'avenir national est une chose autrement
importante que l'avenir littéraire."

Those sociological interests were steadily emphasized.
Faguet became, not less in love with great books, but
more inclined to turn from their technical to their ethical
value. He became himself a moralist, after having in so
many eloquent volumes analysed the works and the
characters of the politicians and teachers of the nineteenth
century. He possessed a finished faculty for amusing and
pleasing while he instructed, and it was remarkable that
in these treatises of his late middle life he addressed a
much wider public than he had ever reached before. His
Commentaire du Discours sur les Passions was a link
between the earlier purely literary treatises and the later
analyses of psychological phenomena, but it was highly
successful. Even more universally popular were the little
books on *Friendship* and *Old Age*, which enjoyed a
larger circulation than any other contemporary works of

their class. Faguet was pleased at his popularity, and felt that he was recognized as belonging to that "vieille race de moralistes exacts et fins" of whom La Rochefoucauld had been the precursor. Of these moral studies, the most abundantly discussed was that which dealt with *Le Culte de l'Incompétence* (1910), a book which bears a very remarkable relation to the state of France when war broke out.

Towards the end of his life, Faguet became a great power in France. He exercised, from that book-bewildered room in the Rue Monge, a patriotic, amiable, fraternal influence which permeated every corner of the French-speaking world. But his health, which had long been failing, gave way under the strain of the war. He had never given himself any rest from perpetual literary labour, and he had always said that he knew that before he was seventy years of age he should be "buried and forgotten." A third stroke of paralysis carried away the greatest living friend of literature in France on the 7th of June, 1916, in his sixty-ninth year. Buried he is at last, to their sorrow, but his compatriots will not readily forget him.

It is not easy to find common terms in which to describe Faguet and his remarkable contemporary, Remy de Gourmont. Their two circles of influence were far-reaching, but did not touch. In the very extensive literature of each the other is perhaps never mentioned. We may suppose that it would be almost impossible for a French observer to review them together without allowing the scale to descend in favour of this name or of that. But here may come in the use of foreign criticism, which regards the whole field from a great distance, and without passion. The contrast between these two writers, both honest, laborious and fruitful, both absorbed in and submerged by literature, both eager to discover truth in all directions, was yet greater than their similarity. We have briefly observed in Faguet the university professor, the great public interpreter of masterpieces. In Remy de Gourmont, on the other hand, we meet the man who,

Two French Critics

scornful of mediocrity and tolerant of nothing but what is exquisite, stands apart from the crowd, and will scarcely share his dream with a disciple. Faguet, like a Lord Chancellor of Letters, is versed in all the legislation of the mind, and lives in a perpetual elucidation of it. Gourmont, standing in the outer court, attracts the young and the audacious around him by protesting that no laws exist save those which are founded on an artist's own eclecticism. Together, or rather back to back, they addressed almost everyone who was intelligent in France between 1895 and 1914.

We have seen in Emile Faguet a typical member of the middle class. Remy de Gourmont was an aristocrat both by descent and by temperament. He was born on the 4th of April, 1858, in the château of La Motte, near Bazoches-en-Houlme, in the Orne; during his childhood his parents moved to a still more romantic little manor-house at Mesnil-Villement. These Norman landscapes are constantly introduced into Gourmont's stories. His race was of considerable antiquity and distinction; his mother traced her descent from the great poet, Malherbe; a paternal ancestor was that Gilles de Gourmont who printed in France the earliest books in Greek and in Hebrew character. A passion for the Muses, like a fragrant atmosphere, surrounded the boy from his cradle. He arrived in Paris at the age of twenty-five, provincially instructed, but already of a marvellous erudition. He was appointed assistant librarian at the Bibliothèque Nationale, where for eight years he browsed at will on all the secret and forgotten wonders of the past, indulging to the full an insatiable literary curiosity. In 1890 he published a novel, *Sixtine,* a sort of diary of a very complicated mind which believes itself to be in love, but cannot be quite sure. It was "cerebral," without action of any kind, an absurd book, but ingeniously—too ingeniously—written. The historic interest of *Sixtine* rests in the fact that it led the reaction against the naturalism of Zola and the pyschology of M. Paul Bourget. Gourmont now achieved a single English reader, for *Sixtine* was read by Henry James, but with more curiosity than approval.

Although hardly a book of permanent value, *Sixtine* had a lasting effect on the career of its author. It expressed with remarkable exactitude the sentiments of the group of young men who were now coming to the front in France. Gourmont became the champion of the "vaporeux, nuancé et sublimisé" literature which started about 1890. He accepted "symbolism," and he became the leader of the symbolist movement, of which his stern mental training and curious erudition permitted him to be the brain. He was the prophet of Mallarmé, of Verlaine, of Maeterlinck, of Huysmans, and at the same time he welcomed each younger revolutionary. All this, of course, was not done in a day, but reconciliation with the intellectual conventions was made impossible by a fact which must not be ignored in any sketch of Remy de Gourmont, and indeed ought to be faced with resolution. In 1891 he was dismissed from the public service and from the Library, for an article which he published entitled *Le Joujou Patriotisme,* in which he poured contempt upon the Army, and openly advocated the abandonment of any idea of the "Revanche." The chastisement was a severe one, and had an effect on the whole remainder of Gourmont's life. About the same time his health gave way, and excluded him from all society, for he was invaded by an unsightly growth in the face. His hermitage was high up in an old house in the Rue des Saints Pères, near the quay, and there he sat, day in, day out, surrounded by his books, in solitude, a monk of literature.

For the next eight or nine years, Gourmont, abandoning politics, in which he had made so luckless an adventure, devoted himself exclusively to art and letters. He joined the staff of the *Mercure de France;* and under its director, and his life-long friend, M. Vallette, he took part in all the symbolist polemics of the hour. He defended each new man of merit with his active partisanship; he wrote ceaselessly; verse, art criticism, humanism, novels, every species of fantastic and esoteric literature

Two French Critics

flowed from his abundant pen. These books, many of them preposterous in their shape, "limited editions" produced in conditions of archiepiscopal splendour of binding and type, possess, it must be admitted, little positive value. They are blossoms in the flower-garden of that heyday of sensuous "symbolism," of which we had a pale reflection in our London *Yellow Books* and *Savoy Reviews*. The most interesting of the publications of Remy de Gourmont during these feverish years is the little volume called *L'Idéalisme* (1893), in which he sought to restore to the word "idéal" what he called its "aristocratic value." A passage may be quoted from an essay in this elegant and ridiculous treatise, on the beauty of words, irrespective of their meaning :

Quelles réalités me donneront les saveurs que je rêve à ce fruit de l'Inde et des songes, le myrobolan,—ou les couleurs royales dont je pare l'omphax, ou ses lointaines gloires?

Quelle musique est comparable à la sonorité pure des mots obscurs, ô cyclamor? Et quelle odeur à tes émanations vierges, ô sanguisorbe?

Stevenson—the R.L.S. of "Penny plain and Twopence coloured "—would have delighted in this.

Gourmont became tired of symbolism rather suddenly, and he buried it in two volumes which were the best he had yet published : the *Livres des Masques* of 1896 and 1898. These have a lasting value as documents, and they mark the beginning of the author's permanent work as a critic of letters. In them he insisted on the warning not to let new genius pass ungreeted because it was eccentrically draped or unfamiliarly featured. These two volumes are a precious indication of what French independent literature was at the very close of the nineteenth century, and it is interesting after twenty years of development and change to note how few mistakes Remy de Gourmont made in his characterization of types. He took a central place among these symbolists, grouping around him the men of genuine talent, repulsing pretenders who were

Aspects and Impressions

charlatans and discouraging mere imitators; marshalling, in short, a ferocious little army of genius in its attack upon the conventions and the traditions of the age. Time rolls its wheel, and it is amusing to notice that several of these fierce young revolutionaries are now members of the French Academy.

At the close of the century Remy de Gourmont abandoned symbolism, and the world of ideas took possession of him. He plunged deeper into the study of philosophy, grammar, and history, and he explored new provinces of knowledge, particularly in the direction of ethnography and biology. In the midst of this acquisitive labour he was stirred to the composition of one remarkable work after another, and to this period belong the four successive publications, which, in the whole of Gourmont's vast production, stand out as the most interesting and important which he has written. His reputation stands four-square on *L'Esthétique de la Langue Française* (1899), *La Culture des Idées* (1900), *Le Chemin de Velours* (1902), and *Le Problème du Style* (1902). During the thirteen years which followed he wrote incessantly, and the widening circle of his admirers always found much to praise in what he produced. But now that we see his life-work as a whole it seems more and more plain that he revealed his genius freshly and fully in these four books of his prime, and in a world so crowded as ours the reader who has much to attract him may be recommended to these as broad and perhaps sufficient exponents of the character of Gourmont's teaching.

It has been said by one of his earliest associates, M. Louis Dumur, that Gourmont was always "le bon chasseur du mensonge humain." This is a friendly way of describing his intellectual dogmatism and his restless habit of analysis. He took nothing for granted, and, whether he desired to be so or not, he was a destructive force. He describes himself, in one of his rather rare paragraphs of self-portraiture, as "un esprit désintéressé de tout, et intéressé à tout," and this very accurately defines his attitude. He strikes us as ceaselessly hovering over hitherto

Two French Critics

uncontested facts in the passionate desire of proving them to be fallacies. The epithet "paradoxical," which is often misapplied, appears to be exactly appropriate to the method of Remy de Gourmont, which starts by denying the truth of something which everybody has taken for granted, and then supporting the reversed position by rapid and ingenious argument. He is unable to accept any convention until he has resolutely turned it inside out, examined it in every hostile light, and so dusted and furbished it that it has ceased to be conventional. He was indefatigable in these researches, and so ingenious as to be often bewildering and occasionally tiresome.

He has left no book more characteristic than *Le Chemin de Velours,* which he called a study in the dissociation of ideas. He chose a very illuminating tag from Pascal as his motto: "ni la contradiction n'est marque de fausseté, ni l'incontradiction n'est marque de vérité." The whole treatise is a comparison between the Jansenist and the Jesuit system of morals, as revealed in the *Provincial Letters.* Like many Frenchmen of recent years, Remy de Gourmont liked religion to be championed, but never by a believer. Neither Port Royal nor the Society of Jesus would thank him for his disinterested support, but he defends them, alternately and destructively, with an immense fund of vivacity. No one has defined more luminously the evangelical doctrine of Jansenius, Bishop of Ypres, and for a while the reader thinks that the balance will descend on the Jansenist side. But Gourmont is scandalized to see Calvinism banging the door of salvation in people's faces, while he applauds the humanity of the Jesuits in holding it wide open, and in spreading between birth and death a velvet carpet for delicate souls. He analyses the works of Sarrasa, a Flemish Jesuit, who in 1618 produced an *Ars semper gaudendi* which was, according to Gourmont, neither more nor less than a treatise on the way to make the best of both worlds. Gourmont was endlessly amused by the indiscreet admissions of Father Sarrasa.

Nevertheless, the Jesuit type shocked him more than

the Jansenist. He admired the logical penetration of
Pascal, his rigidity of thought, his unalterable ideal of
duty, more than the easy-going casuistry of his opponents.
He thought that Protestantism, which rests on abstraction,
was a purer type of religion than the mitigated and
humanized Christianity of Catholicism. But he was
irritated by the way in which Port Royal pushed their
spiritual logic to extremes, and he dared to suggest that
Pascal would have been a better and a more useful man
if he had consented to be less holy. Gourmont speculated
ingeniously what would have been the future of philosophical literature if Pascal, instead of retiring to Port
Royal, had joined Descartes in Holland. On the whole
he decides against the Jansenists, because although he sees
that they were noble he suspects them of being inhuman,
and of laying intolerable and needless burdens upon the
spirit of man. Remy de Gourmont considered evangelical
Christianity an Oriental religion, not well fitted for Latin
Europe. In all the schisms and heresies of the churches
he thought he saw the Western mind revolting against a
dogmatism which came from Jerusalem. The Jansenist
is a pessimist; the Jesuit, on the other hand, cultivates
optimism; he pretends, at all events, that the soul should
be free and joyous, to which end he rolls out his velvet
road towards salvation. Remy de Gourmont concludes
that the final effect of *Les Provinciales* is to make the
reader love the Jesuits, and when he comes to sum up the
matter he is on the side of the Society, because nothing
wounds a civilized man so deeply as the negation of his
free will. It will be seen that neither party gains much
from his sardonic and fugitive approbation.

After 1902 a further transformation began to be visible
in the genius of Remy de Gourmont. An improvement in
his health permitted him to mingle a little with other
human beings, and to become less exclusively an anchorite
of the intellect. Having pushed his individualist theories
to their extreme, he withdrew from his violent expression
of them, and he took a new and pleasing interest in public
life. He continued to seek consolation for the disappoint-

ments of art in philosophy and science, and he developed
a positive passion for ideas. He founded the *Revue des
Idées*, which had a considerable vogue in the intellectual
world. But his chief activity henceforward was as a
publicist. His incessant short essays, mainly published
in the *Mercure de France*, became an element in the life
of thousands of cultivated readers. They dealt briefly
with questions of the day, concerning all that can arrest
the attention of an educated man or woman. The author
collected them in volumes which present the quintessence
of his later manner, four of *Epilogues,* three of
Promenades Littéraires, three of *Promenades Philo-
sophiques*, and so forth. These dogmatic expressions of
his conception of life were written in a style more fluid,
more buoyant, and less obscure than he had previously
used, and they achieved a great popularity, especially
among women. Meantime, as a critic, he showed less and
less interest in the exceptional and the unwholesome, of
which he had been the fantastic defender, and more in the
great standard authors of France. In 1905 he opened with
an anthology from Gérard de Nerval a series of *Les Plus
Belles Pages*, which he continued until the war with
admirable judgment.

The war found Remy de Gourmont not totally un-
prepared. He had always unflinchingly avowed himself
an aristocrat and an anarchist; it was his way of expressing
his horror at vulgarity and tyranny. He had chosen to
be disconcerting in his vindictive pursuit of sentimentality
and folly. He had thought it fitting to be a determined
enemy to militarism. It was difficult for a critic with so
fine an ear as his to tolerate patriotic verses which did not
scan. But the ripening years had sobered him, and he
made after 1911 a much more careful examination of the
destiny of his country. He saw that with all his
scepticism he had been the dupe of Teutonic culture, and
he repudiated the Nietzsche whom he had done so much
to introduce to Parisian readers. From August, 1914,
Remy de Gourmont put aside all his literary and scientific
work, and devoted himself wholly to a patriotic comment

on the war. His short articles in *La France* form an admirable volume, *Pendant l'Orage,* by which all his petulance in times of peace is more than redeemed. The anguish of the struggle killed him, as it had killed so many others. Remy de Gourmont was seated at his writing-table, with a protest against the outrage upon Reims half-completed before him, when a stroke of apoplexy put an instant period to his life. This was on the 29th of September, 1915.

In one of his best books, *Le Problème du Style* (1902), Remy de Gourmont remarks in his aphoristic way, "Il y a une forme générale de la sensibilité qui s'impose à tous les hommes d'une même période." This is excessive in its application, but it is sufficiently true to be a useful guide to the historian. Between 1890 and 1905 there was exhibited, not merely in France and England, but all over Europe, a "general form of sensibility" of which Gourmont was the ablest, the most vociferous, and the most ingenious representative. It is important to try to analyse this condition or fashion of taste, since, although it has already passed into the region of things gone by and of "les neiges d'antan," it has not ceased to be memorable. Our comprehension of it is not helped by ticketing it "decadent" or "unhealthy," for those are empty adjectives of prejudice. What was really involved in it was a revolt against sentimentality and against the tendency to repeat with complacency the outworn traditions of art. This was its negative side, worthy of all encouragement. What was not quite so certainly meritorious was its positive action. It was a demand for an exclusively personal æsthetic, for an art severely divorced from all emotions except the purely intellectual ones, the sensuousness of this school of writers being essentially cerebral. It descended in England from Walter Pater, in France from Baudelaire, and it aimed at a supreme delicacy of execution, an exquisite avoidance of everything vulgar and second-hand. The young men who fought for it considered that the only thing essential was to achieve what they called a "personal vision" of life. In the pursuit of it they were willing to be candid at the risk of perversity, while they obstinately denied that there should be any relation between art and morals. But Remy de Gourmont, who had been their leader in aiming at an impossible perfection, lived long enough to see the whole intellect and conscience of France pressing along a path to greatness which he and his disciples had never perceived in all the excursions of their imagination.

1916.

THE WRITINGS OF M. CLEMENCEAU

IN the year 1893, after a succession of events which are still remembered with emotion, M. Clemenceau fell from political eminence, not gradually or by transitions of decay, but with theatrical suddenness like that of a Lucifer "hurled headlong flaming from the ætherial sky." His enemies, rewarded beyond their extreme hopes, gazed down into the abyss and thought that they discerned his "cadavre politique" lying motionless at the bottom. They rejoiced to believe that he would trouble them no more. He had passed the age of fifty years, and all his hopes were broken, all his ambitions shattered. They rubbed their hands together, and smiled; "we shall hear no more of *him!*" But they did not know with what manner of man they were dealing. What though the field was lost? All was not lost:

> The unconquerable Will,
> And study of revenge, immortal hate,
> And courage never to submit or yield;
> And what is else not to be overcome?

So brilliant an array of mingled intelligence, pertinacity, vigour, and high spirits have rarely been seen united, and the possessor of these qualities was not likely to be silenced by the most formidable junta of intriguers. As a matter of fact, he turned instantly to a new sphere of action, and became the man of letters of whom I propose to speak in these pages. But for his catastrophe in 1893, it is probable that M. Clemenceau would never have become an author.

A brief summary of his early life is needed to bring the series of his published works into due relief. Georges

Aspects and Impressions

Clemenceau was the second son of a family of six; he was born on the 28th of September, 1841, and was therefore a little younger than Joseph Chamberlain and Lord Morley, and a little older than Sir Charles Dilke. His birthplace was a hamlet close to the old and picturesque town of Fontenay-le-Comte, in the Vendée, where his father practised as a doctor. There can be no doubt that Benjamin Clemenceau, an old provincial "bleu," materialist and Jacobin, exercised a great influence on the mind of his son, who accepted, with a docility remarkable in so firm an individual, the traditions of his race and family. We are told that the elder Clemenceau "communicated to his son his hatred of injustice, his independence, his scientific worship of facts, his refusal to bow to anything less than the verdict of experiment." There was also a professional tradition to which young Georges Clemenceau assented. For three hundred years, without a break, his forebears had been doctors. I do not think that any of his biographers has observed the fact that Fontenay-le-Comte, though so small a place, has always been a centre of advanced scientific thought. It has produced a line of eminent physicians, for Pierre Brissot was born there in the fifteenth century, Sébastian Collin in the sixteenth, and Mathurin Brisson in the eighteenth. There can be little doubt that these facts were in the memory of the elder Clemenceau and were transmitted to his son.

Fontenay-le-Comte is on the western edge of the Bocage of Poitou, not to be confounded with the delicious woodland Bocage which lies south and west of Caen. The Poitou Bocage is a more limited and a more remote district, little visited by tourists, a rolling country of heatherland clustered with trees, and split up by little torrential chasms. It is often to be recognized in M. Clemenceau's sketches of landscapes, and is manifestly the scene of part of his novel, *Les Plus Forts*. The natural capital of this Bocage is Nantes, lying full to the north of Fontenay, and thither the young man went at an early age to study at the Lycée. It was at the hospital at Nantes that his first introduction to medicine was made. Thence he

The Writings of M. Clemenceau

finally departed in 1860, another *déraciné*, to fight for his fortunes in Paris. He brought little with him save a letter of introduction from his father to Etienne Arago. For five years he worked indomitably at his medical studies, refreshing his brain occasionally by brief holidays spent at his father's rough and ancient manor-house of Aubraie, in his native Bocage.

He took his degree of M.D. in 1865, and presented a thesis *De la Génération des Eléments anatomiques,* which was immediately published, and which caused some stir in professional circles. It is said to contain a vigorous refutation of some of the doctrines of Auguste Comte, and in particular to deprecate a growing agnosticism among men of science. The axiom, "Supprimer les questions, n'est pas y répondre," is quoted from it, and again the characteristic statement, "Nous ne sommes pas de ceux qui admettent avec l'école positiviste que la science ne peut fournir aucun renseignement sur l'énigme des choses." The thesis dealt, moreover, according to M. Pierre Quillard, who has had the courage to unearth and to analyse it, with "les organismes rudimentaires des néphélés, des hirudinées et glossiphonies," subjects the very names of which are horrifying to the indolent lay reader. The young savant, shaking off the burden of his studies, escaped to London, where he appears to have made the acquaintance, through Admiral Maxse, of several Englishmen who were about to become famous in the world of politics and letters. But perhaps these friendships are of later date; as the memoirs of the mid-Victorians come more and more to light, the name of M. Clemenceau will be looked for in the record.

He went to the United States in 1866, and took an engagement as French master in a girls' school at Stamford, in Connecticut, a seaside haunt of tired New Yorkers in summer. A little later, Verlaine was under-master in a boys' school at Bournemouth. How little we guess, when we take our walks abroad, that genius, and foreign genius too, may be lurking in the educational procession! M. Clemenceau appears to look back on Stamford with

Aspects and Impressions

complacency; he accompanied "dans leurs promenades les jeunes misses américaines: c'étaient de libres et délicieuses chevauchées, des excursions charmantes au long des routes ombreuses qui sillonnent les riants parages" of Long Island Sound. He declares that the happy and light-hearted years at Stamford were those in which his temperament "acheva de se fortifier et de s'affiner." It was in the course of one of the "suaves équipées" that he ventured to propose to one of the young American "misses." This was Miss Mary Plummer, whom he married after a preliminary visit to France.

For the next quarter of a century Clemenceau was exclusively occupied with politics. In 1870 he was settled in Montmartre, in a circle of workmen and little employés whose bodily maladies he relieved, and whose souls he inflamed with his ardent dreams of a humanitarian paradise when once the hated Empire should fall. Suddenly the war broke out, and the Empire was shattered. The government of defence nominated Dr. Clemenceau Mayor of Montmartre, the most violent centre of revolutionary emotion, where the excesses of the Commune presently began. He represented Montmartre at Bordeaux in 1871, and in 1876 Montmartre, which had remained faithful to its doctor-mayor, sent him again to the Chamber of Deputies as its representative. This is not the occasion on which to enter into any detail with regard to the ceaseless activity which he displayed in a purely political capacity between 1870 and 1893. It is enshrined in the history of the Republic, and will occupy the pens of innumerable commentators of French affairs. We can only record that in 1889, M. Clemenceau, who had refused many pressing invitations to leave Paris for Draguignan, consented to take up his election as deputy for the Provençal department.

The career of M. Clemenceau as deputy for the Var came to an end in 1893, after the explosion of the Panama scandal. On the 8th of August in that year he pronounced an apologia over his political life, an address full of dignity and fire, in which the failure of his ambition was acknowledged. His figure was never more attractive than it was at that distressing moment, when he found himself the object of almost universal public disfavour. He had, perhaps, over-estimated the vigour of his own prestige; he had browbeaten the political leaders of the day, he had stormed like a bull the china-shops of the little political hucksters, he had contemptuously exposed the intrigues of the baser sort of political politician. He disdained popularity so proudly, that one of his own supporters urged him to cultivate the hatred of the crowd with a little less coquettishness. But he was a political Don Quixote, not to be held nor bound; he could but rush straight upon his own temporary discomfiture.

The means which his enemies employed to displace him were contemptible in the extreme, but their malice was easily accounted for. He had excited the deep resentment of all the supporters of General Boulanger, who accused him of being the cause of their favourite's fall, and with having betrayed him in 1888. The fanatics of the Panama scandal endeavoured to prove that his newspaper, *La Justice*, had supported the schemes and accepted the cheques of the egregious Cornelius Herz. The Anglophobes, who unhappily numbered too many of the less thinking population of France at that time, accused him of intriguing with the English Government to the detriment of the Republic, and they went so far as to produce documents, forged by the notorious mulatto, Norton, which they pretended had been stolen from our embassy in Paris. "Qu'il parle anglais," was one accusation shouted at Clemenceau in the Chamber on the 4th of June, 1888. Calamities of every sort, public and private, gathered round his undaunted head. At last he could ignore these attacks no longer, and on a fateful day he rose to put himself right before Parliament. It was too late; his appearance was greeted by an icy silence, and, as he said himself, he glanced round to see none but the hungry faces of men longing for the moment when they could trample on his corpse. Magnificent as was his defence, it availed him nothing against such a combination of malignities;

even his few friends, losing courage, failed to support him. The legislative elections were at hand, and the enemies of M. Clemenceau very cleverly organized a press propaganda, which presented him to the French public in an absolutely odious light. He went down to address his Provençal constituents, and in the little mountain town of Salernes he delivered the remarkable speech to which reference has been made. All in vain : on the 20th of August, 1893, he was ignominiously rejected by the electors of the Var in favour of a local nonentity, and his career as a member of parliament ended.[1]

These circumstances, which paralysed for many years the parliamentary activity of Clemenceau, have to be borne in mind when we examine his literary record. Without delay, in that spirit of prompt acceptance of the inevitable which has never ceased to mark his buoyant, elastic character, he threw himself into a new employment. He became, in his fifty-third year, one of the most active and persistent journalists in France. His fiery independence and his audacious vivacity pointed him out at once to editors who had the wit to cater for the better, that is to say for the livelier, class of readers. M. Clemenceau, a free lance if ever there was one, became the terror and the delight of *Le Figaro, La Justice,* and *Le Journal,* while to *La Dépêche de Toulouse* he contributed articles which presupposed a wider horizon and depended less on the passion of the moment. Future bibliographers, it may be, will search the files of these and other newspapers of that day for more and more numerous examples of his fecundity, since he embraced all subjects in what he called the huge

---

[1] A very interesting account of the events which led to the fall of M. Clemenceau is given in the autobiography of the late Mr. Hyndman, who had the advantage of enjoying M. Clemenceau's friendship from an early date. He considers that the French statesman might have faced the storm with success if he would but have consented to make terms with the Socialists. But he would not do so : he replied to Mr. Hyndman—" It is as useless to base any practical policy upon Socialist principles as it is chimerical to repose any confidence in Socialist votes." When Mr. Hyndman urged that this attitude of hostility to all parties might lose him his seat in the Var, Clemenceau " laughed at the very idea of such a defeat." Nor has the conflict between him and the revolutionary Socialists ever ceased.

The Writings of M. Clemenceau

forest of social existence. An exhibition of pictures, a new novel, an accident in the suburbs, a definition of God by M. Jules Simon, a joke by M. Francis Maynard, the effect of champagne upon labour unrest, the architecture of Chicago—nothing came amiss to the pen of a man whose curiosity about life was boundless, and whose facility in expression was volcanic.

But there was a certain group of subjects which, at this critical hour in his career, particularly attracted the attention of M. Clemenceau, and these give a special colour to the earliest, and perhaps the most remarkable, collection of his essays. A student of the temperament of the great statesman, as he has since then so pre-eminently shown himself to be, is bound to give his mind to the volume called *La Mêlée Sociale* which M. Clemenceau published in 1895. This was practically his earliest bid for purely literary distinction, since the juvenile theses on anatomical subjects, and the translations from John Stuart Mill, hardly come within the category of literature. Between 1876 and 1885 M. Clemenceau had printed, or had permitted to be circulated, a certain number of his speeches in the Chamber; I have traced eight of these in the catalogue of M. Le Blond. These formed a very small fraction of his abundant eloquence in Parliament, and they were not particularly finished as specimens of lettered oratory. But between 1885 and 1895 we do not find even such slender evidences as these of the politician's desire to pose as an author. The publication of *La Mêlée Sociale,* therefore, was, to speak practically, an expériment; it was the challenge of a new writer, or at least of a publicist who had never before competed with the recognized creators of books.

It is obvious that in making this experiment M. Clemenceau exercised a great deal of care and forethought. The articles reprinted are not presented haphazard, nor without an evident intention of producing the best effect possible. They are selected on a peculiar system from the mass of the journalist's miscellaneous output. The collection has a central idea, and this is developed in a very remarkable preface, which remains one of the author's most philosophical and most elaborate compositions. This central idea is the tragical one of the great vital conflict which pervades the world, has always pervaded it, and must ever remain unaffected by the superficial improvements of civilization. All through the universe the various living organisms are in a condition of ceaseless contest. Everywhere something conquers something else which is conquered, and life sustains itself and ensures its own permanence by spreading death around it. Life, in fact, depends on death for its sustaining energy, and the fiercer the passion of vitality the more vehemently flourishes the instinct of destruction.

The imagination of the author of *La Mêlée Sociale* broods upon the monstrous facts of natural history. If he traverses a woodland, he is conscious of a silent army of beasts and birds and insects, and even of trees and plants, which are waging ceaseless battle against others of their kind. If he begins to stir the soil of a meadow with his foot, he refrains with a shudder, since millions of corpses lie but just below the surface of the fruitful earth. He peers down into the depths of the sea, only to recognize that a prodigious and unflagging massacre of living forms is necessary to keep the ocean habitable for those who survive. Everywhere, throughout the universe, he finds carnage triumphant; and eternal warfare is the symbol of the instinct of self-preservation.

It will be seen that the new author approached literature definitely from the scientific side, but also that he placed himself almost exclusively under the direction of English minds. M. Clemenceau, in that intense and unceasing contemplation of life which has been his most remarkable characteristic, has always been inspired by English models. In his early youth he was deeply impressed with the teaching of J. S. Mill, and in later years he was manifestly under the successive sway of Sir Charles Lyell and of Herbert Spencer. But by the time he collected his essays in *La Mêlée Sociale*, he was completely infatuated by the system of Darwin. He had long been

The Writings of M. Clemenceau

familiar with *The Origin of Species* and *The Descent of Man;* the death of Darwin in 1882 had deprived him of a master and, as it seemed, a friend, while the publication of the *Life and Letters* in 1887 had given a coherency and, we may say, an atmosphere, to his conception of the illustrious English savant. When, therefore, M. Clemenceau put together the material of *La Mêlée Sociale,* he did so in the quality of an advanced Darwinian, and he produced his first book almost as a tribute of affection to the memory of the greatest exponent of the tragedy of natural selection. But the habit of his mind, and no doubt the conditions of his own fortunes, led him into a field more tragical than any haunted by the spirit of the placid philosopher of Down. Charles Darwin refrained from pushing his observations to such sinister conclusions as this:

La mort, partout la mort. Les continents et les mers gémissent de l'effroyable offrande de massacre. C'est le cirque, l'immense Collysée de la Terre, où tout ce qui ne pouvait vivre que de mort, se pare de lumière et de vie pour mourir. De l'herbe à l'éléphant, pas d'autre loi que la loi du plus fort. Au nom de la même loi, le dernier né de l'évolution vivante confond tout ce qui est de vie dans une prodigieuse hécatombe offerte à la suprématie de sa race. Point de pitié. Le pouce retourné commande la mort. L'âme ingrate répudie l'antique solidarité des êtres enlacés en la chaîne des générations transformées. Le cœur dur est fermé. Tout ce qui échappe au carnage prémédité, voulu, s'entretue pour la gloire du grand barbare. La splendeur de la floraison de vie s'éteint dans le sang, pour en renaître, pour y sombrer encore. Et le cirque, toujours vidé, s'emplit toujours.

This passage may be taken as characteristic of the manner of M. Clemenceau in his most reflective mood, in the "style bref, mais clair et vibrant," which Octave Mirbeau commended. This way of writing would err on the side of rhetoric, were it not so concise and rapid, so full of the gusto of life even in its celebration of death. For, in the pages of *La Mêlée Sociale,* M. Clemenceau

Aspects and Impressions

shows himself interpenetrated by the sorrows rather than sustained by the possibilities of the tormented inhabitants of earth. Recent events, in his own life and in the history of the French nation, had impressed on his consciousness the inherent cruelty of human beings to one another. Like Wordsworth, and with a far sharper personal pang, he had good reason to lament what man has made of man. Moreover, the months which had extended between M. Clemenceau's political fall and the publication of *La Mêlée Sociale* had been marked by violent unrest and by a succession of political crimes. Anarchism, hitherto more a theory and a threat than a practical element in the existence of the people, had taken startling prominence. In quick and formidable succession the crimes of Vaillant, of Emile Henry, of Caserio and others, had filled the minds of men with alarm and horror. These events, and the strikes in various trades with their attendant sabotage, and the unrest among the miners, and the earliest germination of that new disease of the State, syndicalism,—all these and many other evidences of renewed bitterness in the struggle for life created in the mind of M. Clemenceau an obsession which is reflected in every chapter of *La Mêlée Sociale*. As a physician, no less than as a publicist, he diagnosed the "misère physiologique" of the age, and he railed against those in power who touched with the tips of their white kid gloves the maladies which were blackening the surface and substance of human society. In the memory of the attempt made last February to assassinate M. Clemenceau, a special interest attaches to his discussion of this class of murders, of which he gave a remarkably close and prolonged analysis, little conceiving, of course, that he would live to be himself the object of a crime at which the whole world would shudder.

The reader who wishes the literary aspect of M. Clemenceau's mind to be revealed to him in its greatest amenity may next be recommended to turn to the preface of the volume entitled *Le Grand Pan*, which appeared in 1896. The book itself consists of seventy little essays,

The Writings of M. Clemenceau

reprinted from the *Figaro*, the *Echo de Paris*, and other newspapers. These have nothing or very little to do with Pan, but they are eked out and given determination by a long rhapsody in honour of the goat-foot son of Callista, treated as the symbol of natural, as opposed to supernatural science. Everybody knows the famous passage in Plutarch which describes how Thamous the pilot, sailing out of the Gulf of Corinth towards the Ionian Sea on the eve of the crucifixion of Christ, heard a voice announce that "Great Pan is dead!"

> And that dismal cry rose slowly
> And sank slowly through the air,
> Full of spirit's melancholy
> And eternity's despair!
> And they heard the words it said—
> Pan is dead—Great Pan is dead—
> Pan, Pan is dead.

In a passage of rare picturesque beauty M. Clemenceau reproduces the animated and mysterious scene. He had himself lately returned from a visit to Greece, which had deeply stirred the sources of his sensibility. He recalled how the sun, in a transparency of pale gold, sank behind the blue mass of Ithaca, tinged with rose-colour the crags of the Echinades, and bathed the mountains and the sea in the delicate enchantment of sunset. He was sensitive to the paroxysm of pleasure such an experience produces, and he conceived himself standing by the side of the grammarian, Epitherses, on board the merchant-vessel, at the very moment when there sounded three times from the shore the name of Thamous, the Egyptian pilot, who answered at length, and received the mysterious command, "When thou art opposite Palodes, announce that the great Pan is dead!" The recesses of the mountains, the caves on the island, the solitude of the drear battle-field of Actium, took up the hollow cry and reverberated it in a thousand accents of despair, with groans and shrieks of sorrow and confused bewailing, while all nature united in the echoing lamentation, "Pan, great Pan, is dead!"

In this strange way M. Clemenceau opens an essay in defence of a purely positivist theory of human existence. He describes the doctrine of the pagan divinities, under the tyranny of Christianity, and he predicts their resurrection under clearer and calmer auspices. For M. Clemenceau, Pan is the symbol of life in its harmonious and composite action, and science is the intelligent worship of Pan. This despised and fallen god, who seemed for one dark moment to be dead, survives and will return to his faithful adorers, has indeed returned already, and turns the tables on his priestly persecutors. The apparent death of Pan was but a sleep and a forgetting; the spirit of humanity, dominated for a moment by superstition and ignorance, seemed to be lying bound and mute, but it is vocal again, and its powers prove to be unshackled. The Orphic hymn, in dark numbers, had pronounced the sky and the sea, earth the universal and fire the immortal, to be the limbs of Pan. Under the early sway of Christianity the office and meaning of the pagan gods faded into mist; they seemed to disappear for ever. Darkness gathered over the sweet natural influences of the physical world, and reality was bartered for a feverish dream of heaven and hell.

But the gods were only preparing in silence for their ultimate resuscitation. Lactantius said that "Idols and religion are two incompatible things"; in his famous *De Origine Erroris*, conscious of the necessity of recognizing a central force of energy in nature, the earliest Christian philosopher repulsed the notion of polytheism, and insisted that piety can exist only in the worship of the one God. He, like the Christian Fathers before him, shut up the spirit of man in a prison from which there seemed no escape. But the polytheists, thus violently Christianized against their will, remained pagan in essence, and they escaped, as by a miracle, from the furies of the Gospel and the Koran. The revolt was held in check through the Middle Ages; in the Renaissance it

The Writings of M. Clemenceau

became victorious, and the first activity of man in liberty was an unconscious but none the less real restitution of the old liberating deities. The shepherds of Arcadia saw the blood come back into the marble face and hands of their dead god. Pan was moving on the earth once more, for he had triumphed over the sterile forces of dissolution. Pan, as ancient as social order itself, radiant master of the beneficent powers of light, has once more become the supreme deity. This, put briefly, is the thesis of M. Clemenceau.

The influence of Renan is manifest through the whole of this rhapsody, which is unique among the writings of its author. M. Clemenceau had followed the track of Pan through the valleys of Arcadia, and up the rocky pathways that rise abruptly from the stony bed of Alpheus. An actual visit to Greece, the date of which I have not verified, appears to have influenced his imagination; he says, "je l'ai voulu chercher, moi-même; au dépit de Thamous, près des antiques sources dolentes," and he tells us how an avalanche of falling stones and a clatter of cloven hoofs overhead often made him fancy the deity almost within his grasp. In these passages M. Clemenceau reveals himself more plainly than anywhere else as an imaginative positivist, who permits his fancy to play with romantic and even fantastic visions, yet who is none the less essentially emancipated from everything but reality. He is never the dupe of his own symbol. He rejects natural religion no less firmly than revealed religion, and he will not submit his conscience to any supernatural authority. The reader, if he has the patience to do so, may follow the close parallelism of the purely intellectual positivism of the author with the charming, supple, elusive philosophy of Renan in his *L'Avenir de la Science.*

In no other of his writings is M. Clemenceau quite so emancipated from the prejudice of the moment as he is in the preface to *Le Grand Pan.* His central idea is one of satisfaction in the survival of the spirits of the dead gods, to whom, of course, he gives his own formula of definition. Nothing in history seems to affect him more painfully than the tragedy of the massacre of the sacred statues under Theodosius, when, as Gibbon has so eloquently described, the most high gods were exposed to the derision of the crowd, and then melted down. Where M. Clemenceau's emotion seems to be slightly deficient in logic is the parallel between these ancient gods who retain his sympathy, and the strictly impersonal forces of which he acknowledges them a symbol. He delights in Apollo, Pan, and Jove, and speaks of them almost as though they were individuals, yet he admits no sentimentality with regard to what they represent. On the whole, his attitude is not one of benignity. He confesses that nature reveals nothing but a system of forces interacting upon one another; it is not moral and it is not beneficent. Here the tone of *Le Grand Pan* becomes identical with that of *La Mêlée Sociale*. But we demand a clear definition of the central symbol. What does M. Clemenceau really mean us to understand by Pan? We push him up into a corner; we refuse to let him take refuge in his Renanesque imaginations, and we extract an answer at last. Pan is the source of all moral and intellectual action :

Pan nous commande. Il faut agir. L'action est le principe, l'action est le moyen, l'action est le but. L'action obstinée de tout l'homme au profit de tous, l'action désintéressée, supérieure aux puériles glorioles, aux rémunérations des rêves d'éternité, comme aux desespérances des batailles perdues ou de l'inéluctable mort, l'action en évolution d'idéal, unique force et totale vertu.

The career of M. Clemenceau has been marked throughout by sudden and spasmodic crises, rather than by slow evolution of events. If this is true of his political history, it is repeated in his literary record. We need not, therefore, affect surprise at finding him, at the age of fifty-seven, and in the midst of the most bewildering distractions, produce his one and only novel, a modern

The Writings of M. Clemenceau

story deliberately conducted to its close in four hundred pages. When *Les Plus Forts* was published, in 1898, its author was extremely out of the fashion, and it passed almost unobserved from the press. Not a single Parisian critic, so far as I have discovered, gave it any serious attention, and it sank at once into an obscurity out of which the immense recent vogue of M. Clemenceau has only lately drawn it. *Les Plus Forts* was issued at the darkest moment of the statesman's reversal, when he was repudiated by the great majority of those who adore him to-day. He had actually gone so far as to speak of his own as a "vie manquée," when a fresh opportunity of perilous service to the State fell in his way.

In October, 1897, M. Ernest Vaughan, who had laid by a very considerable sum of money for the purpose of founding an efficient social and literary newspaper, approached Clemenceau with the offer of the editorship in chief. The famous *L'Aurore* came into existence, and it set sail at once in the stormy waters of the Dreyfus affair. Terrific was the clash of passions around the name of the mysterious Jew, whose exact character and definite purpose will perhaps never be completely elucidated. M. Clemenceau did not hesitate to throw the weight of his pen into the unpopular scale. When Esterhazy was acquitted he almost lost his self-control; with furious irony and snarling invectives he lashed the populace into a frenzy. Then followed (on the 13th of January, 1898) the famous intervention of Zola, in a manifesto which rang from one end of the civilized world to the other. This was *J'accuse,* the admirably effective title of which, so M. Maurice Le Blond assures us, was the invention of Clemenceau. Next month, at the Zola trial, Clemenceau defended the cause of justice in the teeth of enemies who did not refrain from threatening his very life, and for two years *L'Aurore,* in the midst of the frenzied Dreyfus hurly-burly, was unflagging in its attacks and its rejoinders.

At such a moment M. Clemenceau sat down to write his solitary novel. It would be fulsome to represent *Les*

Aspects and Impressions

Plus Forts as a masterpiece of fiction, though in the present flush of the author's celebrity some have dared so to describe it. As a matter of fact it owes the interest which it possesses almost entirely to the light which it throws on the character of its author. As a mere romance, *Les Plus Forts* suffers from the fact that its author, gifted in so many other directions, is not an effective narrator. As Dr. Johnson mischievously said of Congreve's one novel, *Incognita,* it is easier to praise *Les Plus Forts* than to read it. The scene is laid in a village deep in the heart of Poitou, and commentators have recognized a close reproduction of Mouilleron-en-Paradis, the hamlet near Fontenay where M. Clemenceau was born. At the moment of his fiercest struggle in Paris, his thoughts turned back to the cool woods and the still waters of his old home in the west, to the land of hollow valleys, and to the inexpressive sixteenth-century château which the doctor's child learned to regard as the symbol of rapine and tyranny in the past.

We are introduced to M. Henri, marquis de Puymaufray, a man of over sixty, solitary, a confirmed bachelor, not so good a shot as he used to be. The lonely old man comes back, defeated by life, to his château in Poitou. The mise-en-scène is lugubrious in the extreme, punctuated by the shrieking peacocks at noon and the hooting owls at night. When this impression has been sketched in, we turn back to the hero's early history, and follow the adventures of a young buck of the Second Empire, brought up to despise science, modern thought, the action of democracy in every form. He begins as a pontifical zouave in bondage to Rome; he ends as a sort of anarchist. The biography of the young and stupid nobleman is thus made a peg on which to hang dissertations on all the principal maladies which affected French society a quarter of a century ago. There is an exaggerated forceful woman, the Vicomtesse de Fourchamps, who plays a sustained but obscure part in the intrigue. What does she want? It is difficult to say; she is always "preparing for the battle" or attempting to "conquer" somebody. "Il faut conquérir," she incessantly repeats; she is a kind of tigress, and she seems to be, in petticoats, a type of every social and political movement of which M. Clemenceau disapproves.

The Parisian scenes in M. Clemenceau's novel are not very amusing, and, oddly enough, they are weighed down by a sort of heavy gorgeousness, somewhat in the mode of Disraeli not at his best. All the characters preach, and the reader comes to sympathize with the vicomtesse when she declares herself "agacée des sermons du marquis." The young girl, Claude Harlé, is a somewhat shadowy heroine. She passes as the daughter of a rich industrial, but she is in reality the child of Puymaufray, who was the lover of her mother, since deceased. It is easy to understand that M. Clemenceau has taken this pathetic and tremulous figure as representative of what is chimerical in the society of the day. In her original condition, he puts into her mouth the crude sentiments which are supposed to be nurtured by the enemies of democracy. Claude calmly states that "the good God has instituted two classes of human beings, the rich and the poor, and it is our duty to maintain our inferiors in the practices of religion." A good deal of art is required to remove from such speeches as these the crude appearance of falsity; and it may be remarked that the pious characters in *Les Plus Forts* are not more like real human beings than are the atheists in M. Paul Bourget's later romances.

What is of extraordinary interest in *Les Plus Forts* is not the story itself, which is thin, nor the conduct of the adventures, which is stilted, but the temper and attitude of the writer. If we ask ourselves what is the principal characteristic of this novel, the answer must be —the intensity of action of the personages; they seem to have springs of steel in their insides; they run when other people walk, and cannot move without leaping in the air. "Il faut aux conquérants la pleine sécurité de leur corps. Où l'âme conduit, la bête doit suivre." The book is full of strange utterances of this order, which reveal the violence of the author's temperament in flashes of odd light.

Aspects and Impressions

The episodes, the conversations, are little more than a series of irregular theses on various aspects of the struggle for life. The world is regarded as simply "le syndicat des plus forts," and this idea underlies the title of the book. We are not allowed to forget it, even when our attention is being switched away to the discipline of little Chinese children in a missionary settlement, or to the importance of encouraging a manufacturer of paper in Ceylon.

What is perhaps the most characteristic passage of M. Clemenceau's single novel may be quoted as an example both of his philosophy and of his style. It occurs in the course of a long conversation between father and daughter.

> Certes non, l'argent n'est pas tout. Il est trop, simplement. L'argent n'est pas tout, mais il a le genre humain pour clientèle, car il est devenu, de force libératrice, l'egoïsme tangible en rondelles de métal. Voilà pourquoi tout cède à l'universelle attraction qui n'est pas suffisamment contre-balancée par d'autres. L'argent n'est pas tout. Pourtant autour de lui se rassemblent toutes les autres puissances sociales, et celles-là même qui s'annoncèrent protectrices des hommes, aussitôt installées, par lui se sont agglomérées en tyrannie. Il a remplacé la force brutale, dit-on . . . à la condition de l'exprimer par d'autres signes. Contre l'expression du monde, il y avait Dieu autrefois, a dit quelqu'un. Peut-être. J'ai toujours trouvé Dieu du côté des plus forts.

M. Clemenceau did not pause, meanwhile, from his journalistic labours, and he continued to offer to the public of Paris successive selections from the mass of his productions. On each of these occasions a preface, composed with more than usual care, gave the keynote to the series of essays, or rather suggested a tone of mind in which the reader would do well to study them. In the introduction to the volume of 1900, called *Au Fil des Jours,* the author returned to his favourite theme, the struggle against the universally destructive forces of Nature. The life of man is concentrated on resistance to the persistent attacks upon it made by an army of inimical forces. The pride of existence is humbled by the inevitable fatality which governs the fortunes of the Olympian gods themselves. And it is useless to appeal, with the sentimental pantheists, to the beneficence of Nature, for Nature is the most relentless, the most indomitable of our enemies. In that extraordinary little tragedy of Victor Hugo, *Mangeront-ils*, the vain appeal is made :

> Est-ce pas,
> Nature, que tu haïs les semeurs de trépas,
> Qui dans l'air frappent l'aigle et sur l'eau la sarcelle,
> Et font partout saigner la vie universelle?

With the clairvoyance of the biologist, M. Clemenceau divines the vanity of these remonstrances, and from the terrible cruelty of Nature he sees no relief save in vigorous action. "Toute âme haute veut être de la mêlée." The most troublous epochs are battles for the ideal, even at their worst moments. The only way to resist the destructive fatality of Nature is to strive for an amelioration of the lot of the human race. In all this, the texture of which is occasionally a little stretched when it is made to cover newspaper articles on the lighting of Paris or a show of prize pigeons, M. Clemenceau displays his eager wish to subordinate all his writing to a set of philosophical ideas. He has always held that the general impulses on which our daily existence depends reach us through the channels of thought. He is, therefore, a philosopher by determination, and he bases his own intellectual system on Pasteur and Spencer, on Darwin and J. S. Mill, on Taine and Renan. I have already spoken of the immense influence evidently exercised on Clemenceau by Renan's early and least ripe work *L'Avenir de la Science*. No doubt it was the reading of that remarkable book which led Clemenceau, already biassed in favour of materialism, to transfer to science all the passion which an earlier generation, and since his middle age a later generation, gave to religion. It must be understood that he does not belong in habit of mind or intellectual aspiration to the characteristic French tradition of to-day.

The great merit of M. Clemenceau, in the agitated years when he wielded a pen that was like a rapier, consisted in his fearless and disdainful audacity. He fought in literature exactly as he has always fought in politics, with the air of one who had no wish to conciliate his opponent, but always to browbeat him, to crush him by the weight of his argument, and then run him through the body with his irony. When we turn over the pages of his books, which suffer an inevitable loss from the fugitive nature of the themes on which they mainly expatiate, we are astounded at the ceaseless agility of the lucid, restless brain of the man. He is an acrobat, incessantly flinging himself with aerial lightness into some new impossible position. An article a day for twenty-five years—what an expenditure of vital force that seems to sum up; and yet to-day, at the age of seventy-eight, the indefatigable brain and body seem as elastic as ever! The fullness of the material in M. Clemenceau's articles has always been a matter of amazement to those who know how much clever journalism is of the kind Francisque Sarcey described when he said, "You may turn the tap as much as you please; if the cistern is empty, nothing but wind comes out!" But M. Clemenceau seemed always full, and copious as was the output, the reader had always the impression that there was much more behind.

We may regret that while the great politician was chiefly engaged in writing, namely between 1893 and 1903, he was obliged by circumstances to expend so much of his experience and his condition upon occasional issues. In turning over his pages, we must not forget that he wrote, not in the calm retirement of a study, but out in the street, in the midst of the battle and heat of the day. His insatiable appetite for action drove him forth into the madding crowd. There has always been something encyclopædic about his passion for knowledge, for practical acquaintance with the actual practice of life. He has cultivated a genius for observation, and his feverish career

The Writings of M. Clemenceau

has been spent in pursuing knowledge day by day, without giving himself time to arrange the trophies of his pursuit. He has published no systematic scheme of his philosophy, but has left us to gather it as well as we may from his prefaces, and most of all from *Le Grand Pan*. As an author, we may sum him up as the latest, and in some respects the most vigorous and agile, of the disciples of the Encyclopædists. Like them, through a long and breathless career, he has ceaselessly striven to struggle upward into the light of knowledge.

1919.

A VISIT TO THE FRIENDS OF IBSEN

IN the summer of 1872 I received special leave from the Principal Librarian of the British Museum to visit Denmark and Norway for the purpose of reporting on the state of current literature in those countries. Of my Danish experiences I have given an account in my book called *Two Visits to Denmark* (Smith, Elder & Co., 1911); but hitherto I have not published any of my Norwegian adventures. I am led to do so now, in consequence of a letter which I have just received from Rektor Frederik Ording, of Holmestrand, who is engaged on a biographical study of "Henrik Ibsen's Ungdomsvenner," and who tells me that it has become almost impossible to obtain information about the particular group of men of letters whom I conversed with more than forty-five years ago. They are all long since dead, and no one survives who recollects them in their prime. No one—so it appears—but me! The fact is a solemnizing one. I feel like the Moses of the poet :

> Je vivrai donc toujours puissant et solitaire?
> Laissez-moi m'endormir du sommeil de la terre ;

but before I am allowed by Norway to do that, it seems that I am called upon to disgorge my recollections. They are, I am afraid, though founded on a full journal, rather slight.

Ibsen, as is well known, was at that time, and had long been, an exile from his native country, where his plays were ill received and his character subjected to a great deal of stupid insult. But there was a small circle of his early friends who remained true to the devotion which his genius had inspired in them. When I was in Copenhagen, it

Aspects and Impressions

was impressed upon me that these men formed the real Norway, the fine flower of Norse culture and intelligence, and it was to them that I took introductions. They were mainly jurists, archæologists and historians, whose studies into the annals of their country had given them a determination to support existing institutions. They were called "Conservatives," and by the radical press were treated as though their ideas were desperately retrograde. But in any other country but Norway, fifty years ago, they would have been called advanced Liberals. They desired to introduce broad and sweeping reforms, and they were particularly desirous to follow the example of England. If I understand their position aright, they were rather Constitutionalists than Conservatives, for their first idea always was to bring their views into line with the Constitution.

A short time before my visit, the barrier which surrounded and isolated the group of men of whom I speak had been emphasized by the development of the Venstre, the national radical party, which was urged on and supported by the Peasants' party. The debates in the Storthing in 1871 and 1872 had been very bitter, and public opinion was sharply, but unequally, divided over the burning question of the admission of ministers to the national assembly. Without going further into the obscurity of foreign politics, it is enough to say here that the group into which I was for a short time admitted as an indulged and attentive guest, had the hope that, with all its talents and knowledge, it would be called upon to take over the government of the country. It was thought that Aschehoug would oust the radical Sverdrup as the next Prime Minister. The reign of constitutionalism would begin; the peasant leaders would be sent back to their farms; and Norway would open a splendid period of conservative re-action. In this, the friends were supported by the most powerful newspaper of the country, *Morgenbladet,* which like themselves had long been frankly democratic, but had recently taken a very strong line in opposition to the Left. *Morgenbladet* was boisterously

A Visit to the Friends of Ibsen

attacked by *Dagbladet,* the rival newspaper, edited by Samuel Bætzmann, a bearded and very tall young man, who was pointed out to me in the street, with execration and contempt, by Jakob Lökke.

The hope of my friends was not realized. The whole tendency of Norwegian life was in the opposite direction, and a few days after I left Christiania, the death of King Carl had the effect of still further encouraging the Liberals. The group I had known were swept out of public life by the tide of radicalism, and suffered the obscuration which awaits the unsuccessful politician. Now, as it appears, when all passion has died down, there is a great curiosity about men whose talents and accomplishments, as well as their high patriotism, were an asset in the civilization of Norway at a critical moment. Hence, when it is almost too late, and when I am left the only survivor, I am appealed to for my recollections, pale and slight as they must be.

Late, then, in the summer of 1872 I arrived in Christiania, armed with cards and letters of introduction from friends in Copenhagen, and with a recommendation from Tennyson to Professor Ludwig Kristensen Daa, who had been very civil to the poet when he visited Norway. I arrived in the midst of the excitement caused by the recent celebration of the 1,000 years' festival, and in particular we crossed Prince Oskar who was returning to Stockholm from being present at Haugesund on that occasion, when he had unveiled a colossal symbolic statue of Harald Fairhair. Before my first evening closed in, I hastened to explore the length of the city right up Carl Johans Gade to the New Park; and in the Eidsvoldplads, a square opposite the Storthing House, I received a little shock, for gazing up at the new bronze statue of Harald Fairhair, I saw the drapery rise and flutter in the wind. This was not a replica of the national statue at Haugesund, but an independent design, put up in lath and plaster to see whether public opinion approved of it. It occurred to me afterwards that it was the symbol of the stalwart conservatism of the group of friends of whom I am about to speak, who

trusted to their heroic attitude to impress public opinion—
and failed.

Early next morning I called on Jakob Lökke (1829-
1881), who was head-master of the Christiania Cathedral
School, and the leading educational authority in Norway.
I had been able to be of some assistance to Lökke in
London during the year 1871, and his hospitable and genial
acquaintance was now very valuable to me. Close to the
great church of Our Saviour, in the centre of the city, in
the first house on the left-hand side of the Stor Gade, Mr.
and Mrs. Lökke had an apartment on the third storey in
which they received a small, but extremely distinguished,
circle of guests. Lökke was pompous in manner and a
touchy man, but full of warmth and generosity under a
somewhat difficult surface. His hospitality to me, on this
occasion, was untiring, and it was wholly owing to him
that I was admitted to the remarkable group of Norse
Tories who were making so resolute and so vain a struggle
to stem the rising flood of radicalism. Lökke's "tredie
étage" in Stor Gade was a typical home of lost causes, and
the group of friends were all ardent supporters of Ibsen,
whose satirical temper was then looked upon askance by
the various popular parties.

The first person to whom Lökke presented me was
Emil Stang (born 1834), the son of the then prime
minister of Norway, Frederik Stang, and a leading
advocate. He became very cordial when he learned that
I was bent on introducing Ibsen to the English public,
and had begun to do so; and he told me that he held a
brief for the poet at that moment. It will be remembered
that Ibsen then resided in Dresden. Taking advantage
of this exile, a Danish publisher of the baser sort had
produced a pirated edition of the *Warriors of Helgeland,*
with an announcement that a similar reprint of *Madam
Inger at Osterraad* would follow. Stang laughed as he
told me of Ibsen's gigantic anger at this offence; he had
immediately put the matter into Stang's hands, and had
desired him to get a full indemnity from the Danish publisher. But it was the usual case of trying to bleed a

A Visit to the Friends of Ibsen

stone. The man would not even withdraw his edition, though no more was said of the projected piracy of *Madam Inger*. Mr. Stang told me that the case was still dragging through the courts; I never learned the result.

Lökke took me to the University Library to see the Librarian, Ludwig Daae (not to be confounded with Daa), who was born in 1834 and died in 1910. The visit was untimely, for Daae had not arrived, and only one single clerk was on duty. This man was ready to be friendly, but he was being bullied by the Principal Librarian of the University of Stralsund, a typical loud-voiced Prussian, to whom I took a violent dislike. The librarian was acquainted with Lökke and attached himself to us; he spoke with great contempt of the Library of the British Museum, which he said he knew very well. We proceeded to the Record Office, in order to see Mr. Michael Birkeland (1830-1897), the Master of the Rolls, of whom I shall have much to relate. The Record Office (Riksarkivet) was then in the same clump of buildings as the Storthing House. We did not find Birkeland in, but we found an even more illustrious person, J. E. W. Sars (1835-1915), who was already deep in the preparation of those works which have made him famous as the most philosophical of Norwegian historians. He was shortly after my visit appointed Professor of History in the University of Christiania.

My introduction to Ludwig Daae was only postponed. The next time I called at Lökke's house, a little shabby man with a beard, with woefully dishevelled hair and snuff-coloured old coat, was dancing a sort of lonely pirouette in the middle of the floor, while he talked. He stopped at my entrance, and Jakob Lökke, coming forward, presented me to him as to "the Librarian of the University, Ludwig Daae." "The author of that delightful *Gamle Kristiania*?" I asked. "Ah, do you know my book?" he said, and seemed pleased. I felt very much drawn to Ludwig Daae from the first, and he spoke Norwegian so plainly and elegantly that it was particularly easy for me to follow him. All through the rest of my

Aspects and Impressions

visit to Christiania I had the benefit of his kindliness and wit, his ingenuousness and his fund of knowledge. His book, *Gamle Kristiania,* a picturesque series of essays on the history of the city up to 1800, was familiar to me, and I had written a long review of it in the *Spectator* for Richard Holt Hutton, in which I had ventured to say that it would be impossible for any one in future to attempt a history of modern Norwegian affairs without the help of Mr. Daae's admirable book.

The name of this gentleman offered much difficulty, because, by a very odd coincidence, there were at that moment three unrelated persons whose names were in sound identical. There was Ludwig K. Daa, and there were two Ludwig Daaes, my friend, and a politician whom I did not meet. Norwegians themselves found the identity of the three very confusing. My Ludwig Daae had begun his literary career with an ecclesiastic history of the diocese of Throndhjem, published in 1863, and had gradually extended his range from church to general history, but his gift really lay in the picturesquely biographical. He had just been made lector in æsthetics in the Cathedral School when I saw him, but he held this but a very short time, being soon after my visit appointed Professor of History at the University.

I had now the honour of being admitted every day to the company of Daae and his friends, and it was clearly explained to me that they formed a compact and still influential body of resistance to the subversive policy of Björnson, Sverdrup and the terrible peasant Jaabæk, whom they regarded with peculiar apprehension. Hans Christian Andersen had given me a note of introduction to Björnson, and in spite of the objections of my new friends, I found that I could not resist the temptation to use it. Accordingly I went to the house in Munke-damsveien which Björnson shared with the philosopher G. V. Lyng (1827-1884) whom I had met in Denmark. They occupied a small house in a long suburban lane on the edge of the city. I had been told that the poet was very formidable, and as I waited in the hall, I heard him

A Visit to the Friends of Ibsen

growling "Saa! saa? saa!" over the card and note I had sent in. I quaked, but I plunged; I was ushered into a pretty room with trellised windows, where a large and even burly man (Björnson was then under forty), who was sitting astride the end of a narrow sofa, rose vehemently to receive me. His long limbs, his athletic frame, and especially his remarkably forcible face, surrounded by a mane of wavy brown hair, and illuminated by full blue eyes behind flashing spectacles, gave an instant impression of physical vigour. He was truculently cordial, and lifted his ringing tones in civil conversation. Resuming his singular attitude astride the sofa, he entered affably into a loud torrent of talk, lolling back, shaking his great head, suddenly bringing himself up into a sitting posture to shout out, with a palm pressed upon either knee, some question or statement.

His full and finely modulated voice, with his clear enunciation, greatly aided his not a little terrified visitor in appreciating his remarks, but he spoke at great speed, and it strained the attention of a foreigner to follow his somewhat florid volubility. He expressed himself highly pleased with the reception his romances had received in England, but seemed surprised that his dramas were not known. He recommended to me a new viking-play, called *Sigurd Jorsalfar*, which he had just sent to press, and which had been refused "though with the loveliest music by Grieg ever heard out of a dream" by the Royal Theatre in Copenhagen, a repulse which Björnson flatly attributed to the malignity of the manager, Molbech. He promised to send me to London a copy of *Sigurd Jorsalfar* as soon as it was published, and he was so amiable as to keep his word.

This little adventure in the headquarters of the opposition was not at all well regarded in Stor Gade. Accordingly I was taken, as a counterbalancing influence, to be presented at his country parsonage of Vest Aker to the old poet and folk-lorist Jörgen Moe (1813-1882). Lökke and Daae were my companions on this visit to the celebrated collector, in common with Asbjörnsen, of the so universally admired Norse legends and fairy-tales. The situation of Vest Aker is magnificent; as we drove past the little church to the court of the "præstegaard," the whole of the head-waters of the Christiania Fjord wound and sparkled below us, golden in the blue circle of the hills. Moe, dressed in clerical black, with the white ruff round his throat, greeted us delicately. He was a charming man, with his soft voice and beautiful stag-like eyes; a perfectly gracious and venerable figure, not incapable, however, of receiving a mild excitement from the fact that his poems were presently to be introduced to the English public. Almost immediately after my visit Jörgen Moe was appointed Bishop of Christianssand. As we came back from Vest Aker, my guides showed me the grave of the biographer and bibliographer, Botten-Hansen (1824-1869), and the famous grotto of Wergeland, once in the country, but, already in 1872, touched by the outskirts of the city. As we were crossing the streets in the neighbourhood of the Uranienborg Church, a pale old face appeared for a moment at an upper window. Daae said this was the house where Johan Sebastian Welhaven (1807-1873) was being nursed, and he thought that it was Welhaven we had seen. Lökke did not think it was, so that I shall never know whether I did, or did not, catch a glimpse of the illustrious and the dying author of *Norges Dæmring*. My companions were much amused, and I think gratified, by my eager interest in all these literary associations.

I now left the capital for a little tour by myself in Ringeriget and Gudbrandsdalen, where I had an invitation to meet Asbjörnsen, with whom I had corresponded from London. He had been staying at Ringebo, at the parsonage of the Dean (*Provst*) of Gudbrandsdalen, Dr. Neils Christian Hald (1808-1885). I did not, however, go thither directly, but at the advice of Daae, posted over the hills to Drammen, a magnificent drive by a very circuitous route. Daae had given me letters of introduction; he had passed his youth in that town, and was Professor of History there until he was brought to Christiania. His

A Visit to the Friends of Ibsen

friends received me with generous hospitality, and among the merchant princes of Drammen I found a greater appearance of luxury than I happened to meet with in the capital. When I finally reached Ringebo, I was disappointed to find that Asbjörnsen had been obliged to leave for Romsdalen, on his duties as Torvmester or Forester-General. I was equally unlucky in an attempt to see the poet Kristoffer Jansen (1841-1899) at his schoolhouse at Fykse-in-Gausdal, for he was spending the holidays at Tromsö, in Finmark. After a most enjoyable stay in the picturesque parsonage of the kind Halds, I returned to Christiania.

On the 7th of August I was back in Stor Gade, and was helping Lökke with the notes to a school-book in English literature which he was just publishing; afterwards we called on the Hellenist, Frederik Ludwig Vibe (1803-1881), who was Librarian of the Cathedral School, and a great ally of Lökke and Daae. I was shown his translation of Æschylus into Norse. My acquaintance with the group of Ibsen's friends was now further extended, for on the evening of the next day (August 8), Ludwig Daae asked me to supper, and, when I arrived, I found, beside the host, Michael Birkeland and Dr. Oluf Rygh.

I have already mentioned Birkeland's position at the Rolls Office, which he had entered in 1852, and now commanded. He was not, I think, ambitious of literary fame, and he had at that time published, of an original kind, little except pamphlets. His best-known work was his minutely executed *Reports of the earliest sessions of the Storthing,* but this was only a part of his multifarious research into the whole political history of the country. Birkeland was the life and soul of the *Norske historiske Forening* (Norwegian Historical Society), which then and since did so much for the science of history. He was constantly publishing for the government inedited matter from the very copious archives under his charge. Underneath the mask of the archivist he barely concealed a burning political ambition to be a part of the new constitutional life of Norway. The Master of the Rolls was one of the most attractive men I met in Scandinavia. He was still, in early middle age, very handsome, well set-up, with a fine head excellently poised above broad shoulders, and with brilliant, dancing eyes. The fault of Norwegians in that day was their deadly seriousness, and their excessive sensitiveness to the slightest indication of criticism. But Birkeland was superior to this local weakness, and was genial, without the least pomposity. The fourth member of our party, Oluf Rygh (1833-1899), was united with Birkeland in his devotion to archæology. He also had at that time published very little, but I was told that his investigations were of the highest value, as indeed they amply proved to be. He was the bosom-friend of Birkeland, with whom he formed a singular contrast, being as reserved as the other was effusive, and a small, squat figure, with a round bald head and a bare face, horny and spectacled, which reminded my pert fancy of the shell of a crab.

Daae's house, where we met, was in the country, to the west of Christiania, on the Drammensvej, and close to the sea, with a fine view across the fjord to the royal palace of Oskarshal. There was much conversation at supper about politics, and my companions were emphatic in their conviction that the only hope for a healthy development of the Norwegian nation was a return to conservative methods. Daae spoke with deep resentment of the "fanatical measures of the Radical party," and with horror of the present leader Sören Jaabæk (born 1814), who had just become very prominent owing to his being refused Holy Communion by his parish priest, Pastor Lassen, as a protest against his republican views. My friends thought that the incumbent of Lyngdal had behaved with courage and propriety in "fencing the table" against him. When the meal was concluded, Birkeland proposed my health, and, standing up in the Norse fashion, made a little speech. He said "Englishmen often come to us that they may climb our mountains or fish in our lakes, but it is rare indeed for a young man of letters to visit us that he may investigate what is most dear to us, our native

A Visit to the Friends of Ibsen

literature, the labour of our hearts and our heads." He also spoke at length with regard to the 1,000 years' festival, which appeared to occupy the thoughts of the whole group.

We all came away together, Daae accompanying us to the boundary of the city. At this western end, Christiania then (1872) consisted of very new and fantastic villas whose inhabitants, Daae told me, had never got over the affront which the poet Welhaven had paid them of calling their suburb Snobopolis : which name still stuck to it. It was midnight when we reached the heart of the city, and as the hour boomed forth from the Cathedral, Birkeland held me there in the great square while he discoursed on the history of the building, and on the vestiges of Catholic architecture in Norway.

On the 9th of August, I spent the morning with Lökke in his study, and then we paid a visit to L. K. Daa (1809-1877), the ethnographer and archæologist. I have said that even Norwegians were easily confused between Daae and Daa, and they escaped from the dilemma by calling the younger "Bibliothekaren " and the elder "Grænskeren," the title of the newspaper he had edited. Daa, to whom I presented Tennyson's message, was extremely gracious, and he took me over to the Ethnological Museum, of which he was Director, and showed me some objects recently come to him from Lapland and Finland. Daa was a man of great eccentricity of appearance, tall and gaunt, with limbs flung wildly about, and his fine head recklessly bestrewn with disordered hair, grizzled and reddish. He was very restless and active, and talked English admirably ; he admitted to me that he was a full-blown Anglomaniac. Daa was very much pleased to hear from me that Tennyson recollected their meeting when the poet visited Norway in 1858; Daa had served on that occasion as Tennyson's cicerone. He told me that there was great trouble caused by the English poet's extreme near-sightedness, which made him unable to drive himself in the little karjol which was then the only mode of conveyance in the interior of Norway.

Aspects and Impressions

Next day, I went with Lökke to visit the lexicographer and inventor of the "landsmaal," Ivar Aasen (1813-1896), who lived in one little room, containing a bed, two chairs and a few shelves of linguistic books. He has exercised an immense influence on the language and literature of his country. I found Aasen a prematurely shrivelled little man, with a parchment face, thin, shy and nervous. In conversation he was dull, until Lökke spoke about philology, when his eyes began to sparkle and his cheeks to flush. He talked, then, quite fast, but with a curious inward manner of speech; I confess I could not understand what he was saying.

In the afternoon Lökke and Birkeland took me for a long drive to Frognersæteren, a cottage high up in the mountain above Christiania, whence there is a magnificent view over the whole valley, and even to the Swedish frontier. The fjord, though seven miles away, seems at our feet, and is visible as far down as Moss. Up at the sæter we were received by Professor Torkel Aschehoug (1822-1909), who had been so kind as to wish that I should be presented to him. Aschehoug was the leading jurist of Norway, perhaps of Scandinavia, at that time. His great book on the Laws of Norway, which was appearing in slow instalments, contained in a form never before approached the history and the essence of the national constitution. He had been for a quarter of a century professor of civil law at the University of Christiania; he had taken up, and pushed much farther, the investigations of J. R. Keyser, when that eminent jurist died in 1864. But the extraordinary respect with which Aschehoug was regarded in the group of friends was founded on other qualities than were included in his scientific reputation. He had been drawn more and more definitely into practical politics; for the last four years he had been the leading member of the Storthing for Christiania. I was told that he was "the coming man," the heaven-born leader of the constitutional party which was about to reorganize Norway, and drive back the onset of the horde of radicals and peasants. I was told to observe Aschehoug, for I should live

A Visit to the Friends of Ibsen

to see him the greatest politician in the North of Europe.

When we found him at the sæter, my companions greeted him with a mixture of warm affection and deep respect. He reminded me, in the eyes and mouth, and in his general bearing, of Mr. Gladstone. Aschehoug was very polite to me, but I found him alarming, and was glad that he mainly talked politics with Birkeland. In the evening Birkeland, whose kindness to me was untiring, took me across to the eastern side of Christiania, to Oslo, the city which was destroyed to build the new capital. He showed me what he believed to be the sites of the mediæval palace and cathedral; and, so far as he could judge, the exact scene of the great battle between Haakon and Skule, which Ibsen paints in his *Kongsemnerne*. It was thrilling to go over the vestiges of the ancient city with so enthusiastic and so learned a guide as Birkeland. As it grew late, we supped together at a restaurant, and then Birkeland, in very high spirits, declared he would show me " the night-side " of Christiania. However, we saw nothing very exciting or amusing.

Of the subsequent days of my visit to Christiania, whence I returned to Hull towards the end of August, I find nothing particular to relate. My last evening was spent at the Lökkes', in company with Daae, Birkeland and a very lively Mr. Thoresen, who was a near relative of Ibsen and related amusing anecdotes of the poet's manners. Lökke went down to the quay with me next morning, and stood waving his hat as the "Scotia" slipped down the fjord.

FAIRYLAND AND A BELGIAN ARIOSTO

IT has often been said—it was said in a well-known passage by the elder Disraeli—that in order to appreciate the beauty of fairyland we must make ourselves as little children listening to the wondrous tales of a nurse. But there seems to be a fallacy contained in this explanation of the spell. It cannot be contrived. No sedate, crafty, timid old man of the world can make himself as a little child merely that he may enjoy certain ancient poetry in a melodious stanza. Nor, on the other hand, is it obvious that real children, especially children of the modern sort, possess that ductile *naïveté*, that breathless and delicious credulity, which fairyland demands. I believe, and I speak not without observation, that children, as a rule, like stories best which deal with such themes as dogs that run after ducks, and grown up people that tumble out of motors. They like their tales to be realistic, rather hard, entirely within their experience. Hans Christian Andersen, in his *eventyr*—so falsely translated "fairy-tales"—took advantage of this fact and made a world-wide success by inventing stories in which playthings and articles of furniture and animals come to life and act on the conventional principles of society. That is what children like. They have been so short a time among us that the banalities of experience are still fresh to them, and nothing so amusing as what is pure matter-of-fact.

We may be quite sure that *The Faerie Queene*, which is the main classic of this sort of art in the world's literature, was not written for children. The ordinary infant would be unspeakably bewildered and bored by the visit of Duessa to the Lady of Night, and by the exploits of

Aspects and Impressions

Arthegal and Talus. It might take a faint pleasure in Una being followed by the Lion, as Mary was by the little Lamb; and the fight between St. George and the Dragon (where Spenser appears almost at his worst) might arrest wondering attention. But what is incomparable in Spenser is exactly what would fail to amuse a child. We may be quite sure that it was no audience from the nursery which the poet sought to fascinate. Yet it is true that his poetry appeals only to the child at heart. What we have to do is to define for ourselves what we mean by a child at heart, and we shall soon perceive that the object of our thoughts is not, in the literal sense, a child at all.

Perhaps youth rather than childhood is the image we require. With the advance out of infancy into adolescence, the mystery of existence first becomes palpable and visible to the fingers and the eyes of those who are born to enjoy it. We fall into an error, however, if we imagine that it is given to every one who pleases to arrive at this blissful condition of wonder. The world is very old, and it is troubled about many things; it is full of tiresome exigencies and solemn frivolities. The denizens of it are, as a rule, incapable of seeing or conceiving wonders. If the Archangel Michael appeared at noonday to an ordinary member of the House of Commons, the legislator would mistake his celestial visitant for an omnibus conductor. He would rejoice at having sufficient common sense and knowledge of the world to make so intelligent an error. But those who are privileged to walk within the confines of fairyland are not of this class. They are members of a little clan who still share the adolescence of the world; for, as this world is, in the main, dusty, dry, old, and given to fussing about questions of finance, and yet has nooks where the air is full of dew and silence, so among men there are still always a few who bear no mark upon their foreheads, and move undistinguished in the crowd, in whom, nevertheless, the fairies still confide.

It will be a surprise to many, and it may be a painful surprise, to learn that there are fathers of families, persons "engaged in the City," and holding reputable appoint-

Fairyland and a Belgian Ariosto

ments, who faithfully believe in magical princesses and in fays that dance by moonlight. These persons form the audience in whom Spenser—as, in other times and other climes, such poets as Ariosto and Camoens—seek and find their devotees. It is a fact that there are people of a later age who are still what we call "children in heart," whose hearts are bold, whose judgment is free, whose inner eye is limpid and bright. These men and women are sensitive still, although the searching, grinding wave of the world has gone over them. They live, in spite of all conventional experience, in a state of suspended credulity. They are ready for any amazement. They nourish, persistently, a desire to wander forth beyond the possibilities of experience, to enjoy the impossible, and to invade the inaccessible. Life for them, in spite of the geographers and the disenchanting encyclopædias, and that general suffusion of knowledge (upon all of which we congratulate ourselves)—life, in spite of all these, is still the vast forest, mapped out, indeed, but by them and theirs untraced.

Persons of this fortunate temperament store up an endless stock of good faith wherewith to face the teller of wonderful tales. And of all those to whom they listen, still, after three hundred years, Spenser is the most irresistible enchanter. It has always been admitted that his poetry is the most "poetical" that can be met with; that is to say, that it is the least mingled with elements which are not of the very essence of poetry. More than all other writers, Spenser takes us out of our everyday atmosphere into a state of things which could not be foreseen by any cleverness of our own reflection. He is easily supreme in the cosmogony of his enchantments. He confessed that his verse was no "matter of just memory," and it is evident that he did not wish it to be. He simply resigned himself to the exquisite pleasure of being lost in the mazes of a mysterious and fabulous woodland.

The poets, in successive ages, have delighted in bearing witness to this witchery of *The Faerie Queene*. There is no instance of this more pleasingly expressed, nor more appropriate to our argument, than that of Cowley, who

Aspects and Impressions

says, in his delicious essay *Of Myself:* "There was wont to lie in my mother's parlour (I know not by what accident, for she herself never in her life read any book but of devotion), but there was wont to lie Spenser's Works. This I happened to fall upon (before I was twelve years old), and was infinitely delighted with the stories of the knights and giants and monsters and brave houses, which I found everywhere there—though my understanding had little to do with all this—and by degrees with the tinkling of the rhyme and dance of the numbers." We may doubt whether the child Cowley had not more of a man's taste than the man Cowley had of the heart of a child; but, at all events, he entered with exactly the proper spirit into that miraculous country where "birds, voices, instruments, winds, waters, all agree." And it is in this spirit that hundreds of the elect have read the marvellous poem in successive ages, and will continue to read it until time itself has passed away.

The Faerie Queene is not "about" any thing. There is nothing of serious import to be deduced from its line of argument. The subject wanders hither and thither, awakening fitful melodies in the brain of its creator, as the wind does on the strings of an Æolian harp. The music swells and declines, the harmonies gather to a loud ecstasy or dwindle to a melancholy murmur, under the caprices of a spirit that cannot be discerned and that seems to be under no intellectual control. In saying this, I am not ignorant of Spenser's protestation of a moral purpose, nor do I charge him with the smallest insincerity for having written that apologetic letter to Sir Walter Raleigh, in which he makes what he calls "a pleasing analysis " of the way in which the poem illustrates "the twelve private moral virtues, as Aristotle hath devised." It was necessary that he should have a skeleton of meaning underneath his elaborate dream, not merely for the sake of contemporary decency, lest in that strenuous age he should be cast forth as one that cumbered the ground, but for the sake of his art as well, which needed a steady basis of material as much as a picture needs its canvas or a statue its marble.

Fairyland and a Belgian Ariosto

Moreover, *The Faerie Queene* must celebrate Queen Elizabeth, just as "Orlando Furioso" must praise the House of Este. It was in feudal societies, under the protection of princes, that these romantic enterprises had to be conducted, if they were conducted at all. There was a pleasant confusion, like that of coloured strands in a solemn tapestry, between the laudation of the Sovereign and the celebration of the virtues. Sometimes the monarch was not so virtuous as the poet could have wished; sometimes his Court was as little like fairyland as was humanly possible. That only added to the skill of the poet; that only added rainbow colours to the fabric of the invention.

Then there was always the allegory, with which, in fact, anything on earth could be connected, in the course of which not only could no compliment be excessive, but no attribution could be so certain that it was not able, under pressure, to be denied. Positive persons, in our rash age, do much profane the allegory, which, nevertheless, is essential to all fairy poetry. Without it, what would become of *The Romaunt of the Rose,* or of *The Dream of Poliphile;* what, even, of the *Divine Comedy?* Hazlitt merrily says that people "are afraid of allegory, as if it would bite them. . . . If they do not meddle with the allegory, the allegory will not meddle with them." The fact is, persons who hate fairy poetry make the allegory an excuse for their aversion, which is like saying that you hate the flavour of olives because they have stones in them.

It is a peculiarity of the romance of fairyland that it never introduces us to fairies. Nothing is so prosaic as a fairy, seen in the broad light of Early Victorian illustration. A little being in short skirts and sandals, standing on one toe on the tip of a rosebud, with a spangle in her sleek hair and a wand in her taper fingers—nothing is more repulsive to the Muses. But the whole secret of the great fairy poets is that they are engaged in searching for fairies without ever suffering the disenchantment of finding them. There are none, I think, in the broad pages

of Spenser; even, by a beautiful pleasantry, the Fairie
Queene herself being entirely absent throughout the poem,
at all events as we now possess it.

The personages in *The Faerie Queene,* noble and
miraculous as they are, are not of the fairy persuasion at
all. They wander through the forests in the hope of
coming upon these supernatural denizens, but they never
succeed in doing so. The Holy Grail appeared far oftener
to the Knights of the Round Table than a real fairy was
perceived by Paradel or Blandamour. These men of
chivalry were much interested in the subject, but, as a
rule, they were poorly instructed. It was in the House
of Temperance that Sir Guyon found the book, that hight
Antiquity of Faeryland, which seems to have been a sort
of *Who's Who,* or *Complete Peerage* of the supernatural
world. He flew to the perusal of it, and wherever in it

> "he greedily did look,
> Offspring of Elves and Fairies there he found,"

but he found no examples on the

> "island, waste and void,
> That floated in the midst of that great lake,"

(where it is impossible not to believe that Mr. W. B. Yeats
would have been more successful).

A critic has said that nothing is closer to an intensely
lyrical song than a violently burlesque story. The sense
of beauty immediately evoked by the one is suggested,
conversely, or in the way of topsy-turvy, by the other.
This principle had been introduced into literature—or at
least into modern literature, for the Greeks had it illustrated in Aristophanes—a hundred years before the time
of Spenser, by the *Morgante Maggiore* of Pulci, where
Orlando, the pink of romantic chivalry, comes into collision
with certain "immeasurable giants" and other wild ab-
surdities. The atmosphere of that poem is perfectly
heroic :

Fairyland and a Belgian Ariosto

Twelve Paladins had Charles in court, of whom
  The wisest and most famous was Orlando;
Him traitor Gan conducted to the tomb
  In Roncesvalles, as the villain planned to,
While the horn rang so loud, and knelled the doom
  Of their sad rout, though he did all knight can do;
And Dante in his Comedy has given
To him a happy seat with Charles in heaven.

But, in another turn, we find this splendid Orlando
lifting his sword to give his beautiful lady, Aldabelle, a
smack on the face with the flat of it. This is burlesque,
and Pulci seems to have been the inventor of the *genre*.
He was followed by Boiardo, who wrote of Orlando in
love, and by Ariosto, who described the madness of
Orlando, and by a multitude of other sixteenth century
poets, who described, in this epic mixture of lyricism and
burlesque, various other episodes in the life of the hero.
It was from them, from these Italian precursors, whom
Spenser had read so carefully, that he borrowed the ugly
and violent elements which he introduces, so much to the
scandal of some critics, into the embroidered texture of
The Faerie Queene.

In all this, however, which is very characteristic of the
romance of fairy poetry, we do wrong to be scandalized.
The ugly things, like the misfortunes of Braggadochio
and his Squire (in *The Faerie Queene*), and the fantastic
things, like the journey of Alstolfo to the Moon to recover
the wits of Orlando (in Ariosto), are just as necessary to
our pleasure as the description of the Bower of Bliss, or
of Angelica's flight from Rinaldo. They are all part of
that desire to escape from the obvious and the commonplace features of life which inspires this whole class of
poetry. Those who are naturally conscious that life runs
at a dead level desire to heighten it, and whether this is
done in the lyric spirit or in the burlesque, or in both at
once, matters very little. The essential thing is to lift
the spirit and quicken the pulse.

The only consolation which comes to people of this

fatigued and wistful temperament is that which they receive from a persuasion of the reality of what is marvellous and incredible. Like the theologians, such readers believe certain things to be true because it is impossible that they should be true. They do not ask why, or where, or when, the incidents happened; they are satisfied with the vision and with all its chimerical wonders. In their dreams they see Belphœbe hurrying through the woodland, her hair starred as thick as snow by the petals of the wild roses her tempestuous flight has shaken down upon it, and they do not ask what she represents, nor whither she hastens, nor her relation to fact and history:

> And in her hand a sharp boar-spear she held,
>   And at her back a bow and quiver gay,
> Stuft with steel-headed darts, wherewith she quelled
>   The savage beasts in her victorious play,
>   Knit with a golden bauldrick, which forelay
> Athwart her snowy breast.

Who needs to ask whither Belphœbe goes, or what she means? She is a vision created for the deep contentment of those in whom the longing for noble images and uplifted desires and generous, childlike dreams is perennial.

Critics like to assume that the enthusiasm which breeds this kind of chivalrous poetry is dead and buried in the classics. They no more expect to see a new *Faerie Queene* published than to hear of a new dodo inhabiting the plantations of the interior of Madagascar. But in literature it is always unsafe to say that a door is closed for ever; if we are rash enough to make such an assertion, it is sure to fly open in our faces. It was a commonplace of criticism ten years ago that the epic would never reappear in literature, and behold Mr. Doughty presents us with a *Dawn in Britain* which is as long as the *Lusiads* would be if *Paradise Lost* were tacked on to the tail of it. Last week I read in a very positive volume that the Pastoral can never revisit the cold glimpses of a world that has exchanged its interest in shepherds for a solicitude about

Fairyland and a Belgian Ariosto

miners and chauffeurs. My instant reflection on reading
that opinion was to wonder how soon a young poet
would publish a fresh set of Bucolics, with the contest of
Damaetas and Menalcas set forth to a new tune upon the
Pans' pipes.

For this reason I cannot say that I was astonished,
although much interested, to find a young man—and, I
venture to think, a young man of some genius—reviving
the old music of the magic woodland, which had seemed
to be dead, or closed, since the seventeenth century. It
is a wish to make his work a little known to English readers
which has led me to venture on some remarks to-day about
the Romance of Fairyland. M. Albert Mockel is a
Fleming, and if M. Octave Mirbeau, in a celebrated article
in the Paris *Figaro,* had not called M. Maeterlinck the
Belgian Shakespeare, I should have been tempted to
describe M. Mockel as the Belgian Spenser. I may go
so far as to call him a Belgian Ariosto. M. Mockel has
not enjoyed the same popularity as his eminent country-
man; perhaps he had no Octave Mirbeau to immortalize
him with a gorgeous paradox. But in 1891 M. Mockel,
who must then have been very youthful, published a
poem, entitled *Chantefable,* which was enough to inspire
great hopes of his future among not a few judicious
readers. He has done nothing, in my judgment, to
justify those hopes so fully as he now has in the volume
he has published, called, *Contes pour les Enfants d'hier,*
with ingenious illustrations by M. Auguste Donnay.
These illustrations are very clever, although they would
never have been drawn had it not been for Aubrey
Beardsley's *Morte d'Arthur* (1893). M. Donnay is skilful,
and he emulates Beardsley's wonderful, pure line, without
always perfectly attaining to it.

But the book itself is of a more classic cast, and deserves
longer attention. Here, to quite a remarkable extent, we
find the old stateliness of the fabulous society, the old
ceremonial procession of wonderful events and incredible
people. Here, once more, we enter a world as audaciously
designed as Ariosto's, as intricately splendid as Spenser's.

Aspects and Impressions

Here, again, is what a critic of *The Faerie Queene* has called "the inexhaustible succession of circumstance, fantasy, and incident." The vulgarity of present existence is buried under such a panoply and magnificence of fable that the grown-up children, the blessed *enfants d'hier*, can forget and ignore it.

It would be tedious to retell briefly, in poor words, the brilliant stories which owe so much to the solemn and highly-coloured language in which they are deliberately narrated. But I cannot refrain from giving an outline of the last of them, *The Island of Rest.* In M. Mockel's gallery there is no more magnificent figure than that of Jerzual, Prince of Urmonde. We may call him the Roland of our Belgian Boiardo. All the world is aware of the mysterious end of Prince Jerzual; he went away over the waves of the sea, and nothing was ever heard of him again. But only M. Mockel knows what happened, and he has now consented to reveal it.

Jerzual had loved the ineffable Alise, Princess of Avigorre, and to secure her love he had vowed that he would offer her the suzerainty of the Heights, a mysterious country surrounded by peaks of silver and crystal. Unfortunately, though he searched the habitable globe, the whereabouts of this marvellous region escaped him. One day, in despair, as he rode his magic horse, Bellardian, he came to the edge of a cliff, where the ocean stretched at his feet. Tired of his vain adventures, Jerzual flung the reins on the mane of Bellardian, and spurred him onward. The obedient steed leaped the cliff, and descended on the surface of the waters, which undulated gently beneath him, but bore up both horse and rider. They galloped over the calm sea for hours and hours, for days and days, until at last a fairy island appeared on the horizon, and displayed, as they approached, a silver zone of pure peaks, lifted like a tiara high over the ring of green and golden verdure. This was the land of Jerzual's desire, but neither the white Bellardian nor his incomparable master succeeded in landing upon that exquisite shore without prolonged adventures, which it is not my business to recount.

Fairyland and a Belgian Ariosto

Suffice to say, that they sank in safety on the sands at last.

How they were discovered there by Aigueline, the cruel daughter of the Sea, and sole inhabitant of the island; how the heart of Jerzual fluctuated in the terrible dilemma between his present good fortune and his duty to the Princess; how staunch and uplifted poor Bellardian was, and how strange and pitiful his fate; how the enchantments of Aigueline were broken at last; and how, when the disillusioned Jerzual walked in frenzy upon the sands of the island shore, he saw the shallop of the Princess of Avigorre sail by, with banners flying from it which were not his, but those of his rival, Ellerion, Prince of Argilea; this, and much more, and all of it equally gorgeous and convincing, must be read in the delightful pages of M Mockel's *Contes pour les Enfants d'hier.*

SOME RECOLLECTIONS OF LORD WOLSELEY

THERE is at present no record of Lord Wolseley, who died just too recently to be included in the latest Supplement of the *Dictionary of National Biography*. His memory loiters in the limbo which always surrounds the famous dead for a few years after their decease. Then follow, in due course, the official Life and the selected correspondence; and so finally the monument is unveiled for the pigeons of the Press to perch upon. To my friends, Sir Frederick Maurice and Sir George Arthur, have been entrusted the duty of arranging the memoirs of our greatest modern soldier, and their work will be formidable, for the Great War, of which Wolseley, in flashes of genius, had prescience, has swept over us, and has confused the landmarks of our memories. I feel sure that they will bring judgment and discretion to their task, which is a noble one. But they will certainly, and properly, be inclined to concentrate their effort on the military aspects of their subject, since Lord Wolseley was a soldier before everything else, and so completely a soldier that other aspects must be dwarfed in contemplation of his military glory. These may easily, indeed, be excluded altogether, and I therefore venture to recall, before it is too late, certain scenes which I observed during a prolonged and delighted acquaintanceship, in which the sword ceased to be "vambrashed," as the Elizabethans used to say, and in which the great general was simply an amateur of letters, eager to talk about books and even ambitious to write them. I shall not fall into the error of describing him as a great author, but I think that it may be amusing to preserve some intellectual sketch of a

273

character essentially imposing in very different surroundings.

Lord Wolseley was not prominent before the world as
a man of letters, and I shall not pretend that he could
claim that particular distinction, though he wrote easily
and well. Of his best books I shall have something
presently to say. But I think it is known to only a very
few survivors that he had a predilection and even a passion
for literature, which he shared, I should think, with no man
of action of his time. He was an insatiate reader, and his
reading covered a surprising range. For a man to whom
life offered excitement and animation in almost every
direction, it was notable how much time he found to spare
for intellectual amusement. He attributed his love of
reading to the influence of his Irish mother. He said once
to me, "I would sooner live upon porridge in a book-
room than upon venison and truffles where books were
not," and this meant much from one who was by no means
indifferent to the truffles and the venison of life. The
curious thing is that this obsession with literature nowhere
peeps out in his published works, and is notably absent in
his autobiography, *The Story of a Soldier's Life,* where
we should particularly expect to find traces of it. For this
defect in the general portraiture of that book there are
reasons, upon which I may touch later on. It is a useful
chain of military records, but it is a portrait of its author
in full uniform, with cocked hat and sword. It was my
good fortune to see him always in mufti, and if I essay a
snapshot of him I am bound to show him with a book in
his hand.

My acquaintance with Lord Wolseley began in 1888,
and I owed it to a common friend whom I never cease to
deplore, the ever-ingenious Andrew Lang. I have forgotten how these two came together, but they had a great
appreciation of each other's company. Wolseley was now
just fifty-five, but he looked much younger, and he
flashed about as though the spirit of April still laughed at
him. The first thing which struck an observer on meeting him was that he had the gestures of a boy; the elastic

Some Recollections of Lord Wolseley

footstep, the abruptly vivid movements, one would almost say were those of a happy child. In 1888 Lord and Lady Wolseley were still inhabiting a small house in Hill Street, but immediately after I first knew them they moved to the Ranger's House in Greenwich Park, the scene for me of delightful memories during the next two years. Wolseley was at that time Adjutant-General of the Forces, under Stanhope, and afterwards Commander-in-Chief in Ireland under Campbell-Bannerman. He worked hard every day at the War Office, and came down to Greenwich in the afternoon like any civil servant or bank clerk. His life at that time was marked by the serene and unaffected simplicity which always seemed to me the cardinal feature of his personal character. Much in Wolseley had an appearance of inconsistency. For instance, it cannot be questioned that he demanded a great deal from those who worked under him professionally, nor that he was careful of his own prestige. But when he was released from his military work, he became the least assuming of mankind. Moreover—and this makes the attempt to paint him particularly difficult—he was not, to the public eye, conspicuous, as other great generals have been, through demeanour or appearance. I used often to be surprised, when we were walking together in the street, to notice how few people recognized him, although he was then at the height of his celebrity.

In September, 1889, when my wife and I were going over to the Continent, we observed a shortish gentleman, in tourist dress, pacing the deck of the steamer, and we said to each other: "Does not that man remind you of somebody?" Presently he stopped before us, smiling, and it was Wolseley. He was going alone to Metz, from which point he proposed to make a tour of personal observation round all the battlefields of 1870. He said that there were inconsistencies in the published accounts, and that he had meditated over them till it was impossible for him to rest until he had settled his difficulties by independent inspection. He told us not to say we had met him, and it was an example of that want of conspicuousness, which I have noted, that, although it was broad day-light, and he then one of the most famous figures in England, no one else did seem to recognize him. He had theories about the Franco-German campaign for which he sought confirmation. I begged him to let me know what the result might be, and so he wrote to me, from Bruns-wick, on October 4th :

I postponed writing to you until my tour round the battle-fields should have finished, as I could not tell what to write upon the subject until I had studied the ground. I need scarcely tell you that I knew the chief episodes of each great fight very well before I came abroad. The German account of the events is so full and truthful that no student of war has any excuse for ignorance. With that book, and maps and plans, I have carefully studied every phase of every battlefield from Sedan in the North to Strasburg in the South, and I find I could not write upon the subject without expressions of opinion that would be very unpleasant to many men now alive. The Germans outnumbered the French in nearly all those battles to a large extent, and though the French allowed them-selves to be surprised, and their leaders committed every possible mistake, the errors of the Germans were very glaring upon many occasions. Almost all their battles were not only fought in a manner entirely different from what was intended, but, in nearly every case, they were brought on without, and on some occasions contrary to, the positive orders and intentions of the Generals.

When I saw him at Greenwich soon after his return he spoke more plainly still. He said that he had found, to his great surprise, that the Germans, whose luck, he declared, had been incredible, had been very nearly defeated more than once or twice. He had been particularly excited by his inspection of the battlefield of Gravelotte. If that battle had not, he said, been won by what was really "a fluke," the day would have closed upon the German Army in about the most unfortunate position an army could possibly be placed in. All this struck me, ignorant of tactics as I am, as so very interesting that I entreated him to change his mind and write a complete record of his observations on the battlefields. But he said that the praise of German strategy had reached such a pitch of infatuation in England that he should be "accused of all sorts of things." Nevertheless, I pressed him to write down his experience, even if he kept it private. He finally promised that he would do so that winter, but I never heard any more about it. His last words were "I dare not publish my views," and presently he had to go off to Newcastle on military business, which quite diverted his thoughts. It must be observed that we trusted in those days wholly to German historians, and that the French account, which confirmed Lord Wolseley to the letter, was not published until ten years later.

It was while I was walking with him in Greenwich Park one afternoon about this time that I first realized that he had any literary ambition. He acknowledged a constant temptation to use his pen. I had thought of him as a reader, but hardly as a writer, although he had published his soldiers' *Pocket-Book for Field Service* some twenty years before. I learned afterwards, from Andrew Lang, that Lord Wolseley had produced a novel, under a feigned name; this I had never seen, and Lang did not encourage me to hunt for it. But now, with considerable leisure, he was ready to be encouraged to write on matters at the fringe of his daily occupation. He did not, however, see any particular theme lying in wait for him. During a visit I had lately paid to the United States I had enjoyed a good deal of conversation with two of the leading generals of the Civil War, with Philip Henry Sheridan and with William Tecumseh Sherman. It was Sherman who made the celebrated march to the sea from Atlanta to Savannah at the end of 1864; his tenacity and clairvoyance delighted Wolseley, who was nevertheless inclined to blame Sherman for an excess of ruthlessness in his methods. He laughed when I told him that I had heard Sherman, when teased at a supper-party for destroying some town, first deny the charge, and then, when it was daringly repeated, turn round on the railer like an old snow-leopard, and cry: "Next time I'll burn the whole darned city to the ground."

With Sheridan, Wolseley was in much more complete sympathy. He set him on the very summit as a fighting general, and he said that he had contrived a mobility of cavalry in action which was unprecedented. I think he had known Sheridan personally in his early days on the frontier. I remember his saying that, if he himself were conducting a great battle, he should like nothing better than to have the victor of Opequam on a camp-stool by his side. His memory took fire at what I was able to recall of the conversation of the two great American generals. His chief hero, however, was Lee, and I remember that he put the Confederate general by the side of Marlborough and far above Wellington. I used the occasion to suggest to him that he should write down his ideas regarding the strategic careers of these Americans. He liked the notion, and Mr. Rice, who was then editing the *North American Review,* having been communicated with, an invitation came to Wolseley which he accepted, and wrote, in 1889, one or perhaps several articles, which have never, I think, been reprinted. The life at Ranger's House was very quiet; the Wolseleys rarely dined in town, and the General's existence was almost that of a recluse. I remember we were all very much amused when his valet, a dashing character, suddenly gave warning, his sole cause of complaint being that he was losing caste by remaining in the service of "so very quiet a nobleman, who does not even go to the races! "

All this was completely changed in 1890 when Wolseley was appointed Commander of the Forces in Ireland. He wrote to announce the fact to me in July, and said that it was "rather a wrench going," but that he felt he should like it when he got to Dublin. "A more active, out-of-door life will be good for me," he opined. It was a great business moving all the family possessions, for both husband and wife were ardent collectors of bric-à-brac, and the treasures went by sea. The gallant couple, whose nostrils snuffed adventure as wild horses do their pasture,

Some Recollections of Lord Wolseley

thoroughly enjoyed their position at the beautiful Dublin house, depressingly known as the Royal Hospital. Wolseley took to getting up at 5.30 every morning, and no day was long enough for his activities and his hospitalities. The political crisis was more severe than usual, but Wolseley cared very little about politics, and his buoyant energy and boundless good nature made his house the one bright spot in an otherwise dismal Dublin. That, at least, is how it struck me during an enchanting visit I paid to the Royal Hospital in the midst of the resistance to Lord Rosebery's "predominant partner." Wolseley gave up any thought of periodical literature; when I urged it he said he was "always being attacked for writing." I do not quite know who can have "attacked" him or why, but he had other things to attend to.

He was not, however, unoccupied. It was while he was in Ireland that he composed his *Life of the Duke of Marlborough*, of which he finished two volumes in the spring of 1893 and published them a year later. The notes for it had occupied him for many years, he said, "on board ship, in camp, and often at long intervals of time when on duty abroad and in the field." He made a tour, as I well remember, to the scenes of Churchill's childhood, before he left Greenwich in 1890, and his descriptions of Ash House and the valley of the Axe were jotted down on the spot. The *Life of Marlborough* is Wolseley's principal contribution to literature. It is characteristically written, with that buoyancy and freshness which were inherent in his nature, but which do not appear so vividly in his other publications. The account of the Battle of Sedgemoor, which occupies an entire chapter, is almost a masterpiece; this is Wolseley, the writer, at his highest level. Unfortunately, this admirable book is, and will remain, a fragment, and posterity has a prejudice against what is unfinished. The second volume closes in 1702, when Marlborough's political intrigues had come to an end and William III. was placing him at the head of the allied forces in Flanders. This was, of course, the division of his career, and naturally closed a volume. But the military fun was only just going to begin, and what everybody wanted from Lord Wolseley, of all men in the world, was an account of the great campaigns.

This, however, was never performed, why, we can only conjecture. The book was, on the whole, very well received, but, naturally, everyone noted that it stopped in the middle of the story. In answer to an anxious inquiry which I sent off on receiving my copy of the two volumes, Wolseley wrote :

I hope the book will pay the publisher. If it does, I shall write the military part of Marlborough's life, which, of course, would be to me a more interesting undertaking than describing my hero through a period already well known from the pages of our greatest historical novelist, Macaulay.

This shows that, in April, 1894, no part of the continuation was actually written, but I doubt not that he had made copious notes of some of the 1702-1710 campaigns. Indeed, on one occasion much later, when I was trying to urge him to return to so congenial an enterprise, he told me that the Battle of Malplaquet was actually finished; and Mr. Richard Bentley informs me that this MS. was actually at one time in his father's hands. Wolseley also is known to have described the march along the Danube in 1705, but not reaching the Battle of Blenheim. These fragments must surely exist among Lord Wolseley's MSS., and I urge Sir George Arthur to make careful search for them. They ought to be well worthy of publication. That, at the age of sixty-one, and in active State employment, Lord Wolseley did not feel able to pursue his hero over the innumerable battlefields from Venloo to Oudenarde is easily comprehensible, but that he should have stopped just where he did is lamentable. We may wish that he had been inspired to start, instead of stopping, at 1702.

A side of Lord Wolseley's mental temperament which was little known was his sympathy with the imaginative

Some Recollections of Lord Wolseley

literature of the East. He could not, I suppose, be called a scholar, but he had more acquaintance with Oriental languages than was generally suspected. In particular, the poetry of Persia exercised a great fascination over him. He studied both Persian and Hindustani for a couple of years, and kept a learned Munshi with him all that time as a travelling tutor. This man had a passion for the poets, and, as Wolseley told me, constantly held him in conversation on the subject of Persian history and made him read Persian books. Wolseley learned quotations from the poets by heart, and afterwards, in speaking with exalted or highly-educated natives of India, he found that the apt introduction of such tags from the classics was greatly appreciated, and was made the subject of compliment. Wolseley was very amusing about this.

As I happened to be President of the Omar Khayyám Club in 1897, I thought that a speech from the Field-Marshal at the annual banquet would introduce a charming novelty into that mild orgy of red wine and red roses. Although very busy, for he had lately been made Commander-in-Chief, he "jumped," as we say, at the invitation, and made his appearance as the Guest of the Evening. It was not for me to hint procedure to so illustrious a visitor, but I confess I dreaded lest the clash of swords might jar a little on our floral festivity. I need have had no fear. When the moment came for Lord Wolseley to rise (he had told me that he felt so shy that his "heart was in his mouth," but he showed no sign of discomposure) he assured the company that he had been misrepresented as a man of blood, but that he was, on the contrary, a lover of roses and red wine. He confessed that he knew Omar only in the translation of FitzGerald; I was aware—but kept my counsel—that he had only known that since his invitation to dine. He said that in India he had never heard the name of Omar pronounced, but he expatiated largely on those of Hafiz and Firdousi. The rules of the Club excluded reporters, and I have always been sorry that no record survives of this charming little discourse.

Aspects and Impressions

What does survive is a delicious poem in Austin Dobson's best vein, which was handed round to the guests in privately printed form. This piece described the scene and those present, beginning with

> I note
> Our *Rustum* here, without red coat,

a touch which pleased the Field-Marshal.

Lord Wolseley had taken an active part in the Chinese War of 1860, and I remember his telling me that on his appointment as deputy to accompany Sir Hugh Grant to Hong-Kong he ransacked every library and bookshop in Calcutta for books about China. His account of the campaign, up to the surrender of Pekin in November, 1860, was published in his *Narrative of the War with China*, a work founded on the letters he sent home by each successive mail; it can conveniently be read in chapters XXVII. to XXXI. of *The Story of a Soldier's Life*. But what is not told there is that he preserved to the end of his days a very sympathetic interest in the civic manners of the Chinese, whom he preferred to any other Oriental race, having at one time or another tested them all. In his published writings Lord Wolseley dwells mainly on the perfidy of the ruling classes in China, and on the ease with which Lord Elgin allowed himself to be taken in by the treacherous Chinese Ministers. He expressed horror at the crime of the escort who beheaded Captain Brabazon at the Pa-li-cheaou Bridge, an event which had a peculiar effect on Wolseley, because it was by a mere accident that Brabazon, at the last moment, had taken Wolseley's place in his absence on another business. The want of elementary scruple in the Chinese authorities was shocking to a straightforward British soldier. But, after all, we were at war with them.

On the other hand, what Wolseley loved to expatiate on in private conversation was the sterling virtue of the ordinary Chinese civilian. I recollect how on one occasion, when Sir Francis de Winton was dining at Ranger's

Some Recollections of Lord Wolseley

House, and expressed some views over-indulgent to the Turks, Lord Wolseley turned upon him, sparkling with indignation, and swore that no Turk could hold a candle to a Chinaman, the cleanest, the most temperate, the most philosophical creature in the world. ' In vain did De Winton protest that he meant no dishonour to China. Wolseley was started on his hobby-horse, and gave us no peace till he had delivered quite a little oration on the wonderful merits of the disciples of Confucius. This was in 1889, and long afterwards the zeal for China was eating him up at intervals. I find a letter to myself, dated April 17th, 1901, in which he tells me that he is reading Professor H. A. Giles's *History of Chinese Literature*:

I wonder how deep he has gone in it. The only man I ever knew who had more than dipped into that vast subject was Sir T. Wade, an old friend of mine. I have known many men who spoke Chinese well, some even spoke it fluently —Sir Harry Parkes, for instance—but Wade was the only Englishman I ever met who had probed down deep into the Chinese classics. He often laughed at the notion of any *Fan qui* being well acquainted with them, so great was their volume and so numerous the works to be studied. Indeed very few Chinamen are thoroughly well read in their own classical literature. When we moved upon the Summer Palace in 1860, the Emperor fled in haste, leaving upon a little table the book he had just been reading. I always regretted not having taken possession of it, instead of letting it be destroyed. It was a classical work.

On the night of October 12th, 1899, when the Boer war was declared, my wife and I shared with Lord and Lady Wolseley a box at the performance of Shakespeare's *King John*. Like almost everyone else except Kitchener, the Commander-in-Chief assured us that the war would be a short one; he was radiant and calm on that memorable evening. There were many verses in the play which seemed appropriate to the occasion, and when King John declaimed—

Aspects and Impressions

Here have we war for war, and blood for blood,
Controlment for controlment.

Wolseley whispered "and Victoria for Mr. Krüger!" It was exhilarating, though as it turned out not wholly satisfactory, to listen to King John's proud reply to Chattilion:

For ere thou canst report, I will be there;
The thunder of my cannon shall be heard—
So hence!

But I must not trespass within the circle of our coming disenchantment.

A few months later Lord Wolseley handed over the Command-in-Chief to Lord Roberts, and he presently retired to a farmhouse at Glynde, near Lewes, where he resided for a number of years, more and more secluded from the world, but devoted to his garden and his books. Once more he became a voracious reader of miscellaneous literature. Here he liked to be informed of what was going on in the world of letters, and to see as frequently as he could a few friends who wrote. Among these, I think there was none whom he valued more than Henry James, a very old friend, earlier, I think, than Andrew Lang or myself. It might be supposed that there was little in common between the active soldier and the exquisite and meticulous dreamer, but, on the contrary, their mutual esteem was persistent, and Wolseley delighted in the conversation of Henry James, although he sometimes allowed himself to smile at the novelist's halting and deliberate utterance. Wolseley, on the other hand, was an emphatic, spontaneous talker, not very particular in selecting the very best word or in rounding the most harmonious period. It was amusing to hear them together, the one so short and sharp, the other so mellifluous and hesitating, yet their admiration, each for the other, was continuous.

I do not think that Wolseley was ever more happy than

Some Recollections of Lord Wolseley

in the first years of his residence at Glynde, the world forgetting, by the world forgot. But a certain insidious melancholy soon began to invade him. He gradually cut himself off from all his round of London engagements, and he never once, if I remember right, attended the House of Lords after his retirement from the War Office. He was not in the least degree invalided or deprived of nervous energy, but he felt that in the long, strenuous years of service he had earned a holiday, and now he took it. He made, perhaps, few new friends, but he was careful to cultivate the old ones, and no one was ever more assiduous in the art of friendship. He clung to old associations and to old faces—"they can't escape me," I remember his saying. He liked to see them at Glynde, where they always received a glowing, almost a boisterous, welcome. The house lies in a sort of glen between two ranges of the beautiful Sussex downs, and Wolseley loved to climb these eminences with a familiar companion. He was particularly apt to take such a friend eastward along the lanes to Firle and then up to the summit of the beacon above Alciston. This was one of his favourite afternoon excursions, and from this vantage he would sweep the coastline from Seaford to Pevensey, and dilate on its strategic capabilities.

Of such excursions as these I have the happiest memory. The exercise always seemed to stir the General's brain to especial activity. His rapid, vehement voice rang out in full sonority in the silence of the great rolling Down, and his thoughts seemed to move with more ease than usual in the high, cold air of autumn. His imagination worked with a vitality which almost persuaded his ignorant companion that he also was a strategical genius, so easy did the problems of military movement seem when outrolled by Wolseley's warm voice and punctuated by the sweep of his walking-stick. It was impossible not to feel that "this exceptional combination of mental gifts with untiring physical power and stern resolution" made our wonderful friend unique in his class and time. One was amazed to find one's self entrusted with the professional secrets of

Aspects and Impressions

which one was really so unworthy a recipient. But it was characteristic of Wolseley that, with all his fire and abruptness, he was incapable of the smallest element of patronage. He lifted his friends, in a whirl of generous illusion, up to a level with himself, and insisted on their sharing his conceptions. No one ever possessed a more fascinating gift for persuading the person he talked with that the friend's powers and capacities were equal to his own. The impression could only be momentary, but it was extremely grateful while it lasted.

Few things in private conversation are more winning than lack of discretion. I cannot pretend that Lord Wolseley was a cautious speaker, and I think his company would have been much less entertaining than it was if he had minced his words or hedged his opinions. He had spent twenty years or more of his life in a prodigious enterprise, no less than the entire remodelling of the British Army. He had seen with Napoleonic clearness what sweeping reforms were needed, and he had not felt the smallest hesitation in setting about their introduction. But he had originally been quite alone in this perilous enterprise. Hercules had come to the cattle-yard of Augeas and had found it clogged with the mire of generations. He set about turning the course of Alpheus and Peneus, rivers of Whitehall, and he sent their waters rushing through the stable. With his besom he began to scrub the refuse out of every corner. But the old-fashioned stablemen were not pleased to be disturbed, and Augeas, in consternation, refused to give Hercules his reward. Thereupon there arose loud and lasting clamours, in the midst of which the work, frustrated as far as mediocrity found possible, went forward steadily, but in a wind of exasperation. There was rage on both sides, recrimination, injury; and even the monarch of Elis was not disengaged from the struggle. If these things are an allegory, it is a very transparent one, and it need not be translated. It suffices to say that he would have little insight into human character who should express surprise at any vehemence of expression, with regard to those who opposed his cleansing activities, which the Nemean hero might give way to in private conversation. He was tired with fighting those of his own household and he was sick from the stupidity of persons clothed with brief authority.

If, however, Lord Wolseley expended the treasures of what could at call be a very lively vocabulary on the men who had hindered his life's work, nothing could exceed his loyal memory of the few who had found courage to support him. Among the latter, Mr. Cardwell and Lord Northbrook stood pre-eminent, particularly the former, of whom I remember many tributes of the warmest appreciation. I have often heard Wolseley say that he came back from the Crimea with a sense of horror at all the shortcomings of our military system, and that his criticisms met with none but the most languid attention except from Cardwell. It was a highly fortunate circumstance that these two came together, for Cardwell at home in England had come to the same conclusions as Wolseley had in the four quarters of the globe. He was able, as Secretary for War from 1868 to 1874, to put into practical shape the ideas which Wolseley had, by his high gift of imagination, seen in the field itself to be necessary. Wolseley believed that, but for Cardwell's unflinching support, his enemies would have contrived to have him honourably deported to some command at the Antipodes where his tiresome brain would have ceased to worry the War Office. The fiercest of the fight gathered about the year 1872, when "the old school" would hardly believe that anyone calling himself a gentleman could make himself so intolerably objectionable as did this horrible Sir Garnet Wolseley. At this time Cardwell, in the face of every species of intrigue and resistance, shielded his assistant from his opponents. Later on he helped him to collect around him the ablest soldiers of promise on whom the army of the future depended. I never heard Wolseley speak of anyone with so much regret as of Cardwell, cut off, by failing health, in the midst of his labours.

Aspects and Impressions

It was Lord Northbrook who chiefly aided and abetted Wolseley in his scheme for sending General Gordon off up the Nile. When the tragedy was complete, Lord Northbrook inclined to think that their action had been "a terrible mistake." But Wolseley never would admit that it had been a mistake. He persisted that it was the only thing to do, and that the responsibility for failure rested on Mr. Gladstone and his Government. There was nothing that Wolseley loved better than to recount the adventure of his seeing Gordon off to the Soudan on November 18th, 1883, and his dramatic conversation at the London railway station. Gordon was settled in the train when Wolseley asked: "By the way, General, I suppose you have plenty of money?" "Not a penny!" And Wolseley would recount how he dashed in a hansom to his bank, and brought back the bank-notes just in time for the perfectly indifferent Gordon to slip them into his pocket as the train went off.

Before he left town in 1900 Lord Wolseley had begun, at the suggestion of some of his friends who regretted that so much high experience of life should be wasted, to prepare his own autobiography. As I took a special interest in this project, I was told (December 1st, 1900), that he had "written, at odd moments, many pages for the Memoirs, but, of course, they have still to be pumice-stoned down and put into shape." The sudden cessation from all administrative activity had threatened to be rather disastrous, but, as I have said, he took his retirement to Glynde very serenely, and this business of the autobiography promised to be the best antidote to languor. When one saw him in the next years, it stood always in the background; its progress was reported like the growth of a slow fruit, which stuck on the bough, but was not swelling as it should. At last, in his seventy-first year, I received, not without surprise, the announcement that it was ripe and ready for the market. A little further delay, and there appeared, in two fat volumes, *The Story of a Soldier's Life*. The copy which reached me from the author generously acknowledged the "valuable advice" that I had "so often kindly given." But I dare not take this tribute to my soul, for, as a matter of fact, the book bears no trace of external advice. It is a very strange production, and may be succinctly described as an editing from earlier records by himself of fragments of a story the details of which the author had forgotten.

There is no question that, as an autobiography, *The Story of a Soldier's Life* is disappointing. It was undertaken too late, and it could never have been written at all, save for the fact that Wolseley had, in earlier years, kept copious journals and written long letters when he was abroad on his various campaigns. These letters and journals were collected and typed, and a secretary helped to put them together and give a certain amount of cohesion to the narrative. The book was strangely edited; the preface appears in the second volume, the dedication is repeated twice, there is no account whatever of the circumstances in which the Memoir was compiled. What is more serious is that the personal and intimate life of the author is entirely neglected. When he had not before him letters from the Crimea or the Red River, from China or Ashantee, he had nothing to go upon but the newspapers.

The sad cause of all this cannot be concealed. Although his physical health, and indeed in essentials his mental health, were unimpaired, he had begun to suffer from a radical decay of memory. This was already becoming obvious before he left the War Office, and it grew rapidly in intensity. It was a very curious infirmity, for it dealt chiefly with what I may call immediate memory. For instance, in these later years, if an old friend came to see him on a carefully prepared visit, he would recognize him instantly, with the old ardour, but would say : "I'm delighted to see you, no one told me you were coming ! " If a little later on the same occasion he was called away for a few minutes, he would return with a repeated welcome : "Oh ! how nice to see you—nobody told me you were coming ! " This painful affliction has to be mentioned, if only because it explains the strange construction

Aspects and Impressions

of *The Story of a Soldier's Life*. It grew upon him, until it wove a curtain which concealed him from all intercourse with the world. In perfect physical health, but needing and receiving the most assiduous attention, he lived on, mainly at Mentone, until he completed his eightieth year. But his wonderful and beneficent life had really come to an end ten years earlier.

1921.

INDEX

Index

Index

Index

Index

Index

Index

297

Index

Index

Index